The Trundlers

The Military Medium-Paced Story of Cricket's Most Invaluable Breed

Harry Pearson

ABACUS

First published in Great Britain in 2013 by Little, Brown
This paperback edition published in 2014 by Abacus

A CIP catalogue record for this book
is available from the British Library.

ISBN 978-0-349-13868-8

Typeset in Baskerville by M Rules
Printed and bound in Great Britain by
Clays Ltd, St Ives plc

Papers used by Abacus are from well-managed forests
and other responsible sources.

MIX
Paper from
responsible sources
FSC® C104740

Abacus
An imprint of
Little, Brown Book Group
100 Victoria Embankment
London EC4Y 0DY

An Hachette UK Company
www.hachette.co.uk

www.littlebrown.co.uk

Acknowledgements

When I started playing cricket as a teenager I received a good deal of encouragement from a work colleague of my father's, Harold Thompson. Mr Thompson lived near Acklam Park in Middlesbrough, in those days still a Yorkshire county ground. Following my every failure with bat or ball, or both, my dad would report that Mr Thompson had said to tell me that Sir Leonard got a duck on his debut, or that the great Hedley Verity was once hit for thirty runs in a single over by Jock Cameron.

When Mr Thompson died he bequeathed to me his library of cricket books. I never met Harold Thompson, but his generosity all those years ago has helped shape *The Trundlers*. Among the books in his collection were several by Sir Pelham Warner, H. S. Altham's *A History of Cricket*, many works by Neville Cardus, Ian Peebles's *Talking of Cricket*, Monty Noble's account of the 1928–9 Ashes series, A. A. Thomson's *Hirst and Rhodes* and the autobiographies of Cyril Washbrook, Len Hutton, Alec and Eric Bedser and Maurice Tate. I have used all of them extensively.

Other books that proved invaluable while writing *The Trundlers* were Gerald Brodribb's biography of Maurice Tate and his monograph on under-arm bowlers; *S. F. Barnes: Master*

Bowler by Leslie Duckworth; *On the Spot,* David Matthews's biography of Derek Shackleton, and *The Flame Still Burns,* Stephen Chalke's masterful work on Tom Cartwright. Peter Walker's *Cricket Conversations* and Denzil Batchelor's two anthologies, *The Book of Cricket* and *Great Cricketers,* have also come in handy. My stint reviewing books for *Wisden Cricketer's Almanac* happily coincided with the publication of Martin Wilson's biography of William Lillywhite, Robert Brooke's book on F. R. Foster and Patrick Ferriday's work on the Triangular Test Series of 1912 – all three are worth seeking out.

Cricinfo and the Cricket Archive are invaluable sources of facts, figures and other pleasures for any cricket fan. Had they been available when I was an adolescent it is unlikely I would ever have left the house.

Thanks must also go to my publisher Richard Beswick for supporting the idea of a book about cricket's least celebrated men, my editor Zoe Gullen for sorting out my random grammar and my agent Andrew Gordon and his assistant Marigold Atkey for their bold attempts to prevent me from starving to death.

Finally, when you sit next to an author it is, I believe, never wise to ask what he or she is working on at the moment. They will invariably do one of two things: talk madly about it until it is time to go home, or clam up entirely. I fall into the former category. To all those who have sat next to me over the past eighteen months and politely endured two hours of unstoppable blather about George Hirst, Cliff Gladwin and Robin Singh, I humbly apologise. Especially if you were one of those who took advantage of one of my rare pauses for breath to say, 'Actually, I'm not that interested in cricket.'

Contents

Introduction

It all started with Denzil Batchelor. The library in my village only had a small selection of cricket books and *Great Cricketers* – edited by the veteran writer and bon viveur – was by far the thickest of them. This was Yorkshire, after all: we sought value for money in everything, even if it was free. In fact, especially if it was free.

Great Cricketers contained pen portraits of sixty-three players. That two of them were Sir Leonard Hutton only added to its local appeal. It was not the chapters on the saintly opening batsman that arrested my attention, however, but those on the pacemen. My imagination was fired by the deeds of Ted McDonald, whose wrist at the point of delivery was – Neville Cardus wrote – poised like 'the head of a cobra before the venom was released' and Eddie Gilbert, the Aboriginal Australian who – Ray Robinson claimed – bowled one day at Brisbane 'as if instead of an arm he had a bazooka up his sleeve'. Most of all, though, it was the account of the feats of the Demon himself, F. R. Spofforth, that inspired me.

The great Australian fast bowler was tall and spindly, with a beaky face, thin, angular body, long neck and pronounced

Adam's apple. He called to mind a starving ostrich that had swallowed a snooker ball, but since that was more or less how I looked myself he quickly became my idol.

Determined to emulate Spofforth, I hurtled in at high speed (Frederick had been a sprinter and covered 100 yards in 10.2 seconds), leapt at the crease and hurled the ball down the wicket with all my might. Watching adults shook their heads. 'Stop trying to bowl like an express train and concentrate on accuracy,' they counselled. I ignored them. They were dullards who had followed their own cautious advice and ended up working for ICI and British Steel. I was a flamboyant boy genius bound for glory just as surely as I was bound to go down the garden and retrieve all the tennis balls I'd just flung down the leg-side and into the river.

In the 1974 Easter holidays two friends and I, fired up by reading about Wes Hall, Charlie Griffith and crazy Roy Gilchrist, invented a game called Bumper War. This was played on the concrete strip in front of the garage and involved one player taking the sacrificial role of batsman while the other two bowled at him from ten yards with tennis balls that had first been dunked in a bucket of water. There were no stumps. The aim of the bowlers was not to dismiss the batsman but to hit him, preferably on the head. Hour after hour, fuelled by sugary syrup from my friend's SodaStream and regular packets of nuclear-orange cheese-flavoured corn puffs, we peppered each other with bouncers until the batsmen's protective duffel coats were soaked through and their faces splattered. 'Why don't you try playing proper cricket?' our dads would say when they got back from work. But we had watched proper cricket and since it generally seemed to involve Roy Virgin prodding forward to Geoff Arnold we refused to surrender to its suet-like blandness.

At some point during the summer term that followed I was called into the school under-16s team. Bowling opportunities for thirteen-year-olds at this exalted level were few and far between: youngsters were expected to bat low down, field in the deep, bring on the plastic beakers of weak orange drink in the intervals and keep their mouths shut. Indeed, our most important task was to stand outside the changing rooms while the older boys lit up their fags and hiss 'Nix, nix!' if the games teachers came into view.

I can't now recall who we were playing, but we were so far down the road to a hiding that, with nothing left for it but desperation, the skipper, a boy with nuclear acne and the ability to gob what looked like a spinach omelette down the shirt front of anyone who offended him (and he was highly sensitive on a diverse range of topics), called on me to take my sweater off.

Like my hero Spofforth I elected to bowl round the wicket, tearing in off the nine-pace run-up the Demon had used and sending the ball angling across the batsman. I took a wicket with my third delivery, caught behind. Three more followed, two clean bowled and though the stumps didn't cartwheel I imagined that was only because the groundsman, a gnarled Second World War veteran, had hammered them into the ground using a sledgehammer. In the face of my onslaught the opposition fell to pieces. We won by six runs. Boys who had previously only paid attention to me long enough to jab a compass in my backside were now patting me on the back and calling me by name in not entirely sarcastic voices. As we trooped off I felt elated. Now I was on my way. I would be the English Demon, a latter-day Alfred Mynn or Charles Kortright, the Essex thunderbolt who had once clean bowled W. G. Grace and sent him back to the pavilion with the cry, 'Not leaving us surely, Doctor? There's still one stump standing.'

Yes, they would call me the Teesside Terror and I would bowl so fast and with such mortal venom even pan-faced Aussie bruisers like Keith Stackpole would hide in the toilet with their fingers in their ears rather than face me.

As we reached the pavilion steps the games teacher who had been umpiring came over. 'There you are, Pearson,' he said with a smile. 'See how much better you do when you stop trying to be the next Freddie Trueman and focus on line and length?' There are few things more damaging to the adolescent soul than the kindness of adults.

I didn't give up, though. I carried on tearing in. But it made no difference in the end. Some are born medium-paced, some become medium-paced and others have medium pace thrust upon them.

Sport has a nasty way of reminding us we are getting old. Recently a Swedish friend told me how her father had slipped gradually into senility. 'To be honest,' she said, 'he was never the same once the government revoked his elk-hunting licence.'

The elk is a large and ungainly creature, with a body like a grand piano, gangling, knotty limbs and a cranium over-weighted with antlers in the shape of the sort of giant foam hands people are encouraged to waggle about at T20 matches. Watching one rise from a recumbent position recalls a drunk wrestling with a deckchair. Nobody in Scandinavia wants wounded elk wandering around so, in order to hunt the great beasts, you have to take an annual marksmanship test to prove you can kill them with a single shot.

'When you have hunted elk since you were a young man, and then you fail that shooting exam, well ... ' My friend shrugged glumly. It is plain what she means. Once they strip a person of his or her right to hunt elk the Swedish authorities are effectively handing them a bit of paper that says, 'Now sit down, watch *Cash in the Attic* and wait for your coronary.'

In Britain we have no tradition of shooting large-headed ruminants yet sport still finds a way to deliver unpleasant little hints that we are heading inexorably towards the door marked 'Death'.

It is hard, for example, to avoid the feeling that the grim reaper is sharpening his scythe when, as an opening bowler, you turn at the top of your run and discover the wicketkeeper is standing up for you. Of course the stumper is diplomatic. He does not actually say, 'Thing is, mate, you've slowed up so much recently it's coming through to me second bounce when I stand back.' No, he gives you some guff about noticing how this opening batsman lifts his back foot off the ground when he plays forward, and there might just be a chance of whipping the bails off. You want to believe him, of course you do, but you know in your guts that once a wicketkeeper starts standing up for you he is never going back down again, no matter how many full tosses you fling down the legside in the hope of breaking the patronising little bastard's thumbs.

The slide begins before that, though. It starts the minute the opening bowler finally caves in and says, 'I've stopped striving for all-out pace and begun to focus on accuracy instead.' Abandoning speed for line and length, renouncing the bouncer in favour of 'doing a little bit each way off the wicket': this is the sporting equivalent of that moment when you look at a pair of Italian boots and say, 'Very handsome, but they'd be murder on my corns.' For the vast majority of humanity this is inevitable. We aim for the stars and end up behind the counter in Specsavers.

This is why trundling is what most club cricketers do.

Naturally they dress it up, usually with a faux self-deprecating mutter about 'doing a bit both ways off the track'. For many years I opened the bowling each Sunday with a middle-aged actor whose appearance in various TV advertising campaigns had made him, if not quite a household name then certainly someone the opposition had a funny feeling they knew from somewhere. The actor had a reliable yet vaguely baffled middle-class appearance and was a thoroughly nice chap, a good team player and a dobber of the most fundamental-ist type. His deliveries swung less than an Iranian cleric and refused to deviate off the seam, even on municipal pitches that had apparently been fashioned using several tons of coal cinders and a top dressing of Rottweiler dung. At the other end the bowlers might have the ball moving randomly about the place like a rogue supermarket trolley, but from the actor's end the ball came through straight and flat and true, until someone else replaced him.

The actor was not deterred, however. Nor did he blame himself. To hear him tell it he was just a slight twist in the cli-matic conditions away from being S. F. Barnes. After every game I would sit with him over a beer and listen to him lament the fact that 'I just couldn't get the in-dipper work-ing today, the wind wasn't in the right direction, if the Skip had given me your end . . . ' or 'The away swinger was going much too early this afternoon, the atmosphere was too heavy. Skip should have brought me on later after that shower . . . '

On one occasion he blamed the failure of his leg-cutter to 'go' on a tiny alteration of his bowling action caused by spending the previous week stripping paint off a pine wardrobe. 'Bowling,' he sighed, with more anguish than he ever managed when his boss turned up a day early for dinner in the commercials, 'is a cruel mistress.'

This happened to me longer ago now than I care to remember. Over the years I have adjusted to it. In many ways, being medium-paced is a lot like being middle class: it takes you a long while to learn to stop apologising about it or pretending that actually, you know, your grandfather was a coal miner and you can still shake the batsman up with a quicker one every so often, *if you want to.*

In the case of the high-class medium-pacers of the Test and county scene, people tend to make excuses on their behalf. When it comes to even the most blatant wibbly-wobblyman, writers will often defend their subject from perceived charges of trundling by announcing, 'His deliveries come off the wicket much quicker than batsmen expect', or, 'He was faster off the pitch than he was through the air', or, 'He bowled a heavy ball'. They will then offer the comment, 'Although scientists may say this is impossible, many seasoned observers attest to it', which makes the dobber sound weirdly miraculous, like a bleeding statue of Christ in an Italian cave. But there is nothing magical about the trundlers. Even the great ones such as Barnes and Tate, Bedser and Cartwright were craftsmen, admired for their skill and their diligence, their stamina and patience. They did not, however, quicken anyone's pulse. They are the cholesterol of cricket.

Once you own up and face your inner trundler, accept that this is who you are and things will get altogether easier. Nowadays I look back with regret at how, during my teenage years, I failed to celebrate the endeavours of John Dye and Bob Cottam, and that I may even have voiced the opinion that Ken Higgs was boring. I am older now, and know that a good trundler is something you only come to appreciate later in life – like comfort-fit slacks or repeats of *Baywatch* on Men & Movies.

With the wisdom of years I can see, for instance, that the attack of Viv Richards's West Indies team was unbalanced not by the lack of a top-class spinner, but by the clear absence of an heir to Vanburn Holder, whose elegantly bowed legs and sensible insistence on line and length above pace and bounce brought a hint of the King's Singers to calypso cricket. I can see now why some of the gentlemen who sat around me at Headingley and Scarborough would greet the sight of Vanburn replacing Andy Roberts with the contented sigh of gardeners sniffing the scent of evening drizzle after a hot August day. You could relax with Vanburn.

So what exactly do I mean when I say 'trundler'? That's not easy to answer, as the classification of bowling speeds is more a matter of opinion than an exact science. Some pundits claim there is a distinction between medium-fast (approximately speeds of between 70 and 79mph) and fast-medium (80 to 85mph), while others regard the terms as interchangeable. Fast bowling is variously defined as being above 85mph or above 145kph (which is slightly more than 90mph). Whichever view you hold, this leaves the medium-paced category a little blurred around the upper edge. For what it's worth, I have tried to concentrate on bowlers who delivered the ball at between 55 and 75mph, but establishing which bowlers that includes is also fraught with difficulty. The radar speed gun – now a constant presence in top-class cricket – is a relatively recent innovation. Before speed guns appeared a decade or so ago, tests on the pace of bowlers were sporadic, the methods used variable and the equipment often eccentric – in New Zealand, for example, the speeds of England's Ashes-winning pacemen Brian Statham and Frank Tyson were assessed using a special ball with a metal plate attached to it.

The tests carried out in Perth by scientists from the University of Western Australia in 1979 are more helpful. Under the watchful eye of Dr Frank Pyke, cameras measured the speeds of a variety of bowlers in the nets. One of them was Sarfraz Nawaz. According to the tests, the *fastest* ball that Sarfraz bowled during the session travelled at 75.63mph. This suggests that Sarfraz's stock ball was delivered at *below* that speed (during the same tests Imran Khan's fastest delivery was clocked at 86.77mph). Since Sarfraz played county and Test cricket from the late sixties until the mid-eighties that gives something by which to judge bowlers of the period.

When we go back further into the past, however, it becomes far more difficult to know exactly how fast or slow bowlers were. Rodney Marsh said that the most reliable guide to a bowler's pace is the position the wicketkeeper takes to him. Generally, in the pre-1960s era I have opted to focus only on those bowlers that wicketkeepers stood up to. This includes some of the best Test opening bowlers of all time, including Alec Bedser, Maurice Tate, S. F. Barnes and Amar Singh.

Since wicketkeepers have, in recent times, stood up at the stumps to very few medium-pace bowlers we might reasonably infer that Tate and Bedser were not as quick as, say, Praveen Kumar or Derek Pringle bowling at the same treacly clip as Jeremy Coney and Mohinder Amarnath.

Does that seem likely? We can't be sure. Bowlers nowadays are generally taller and have more muscle mass than in the years before and after the Second World War. Diet is better and cricketers are physically fitter. All kinds of technology including computer analysis exist to help bowlers identify areas that will help them add an extra few feet of speed. I think that bowlers today are, on average, quicker than they used to be. But why wouldn't they be? At the London Olympics in 1948 the men's 100 metres was won in a time of 10.3. In 2012 that wouldn't have been good enough even to make the final. Perhaps more relevantly, the world record for the javelin when 'Chub' Tate was at his peak was 66.62 metres. By the time Bob Willis was leading the England attack it had risen to nearly 100 metres (the design of the missile was changed in 1986 to prevent it flying onto the running track). If javelin-throwers could improve their performance by close to 50 per cent over that period, mightn't bowlers do something similar? I would therefore suggest that people's judgement of what is fast, medium-fast and fast-medium has changed over the years and that what spectators in the twenties thought of as fast-medium would today look more like slow-medium.

Michael Holding once observed, 'Just because a bowler bowls the occasional fast ball, that doesn't make him a fast bowler.' The same is true of trundling. It's not just about speed; it's about attitude too. Medium-pacers are men who bowl within themselves, who do not strain for pace or expect to shock or startle their opponents. For this reason you will find very few of Holding's compatriots in this book. In the early seventies the mainstays of the West Indies attack were the stiff-legged left-armer Bernard Julien who played for Kent and the springy Essex all-rounder Keith Boyce. Neither was anywhere near as quick as Patrick Patterson or Malcolm Marshall, and it's possible that they weren't much faster than county team mates such as Richard Elms and Stuart Turner, but Julien and Boyce both bowled in the Caribbean style. They dug it in; they tried to make the batsman hop around. They might only have been medium pace, but they bowled like fastmen.

The same holds true of the man who was, in many ways,

the last in the long line of great British trundlers, Sir Ian Botham. The all-rounder had been taught to bowl by one of the best and most enduring of all post-war medium-pacers, Tom Cartwright. Like his mentor, Botham could swing the ball both ways and move it off the track. If Beefy had stuck to Cartwright's line and length, and taken the same puritanical approach to speed, he'd have slotted in here just fine. Sadly Botham insisted on striving for pace, on bowling bouncers. And even late on in his career, when the years and back injuries had curbed his pace to the point where – as at the 1992 World Cup – his shorter deliveries rose from the pitch with the lazy hum of a maybug, wicketkeepers still stood back to him. I think this was probably less for tactical reasons than for fear of giving offence to the notoriously touchy Botham. And frankly, if Alec Stewart was frightened of upsetting the Great Man, then there is little chance of me risking it. Trundling is, after all, a state of mind, a philosophy. Even, to some, a way of life.

Back in the seventies there was a profusion of books about pace bowlers – *The Fast Men* by David Frith was one of my favourites as a teenager – and recently a similar number of books have appeared about spinners. Nobody gives the medium-pacer much shelf space, however. What follows is my attempt to rectify that situation.

Admittedly, the response from my friends has not been entirely upbeat. 'Hmm,' they have said when I've outlined what I am up to. 'But aren't seamers – I mean Ken Shuttleworth and so forth – a bit, you know, dull?'

'Indeed,' I have responded cheerily, 'as dull as mashed potato.' And then, in case they should get the wrong idea, added, 'Back in the days when mashed potato was grey and lumpy, nobody had thought of adding olive oil and wild garlic, and even the addition of butter was considered the sort of sensual excess that would lead inexorably to married couples having sexual congress on the sitting-room carpet, on weekday afternoons, with the curtains open. But that,' I have continued with what some may feel is a wild hint of madness, 'is what makes it so brilliant. I mean, what could be more banal than getting all excited about Allan Donald or Anil Kumble? It's like enjoying sunshine, or jumbo prawns. On the other hand, it takes a lifetime's basting in the summer game to truly appreciate the subtle joys of Richard Ellison.'

So this, then, is the book. It is a work that studiously ignores the Indian spin kings Bedi, Prasanna, Chandrasekhar and Venkataraghavan to focus instead on the shine-on-the-new-ball-reducing efforts of Madan Lal and Eknath Solkar, brushes aside Richard Hadlee, Jeff Thomson and 'Typhoon' Tyson in order to cast a closer eye on Jeremy Coney, Max Walker and Cliff Gladwin.

In the past decade cricket has moved forward. New competitions and styles of play have made the sort of decaffeinated cricket offered up by RFMers of my youth such as Teesside genius Chris Old, a man who appeared permanently on the verge of a nosebleed, a thing of the past. These days fast-medium men are not content with hitting the seam in good areas, but are determined to reverse swing the cherry and all sorts of other fancy stuff.

The modern game is chock-a-block with icons and legends; journeymen are in altogether shorter supply.

Chapter 1

Dawn of the Dobber

So who was the first military medium-paced, line and length, do-a-bit-off-the-pitcher? Or, as the traditional seventeenth-century English rhyme asks, 'When Adam bounced and Eve span/Who was then the trundly-man?'

In the early days of cricket bowlers were just that: bowlers. Like lawn or crown green bowlers they rolled the cricket ball along the ground towards the batsman and trusted the batting strip – often bumpy, or 'glibby' as they said in Georgian match reports – would do the rest for them. In short, they bowled what the Australians call 'grubbers'.

The lack of anything in the way of bounce was reflected by the size and shape of the wicket, which in those days consisted of a pair of stumps, each a foot tall, placed two feet apart and topped with a single bail. As the bowler was aiming for a target that was wider than it was tall, elevation was hardly to his advantage. The batsman, meanwhile, wielded a bat that was rather like a hockey stick: ideal for smacking a ball that travelled along the ground.

The action of rolling the ball was sometimes referred to as 'trundling', but these early bowlers were not trundlers in our sense. Since they could not impart spin, or deceive the batsman with flight or by varying length, they relied more or less completely on raw pace.

For those of us who grew up in an era when under-arm bowling was something reserved for French cricket, for use in garden or beach games against the weedier breed of tots, the notion of a lethally quick under-armer is a hard one to grasp. Accounts of cricket in Georgian England, however, make frequent reference to the speed at which bowlers such as the dissolute Yorkshire squire George Osbaldeston could propel the ball. Stumps and shins are splintered, bats knocked from hands. Wicketkeepers and longstops struck in the chest by a ball bumping into the air off a divot are carried away on pallets, and cough up blood for days.

On one occasion George Brown of Brighton, who bowled daisy-cutters at such a ferocious pace his team's wicketkeeper jammed a straw-filled sack up his shirt as protection, was playing at Lord's. He hurled down a lightning delivery that evaded the padded wickie. The fearful fieldsman at fine leg elected not to contort himself into the long-barrier position, but instead to avoid injury by stopping the ball with his coat. The ball burst through the garment and crossed the boundary where it struck a wandering dog, killing it instantly. Even allowing for exaggeration, I think it fair to say that this is not the sort of mayhem associated with Colin Dredge or Roger Binny.

Thus, though it would be amusing to identify the first genuine trundler as Oliver Cromwell – denounced by the Royalist Sir William Dugdale for the cricketing antics of his youth – and speculate on the future Protector bowling military medium of an undeviating line and length, trusting all the while to God and his own piety to do the rest, it would be inaccurate. Instead we must let Thomas Brett and his ilk roll their fizzing 'skippers' at the batsman and await the arrival of the man who, if not quite the father or even the godfather of modern trundling, is certainly the medium-pacers' we-call-him-uncle-but-he's-not-actually-a-relative-he's-just-an-old-and-very-dear-friend-of-mother's.

Edward 'Lumpy' Stevens was born in Surrey in 1735 and began playing professional cricket at the age of twenty-one. A gardener by trade, Lumpy was short, tubby and noted for his good humour and fondness for food. Perhaps it was his pot belly that led to his discovery, for when Stevens bowled he did not stoop low to the ground and roll the ball, he remained upright and lobbed it through the air.

Lumpy's invention – known as length bowling – revolutionised cricket. Bowlers could now spin the ball with their fingers or thumb and deceive the batsman by changing the point at which the ball pitched. Lift, meanwhile, came not just randomly, from hitting potholes or bumps, but from the natural bounce of the ball. Unlike the grubber-merchants, Stevens did not rely on pace but on dogged accuracy (he once won a hundred pounds for his patron, the fourth Earl of Tankerville, by hitting a feather with a ball four times in a row).

Cunning and craft played their parts too. In those days the team that won the toss got to choose whereabouts on the field the stumps would be sited, and Stevens was an expert at selecting the spot that best suited his skills. Normally he chose a strip bisected by the brow of a hill, knowing that when he pitched the ball on the upward slope it would lift, and when on the downward it would 'shoot'.

Like many a later trundler, Lumpy refused to take orders from anyone, even the high and mighty. The Earl of Tankerville was an old-school Georgian aristocrat 'renowned for nothing but cricket-playing, bruising and keeping low company'. His Lordship didn't take kindly to the lower orders answering back and had once been put on trial for thrashing a footman half to death. When it came to cricket, however, even Tankerville did as Lumpy said.

The results of length bowling were far reaching. To tackle the bouncing deliveries of Lumpy and his imitators the once-curved cricket bat became straight and the batsman's stance more upright. The wicket was made taller and narrower too.

Stevens got the better of the best batsmen of his day including the great John Small, the straight-bat stylist from Hampshire and such a devotee of the game that the sign outside his house in Petersfield read:

Here lives John Small,
Makes bat and ball,
Pitches a wicket, plays at cricket
With any man in England.

One memorable tussle between Stevens and the Hampshire gamekeeper led to another far-reaching change to the architecture of the game. Stevens succeeded in bowling Small three times in a single over, but each delivery went through the 'gate' between the two stumps that formed the wicket. As a direct result of Lumpy's ill-luck the third stump was introduced, which to the delight of later generations of purists immediately made slogging across the line far more hazardous.

Stevens played for Chertsey, Surrey, Hambledon, Kent and just about anybody else who would pay him. In 1789 he was selected for an All-England team for what would have been the first ever international cricket tour. Unfortunately the trip to Paris had to be cancelled after revolutionaries stormed the Bastille. Lumpy retired from the game shortly afterwards.

While not a trundler in the truest sense, Lumpy's lack of pace, his accuracy and his ability to 'do a bit off a helpful pitch' are characteristics of the trundler's art that he invented.

As Lumpy's career came to an end pitches started to improve. Flatter wickets, along with better bats, made the bowler's life more difficult and they began to seek ways to even things up. Tom Walker is the man credited with first raising his arm from the perpendicular when delivering the ball, and soon others were following suit, arms gradually rising ever higher until the ball was not being delivered under-arm any more, but round-arm.

In the early 1820s a number of bowlers had begun experimenting with the style, and in 1822 one of them, John Wile of Sutton Valence (who had reportedly learned the art of round-arm from his sister Christina, who had to raise her arm when bowling because of her hooped skirt), had attempted to force legalisation by bowling round-arm against the MCC at Lord's. The umpire no-balled him for throwing and Wile stomped off the field, mounted his horse and galloped out of the history books for ever.

It was around the time of Wile's futile demonstration that the career of the man I think can legitimately be proclaimed the first medium-pacer began. William Lillywhite was just five feet, four inches tall, but compensated for his lack of height by playing in a top hat (the psychological effect on the batsman of imposing headgear is, alas, largely ignored these days, though it was noticeable that Ian Botham's mullet grew ever more refulgent as his pace diminished). Lillywhite was portly with a rubicund face and curly white hair, a combination that along with his tall hat gave him the benign look of the fellow from the Quaker Oats packet. He was born in Sussex in 1792, the son of a brickyard manager. He bowled slow-medium pace with such unfailing accuracy it is said that during a career spanning twenty-six years he delivered only five wides – quite an achievement for a round-armer who always performed in wide cotton braces and a high collar.

The Sussex schemer neither spun the ball nor flighted it, and swing was still something for the future. Bowling round the wicket – so that the movement of his arm naturally carried the ball across the batsman, making his line hard to pick – Lillywhite just nagged away, putting the ball there (he was too accurate to bother with 'thereabouts', though doubtless he could have hit that more nebulous area had he wished to) and trusting the still-uneven wickets of the period to do the rest. It was a simple but highly effective method: in 245 matches Lillywhite took 1570 wickets. Analyses survive for 1355 of these and give him a bowling average of 10.89.

Nicknamed the Nonpareil by his Victorian fan club, Lillywhite's metronomic style was a wonder of the age. At a time when cricketers – like modern-day prizefighters – were expected to drum up business for coming fixtures, Lillywhite merrily played the role of braggart. 'I bowls the best ball in England,' he proclaimed.

Lillywhite was proud of his stratagems, dismissive of the opposition. To hear the great man tell it, it was only his lapses of concentration that allowed batsmen to score at all. 'I suppose,' he once announced airily, 'that if I were to *think* every ball, they should never get a run.' He boasted that he could, at will, pitch the ball on a tiny scrap of paper. When it was put to him that Kent's master strokemaker Fuller Pilch was a match for any bowler, Lillywhite spluttered angrily, 'I wish I had a pound for every time I've taken his wicket.' (By the close of his career he'd have earned £44; Kent paid Pilch £100 a season.)

On another famous occasion, the sporting equivalent of

John Henry's battle with the steam-hammer, Lillywhite engaged in a test against the spring-loaded bowling 'catapult' devised by Pilch's team mate Nicholas Felix. Like the American steel-driving man of legend, Lillywhite emerged victorious over the machine. However, unlike John Henry he did not collapse from his exertions and die.

By 1827 Lillywhite's brilliance and that of his bowling partner, the cunning ('fox-headed' was the term of the day) medium-pacer James Broadridge, had helped make Sussex the best team in England. Their reward was a trial series against an All-England XI. However, the third game in the series was delayed when a number of England's players refused to play against the 'cheating' Lillywhite – the legitimacy of round-arm was still in dispute.

A year later, the MCC finally agreed to legalise Lillywhite's style of delivery. As with any development in the game, from the introduction of the front foot no-ball rule to the arrival of T20, this decision produced a torrent of articles in the press proclaiming the death of all that was noble in the summer game. Notable among them was a piece by the great John Nyren, who announced that, as a result of round-arm bowling, 'the elegant and scientific game of cricket will degenerate into a mere exhibition of rough, coarse horseplay'.

The new rules did not allow the bowler's arm to be raised any higher than his shoulder. Naturally enough, this proved hard to enforce. Many bowlers were accused of bowling with their arms above the horizontal; chief among them William Lillywhite. The belief of some observers was that the Nonpareil did not do this occasionally, or even frequently, but more or less all the time. As a consequence there were those who disregarded Lillywhite's achievements, just as there are those today who refuse to acknowledge the greatness of Muttiah Muralitharan. For such doubters it was not

Lillywhite who was the best bowler of his generation, but another medium-pacer, William Hillyer of Kent. Hillyer was quicker than Lillywhite, though how much quicker is harder to pin down. What is certain is that in 1849 he was the leading wicket-taker in England, with 141.

Whatever the doubts among some of his contemporaries, there are few now who would question the idea that Lillywhite was the pre-eminent bowler of his age. The man himself would not have disagreed, nor, I think, would he have looked too favourably on the trundlers who were to follow in his dainty footsteps. Like many great sportsmen Lillywhite was covetous of his reputation. He had made a handsome living from cricket, dressed in swashbuckling style and took a dim view of younger rivals who had the temerity to challenge him. 'These bowlers might run people out, or stump them out, or catch them out,' he pronounced testily when asked to comment on the coming generation, 'but they can't bowl to bowl anyone out; that bowling isn't nothing but mediocrity.' It was a view that would echo down the centuries from one great veteran bowler to the next. Like Alec Bedser bewailing the fact that modern bowlers pitched too short, or a grumbling F. S. Trueman in the *Test Match Special* commentary box, the Nonpareil simply did not know what was 'going off out there'.

Lillywhite died in 1854. As a consequence, he did not get to denounce a man who was said to be his equal in nagging accuracy. Born in Nottingham in 1842, Alfred Shaw was only a couple of inches taller than the Nonpareil, but further changes in the laws allowed him to bowl with a legitimately high arm. To balance that, Shaw was playing on wickets that were by now flattened with a heavy roller against batsmen who, inspired by W. G. Grace, were playing with fresh and ever greater aggression.

Unlike Lillywhite Shaw varied his pace and flight, and imparted a moderate amount of break on the ball to bring it in to the right-hander off the pitch. Like Lillywhite he bowled at slow-medium pace with extraordinary consistency, pinning batsmen down until, in despair, they gave their wicket away. Shaw rarely bowled a loose ball and seems to have been more or less impossible to score from. During his career he bowled around 16,500 maiden overs and conceded on average a run every four deliveries. He also picked up two thousand wickets at 12.12 runs apiece.

Along with his fellow professionals, the elegant batsman Arthur Shrewsbury and the tearaway paceman John 'Foghorn' Jackson, Shaw made Nottinghamshire the most formidable side in England. Shrewsbury and Shaw were also business partners, and had a strong sense of their own worth. This was an era in which the policy of counties, the MCC and England was to compensate gentlemen amateurs for their loss of earnings and expenses when playing cricket. The result was that 'amateurs' such as W. G. Grace often earned ten times as much from cricket as professional players did.

The situation was ironic, but Shaw for one did not see the funny side. In fact, he was the first top-class trundler to display the militant streak that would become a characteristic of a certain strand of the breed. George Lohmann, S. F. Barnes and Tom Cartwright would all be noted for refusing to toe the establishment line. Jim Cumbes, a medium-pacer with Worcestershire in the seventies, was also a top-class goalkeeper and an active trades unionist. Cumbes is worth bringing up here, if only to recall the time he remonstrated with an Everton team mate who had agreed to spend a summer playing in South Africa by asking, 'What about apartheid?' To which he received the memorable reply: 'All sorted out: three bedrooms with a balcony overlooking the beach.'

Shaw pulled out of an invitation match against the Australians at the Oval because he was only offered ten pounds but wanted twenty, and he and Shrewsbury led the Nottinghamshire professionals in a strike over improved contracts that for a while threatened to destabilise the English game. Eventually the other five professionals caved in and, after a bitter winter, Shaw and Shrewsbury were forced to do the same. The pair's wrangles with the 'gentlemen' continued, however, not least because their organising of lucrative winter tours to Australia with teams of English professionals severely cut into the profits of the amateurs' competing tours. A sharp focus on money would be a feature of Shaw's life, both during his cricket career and after it. His bowling partner 'Foghorn' Jackson took the traditional professional of the day's more laissez-faire approach to fiscal matters, was praised for it by the game's rulers and died penniless in a Liverpool workhouse.

At Melbourne in 1877, Shaw delivered the first ball in Test cricket. Unsurprisingly, it was a dot. W. G. Grace – who dominated batting in the late Victorian era in much the same way Bradman would in the thirties and forties – rated Shaw as 'perhaps the best bowler in England' and made note of the levels of concentration that were necessary when facing him. In all Shaw dismissed the Old Man on forty-nine occasions, more than any other bowler. During a career that ran from 1864 until 1897 the man they called the Emperor of Bowling so dominated the county scene that he spawned a host of imitators, men who bowled at slow-medium pace, pitching the ball just outside off stump to a packed off-side field with the sole intention of keeping the batsmen quiet. Negative bowling became the predominant style in English cricket.

Shaw took the blame for the situation, but that was unfair. His niggardly, conservative bowling had simply awakened something in the national psyche. Despite the hero-worshipping of fast bowlers such as Mynn and, later, Kortright and Tom Richardson, there was something about naked, sweating hostility that did not truly chime with the English. Just as the England selectors would tend to prefer spinners who didn't actually turn the ball all that much to those that did, so true pace would always be regarded on these shores with the ill-disguised suspicion reserved for anything associated with 'temperament'.

If Shaw had been from Kingston, or Perth or Mumbai, it seems unlikely that his influence would have been so pervasive. But he was an Englishman and something in his unfussy, non-fancy style fitted with the national character. From this day forward – no matter what Harold Larwood, Frank Tyson, John Snow or Andrew Flintoff would achieve – military medium would be English cricket's default setting. Like rice pudding or cardigans, it might fall out of fashion occasionally, but when comfort was needed the nation would turn to it again and again and again.

W. G. Grace, the batsman who did most to foster the spirit of negativity in English bowlers, was himself a trundler. In his heyday, the Doctor was rather nippy and took the new ball. As he gradually expanded into the rotund, bearded giant of popular imagination his pace, like his waistline, subsided dramatically until by 1870 he was bowling slow-medium deliveries with a pronounced round-arm action.

Because his slinging style tended to propel the ball naturally towards the off, Grace always bowled round the wicket, bustling in off a short run. By all accounts, WG neither swung the ball nor imparted any kind of cut on it. Instead, like later-period Ian Botham, he seemed to rely

more or less entirely on persistence and force of personality
to get his wickets. According to C. T. Studd, any batsman
facing the Doctor had to be mentally prepared to resist the
great man's positive energy or 'else be hypnotised and
diddled out'.

Leaving aside the psychological, in an attempt to explain
how a medium-pacer of such unexceptional quality accounted
for so many batsmen – for the dobbing Grace took over two
thousand first-class wickets – contemporaries took to praising
WG's mastery of length and line though the fact that so many
of his victims were caught at square leg or midwicket suggests
that his preferred delivery was a long hop: hardly the sort of
thing any expert – then or now – would suggest as a stock ball.
Grace, however, was, as Lord Harris described, a man of
many wiles. Two of the most singular tricks were employed
when bowling. First there was his run to the wicket, which saw
him holding the ball with both hands, high up on his chest.
Other bowlers have attempted to hide their grip on the ball
from the batsman until the last minute by holding it behind
their back or bottom; Grace was the only one who concealed
it in his beard.

WG's second gimmick was more directly effective. After
delivering the ball round the wicket he swerved sharply to
his left so that he finished his follow-through on the off-side.
Thus as the ball arrived at the batsman the umpire's view of
events was completely obstructed by Grace's hulking eighteen-
stone frame.

By all accounts, WG was as fond of appealing as he was
of a roast dinner. His howls for lbw, uttered in his famously
high-pitched West Country burr, were made to umpires who
had only the faintest idea of what had occurred. Swayed
by the ferocity and frequency of Grace's yelping, his absolute
certainty as to the justice of his cause and his gargantuan

reputation, these poor officials frequently raised the finger whether they knew what had happened or not.

Whether he was bowling well or badly, Grace was always easy to hit, reportedly delivering at least one smashable ball every over. Yet he was almost as hard to remove from the attack as he was from the crease, brushing aside a captain's diplomatic call for him to 'take a rest' by calling back, 'I shall have him in an over or two.' In this respect he was a model for many veteran club bowlers, who remain firm in the belief that they could easily dismiss Sachin Tendulkar if only they were allowed three thousand deliveries at the little fellow.

At the Oval in 1882 cricket was changed irrevocably when Australia defeated an England team that included WG by seven runs. The man most responsible for creating the Ashes was my boyhood idol Frederick Spofforth, who returned match figures of 14–90. The Demon had announced his own and his nation's arrival on the international scene at Lord's four years earlier, when he took ten wickets as the tourists skittled out a powerful MCC team for 33 and 19. In the pavilion following the Australians' victory Spofforth apparently bounced around crowing, 'Ain't I the demon? Ain't I the demon?', thus becoming one of a number of sportsmen who invented their own nicknames.

The question that must be asked, though, is how quick was the Demon? WG reckoned him 'terrifically fast' and Neville Cardus likened him to Saul 'breathing out threatenings and slaughter'. But others are altogether less certain. Lord Harris included him in a list of excellent Australian medium-pacers he had faced, and there seems to be a consensus that Spofforth's dramatic run-up and his stupendous delivery-stride pounce, combined with his height, devilish facial hair and diabolic profile, may have served to create more of an impression of speed in the batsman's mind than existed in reality. 'The long arms seemed to be whirling round at much the same speed whether the ball was coming fast or slow,' Ivo Bligh noted.

Tellingly, many of the best wicketkeepers stood up at the stumps when he bowled, in the hope of whipping the bails off. It's unlikely, I think, that AB de Villiers will ever make a stumping off Dale Steyn as Jack Blackham did off Spofforth in 1877. The victim, incidentally, was Alfred Shaw.

Spofforth reportedly cut his pace when he came to England because he found that on the soft, green surfaces it increased his effectiveness, particularly when bowling a ball that jagged back in to the right-hander. He was unfailingly accurate (it was claimed that if you poured water on a six-inch square on a plumb length he would bowl any team in the world out for nothing), possibly mastered in-swing before anyone else (though as we shall see there are other claimants), had well-concealed variations of pace and never tried too hard when conditions were in his favour. Oddly, it seems that the man who inspired my youthful contempt for medium-pacers had in all likelihood been one himself.

Chapter 2

Medium is the Message

Whether or not Spofforth was as quick as his nickname suggested, he undoubtedly had the flamboyance of the true fast bowler. With his angular figure and whirlwind bowling style the Demon caught the imagination of the public and the eye of the satirists. (More than a century later another aggressively moustachioed Antipodean paceman who wasn't quite as speedy as he made out did much the same: Merv Hughes.)

The man who succeeded Spofforth as the greatest bowler on the planet had none of the Demon's febrile flash and did not attract anywhere near the same amount of publicity. Rather, and like many of the greatest trundlers, Charles Turner seemed to fade from popular memory more or less the minute he was gone. Despite his considerable achievements – which surpassed those of Spoff – there were neither cartoons of Turner in *Vanity Fair* nor jokes about him in the music halls.

Turner was as solidly ordinary in appearance as in name. He was of average height, sturdily built with the muscular, almost waistless torso common among nineteenth-century sportsmen. Born in Bathurst, New South Wales, he had a bristling moustache, dark, shrewd eyes, jug ears and a vague facial resemblance to Ian Chappell, Allan Border and quite a few other Australian cricketers you wouldn't care to pick a fight with.

Turner made his debut in Spofforth's final Test, against England at Sydney in 1887, marking the occasion by taking 6–15 as the visitors were dismissed for their lowest-ever total of 45. The newcomer bowled right-hand military medium pace, cutting the ball with fingers and wrist so fiercely it ripped off the wicket and appeared, to mesmerised batsmen, to dart back in at them like a terrier scenting a rat.

Unlike Spofforth, Turner's style was neither dramatic nor classic. He was a country boy and there was something decidedly rustic about his approach. He bounced diligently to the wicket off a long run and delivered the ball chest on, his right arm swinging over at forty-five degrees. His method was his own and it had been learned the hard way. As a teenager Turner had not been good enough even for his grammar school team, and so had taught himself to bowl through long lonely hours in the nets in Bathurst. There Turner would bowl his off-breaker until he had hit the stumps six times on the trot, and then do the same with his straight ball. A perfectionist when most cricketers were still trusting to their physical gifts, he would even water the grass strip so that he could perfect his accuracy on the sort of rain-affected wickets that were then commonplace, especially in England.

Despite his lack of lithe elegance, pyrotechnics or sideways-on orthodoxy, Turner was brutally effective. He snapped up twenty-nine wickets in his opening three Tests and during 1887–8 he became the first – and so far only – bowler to take a hundred first-class wickets in an Australian season.

Off the back of this extraordinary achievement, Turner was selected to tour England with Percy McDonnell's side.

The 1888 Australians were a poor team handicapped by the withdrawal of one outstanding bowler, the off-spinner George Giffen, and the temporary loss to smallpox of Sammy Jones, the finest Antipodean strokemaker of his time, a few weeks after they arrived in Britain. Only one batsman averaged over twenty and *Wisden* caustically dismissed the third best bowler in the team, leg-spinner Harry Trott, as 'too slow to trouble the better batsmen'.

Another great trundler was with the party but, sadly, Harry Boyle's best days were behind him. A tall, burly right-arm medium-pacer who specialised in breaking the ball away from the right-hander, Boyle had grown up in Victoria in the pleasantly named settlement of Peg Leg Gully. A teenage prodigy, he played for his state when he was just seventeen and astounded the crowd at Melbourne in 1873 by bowling W. G. Grace – a feat which up to that point most Australians had considered physically impossible.

In 1878 Boyle had gone to England with the Australians as an understudy to Frank Allan, but he proved to be far more dangerous in English conditions than he was back home and was soon promoted to opening the bowling with Spofforth. In the game against the MCC in which the Demon quite literally made his name, Boyle took 8–17. Not that anyone noticed, with all the furore surrounding Spoff.

On the 1882 tour Boyle was at his finest, taking 144 wickets in eleven-a-side matches and topping the bowling averages ahead of the Demon. In Australia's historic win at the Oval that year, it was Boyle who took the final English wicket. He was back again in 1884, but the summer was hotter and drier than those he was used to and though he got his best Test figures – 6–42 in the Manchester Test – his overall return of 67 was poor. On that same tour Spofforth took 207 first-class wickets.

Boyle had the type of bushy beard that is sometimes called a Lyster, and favoured the sort of striped pillbox hats that give Victorian cricket teams a touch of the chain gang. He was a notoriously courageous fielder at silly mid-on and the sort of fierce competitor Australia would come to be noted for. One contemporary said of Boyle that 'he played the game right up to the handle'. Unfortunately, by 1888 he only had one hand left on the handle and barely featured.

Luckily for McDonnell, his two top bowlers were very good indeed. Alongside Turner was another medium-pacer, Jack Ferris. Ferris was the first in a line of Australian left-arm seam bowlers that runs through the decades via Bill Johnston and Alan Davidson all the way to the explosively erratic Mitchell Johnson, and in terms of numbers and quality so far eclipses that of any other nation as to be almost freakish. Ferris was implacably accurate, had a variation of pace that was on the subtle side and moved the ball both ways off the pitch. On good wickets he was said to be Turner's superior, but in the days of uncovered pitches, in the drizzle of England and an Australia then labouring under the damp effects of La Niña, those were few and far between.

Turner and Ferris have some claim to being the best opening bowlers ever to appear for an Australian touring side – certainly their figures eclipse those of any before or since. On that tour Turner took five wickets in an innings on thirty occasions and ten in a match a dozen times; his total of first-class wickets, 283, was then a record for an English season and has only been surpassed three times since. Ferris, meanwhile, finished the tour just one short of a double century of victims.

Perhaps the most astonishing thing to modern eyes, however, is not the quality of Turner and Ferris's bowling, but the quantity of it. During the course of the twenty-week tour

Turner bowled more than 1700 overs, Ferris a little under 1500. Relishing the wet wickets of England the pair destroyed several county sides in early summer and then ripped through the English batting in the first Test match at Lord's, dismissing a team that included W. G. Grace and Bobby Abel for 53 and 62. Against an England XI at Hastings, Turner took seventeen wickets in the match, fourteen of them clean bowled and two lbw.

Unwilling to allow such mayhem as the province of the moderate medium-pacer, some writers have claimed that Turner was actually rather quick. In this case, there is hard evidence to refute them as Turner was the subject of time trials at the Woolwich Arsenal, where his pace was measured at just 55mph – the speed of a quick spinner. Even allowing for primitive equipment, which had been designed to measure the velocity of bullets and artillery shells, this does not suggest him as a rival to Shoaib Akhtar.

Wicketkeepers stood up to Turner: in his final Test he would have England's notoriously wayward all-rounder Bobby Peel stumped twice for a pair. If he was nicknamed 'The Terror' it was a testament to his ability to terrorise batsmen psychologically rather than physically. Turner cut the ball in viciously from the off and swung it away through the air. It was said that in damp conditions he could be played only 'by guesswork, or by God'.

On the 1890 tour Turner and Ferris again performed wonders, taking 430 wickets between them and receiving just as little support from the other Australian bowlers – who managed 61 between them – as two years previously. The right-hand/left-hand combination was particularly effective, as both men were able to bowl into the other's footmarks. Since they often bowled unchanged through entire innings, those were often considerable potholes. Confronted by the pair on moist green pitches many English batsmen reacted with the same type of eyes-closed-and-prod-forward panic their successors would deploy against Saeed Ajmal.

In some respects Turner was lucky on those first two tours, as both were in exceptionally wet summers even by English standards. When he returned again in 1893 the weather was better, the pitches firmer and he was altogether less of a menace, though he still finished top of the Australian first-class bowling averages with 148 wickets at 13.63.

Like Boyle and a couple of other Australian seamers of later vintage, Bob Massie and Terry Alderman, Turner some-times seems like a man born in the wrong country. Had his parents been living in Derbyshire when he arrived there's no telling how many wickets he might have taken, or how long his career would have lasted.

But, unfortunately for Turner, he was an Australian and the climatic conditions in his own country were on the turn. La Niña had whistled off never, apparently, to return. The weather was now almost exclusively hot and dry, the batting tracks increasingly hard, fast and true. In the 1888–9 season Turner took just twenty-nine wickets, the following season fewer still. As he would later note, the meteorological changes in Australia during the later years of the nineteenth century would alter the country's wickets – and therefore its bowlers – irrevocably. In the twentieth century Australia's star per-formers with the ball would almost exclusively be fast bowlers and leg-spinners.

The Australian selectors noted Turner's lack of effective-ness on home soil. During the 1894–5 series he was dropped, though not before he caused havoc on a sticky wicket at Sydney and became in the process the first Australian to take one hundred Test wickets (he had reached his half-century of victims in an amazing six matches). Turner continued to play first-class cricket for a couple more years, but with ever-diminishing effect.

He was never recalled by his country. Some have suggested that this was down less to any erosion of his talents than to a falling-out with two members of the selection committee, George Giffen and Jack Blackham. It is alleged that Turner, a generally quiet and dignified man, had rebuked the pair after an incident on a train journey in England in 1893 which had left 'the carriage they were travelling in splattered with blood'.

Controversial or not, it was an underwhelming end to an extraordinary burst of brilliance. In 155 first-class matches the trundling Terror took 993 wickets, an incredible average of 6.4 per game, and bagged an even more remarkable thirty-five ten-wicket match hauls. Those who played against him, particularly in England, held him in the highest regard. Sir Stanley Jackson considered him the finest medium-paced bowler he ever played against, and – as we shall see – that was a considerable number; W. G. Grace thought his zip off the wicket was surpassed only by that of George Freeman, while Pelham Warner rated him as one of the twenty-five greatest bowlers of all time.

After retirement Turner worked in banking, but doesn't seem to have had the same stamina off the field as he had on it and never really settled to anything. He flitted from job to job and from wife to wife, frittered away a considerable benefit awarded to him by New South Wales and died of senile decay, aged eighty-one, in 1944.

Turner's main rival as the supreme trundler of the late Victorian era also met with a tragic end. George Lohmann, the handsome Anglo-German professional from Surrey, whose broad shoulders, blue eyes, flaxen moustache and general air of clean-limbed manliness often seemed to give the cricket writers of the day a case of the vapours, would be dead of tuberculosis before he was forty.

Born in Kensington, west London, Lohmann – who according to an Edwardian rhyme was 'neither fast nor slow man' – was the son of a stockbroker's clerk. He was raised in a lower-middle-class household and started playing on Wandsworth Common for a church social group. Here, as a nineteen-year-old, he was spotted by Surrey, who signed him on professional terms in 1884.

Lohmann was an all-rounder who combined dash with imposing height. His athletic figure, good looks and easy charm made him a hero to small boys of all ages. The future England captain and MCC top dog Pelham Warner was one of the young fellows who had watched Lohmann at the Oval and never quite lost the misty glow of seeing that 'handsome man very much of the Saxon-type'. Lohmann was 'a dashing batsman who did not care much about runs unless they were needed', Warner (who as an amateur approved of such carelessness) wrote approvingly, and a brilliant fielder: his catch to dismiss A. C. Bannerman of Australia at the Oval in 1888 was described by the normally diffident *Wisden* as 'miraculous'.

It was his bowling, though, that really caught the eye. His short, easy run-up was not particularly noteworthy, while his action – Warner noted – 'had a suspicion of strain about it', yet when he let go of the ball mayhem invariably ensued. Lohmann was on the slower side of medium; he had great control, clever variations of pace and cut the ball both ways off the pitch. He was a master of flight ('The flightiest bowler I ever saw,' Warner said, suggesting that this trundler may even have 'looped' the ball like a spinner), often fooling the batsmen with a slower delivery that seemed destined to be a long hop, but turned out to be a yorker. He bowled a quick off-break and the occasional faster ball that went away 'with the arm'. On other occasions he deceived the batsman with a ball that looked like it was spun but in fact went straight on. Like Turner, he was at his most lethal on damp wickets, greeting the green grass with the joy of a young bullock let out onto fresh pasture.

Again like Turner, Lohmann was a bowler who unnerved opponents. C. B. Fry commented: 'He was what I call a very hostile bowler; he made one feel he was one's deadly enemy, and he used to put many batsmen off their strokes by his masterful and confident manner with the ball.' When Fry describes Lohmann as hostile he is referring to his attitude of mind. I imagine the Surrey medium-pacer as an early, and much slower, version of Glenn McGrath, a bowler who, at least it seemed to me, had something in his bearing and personality that always made a batsman treat him as if he was much quicker than he actually was.

Lohmann's own views on bowling were set down for *Wisden* around the time that, up in Leeds, George Hirst was mastering swing. The first principles of bowling, Lohmann said, were deception in delivery, variety in method and attack on the batsman at every point.

This attitude of all-out aggression – one Lohmann shared with WG, Turner and S. F. Barnes – is perhaps indicative of the style of the early trundlers. They were not men designed to block up one end while someone else did the damage at the other. They weren't there merely to keep the opposition quiet until the wicket was sufficiently worn to take spin, or the next new ball became available for the quicks. Lohmann and Turner were out-and-out strike bowlers, as unhindered by their lack of raw speed as Shane Warne or Muttiah Muralitharan.

Between 1886 and 1892 Lohmann took more than 150 wickets each season for Surrey – and more than two hundred in three of them. He was just as effective in international cricket. Indeed, he has the best strike rate and the lowest average of any Test bowler in history.

During Lord Hawke's tour of South Africa in 1895–6, bowling on matting wickets that suited his style perfectly, Lohmann picked up 157 wickets at just over six runs each, and in the three Test matches devastated the local batting with thirty-five wickets at just 5.8 runs apiece. In one astonishing game at Port Elizabeth Lohmann finished with a match tally of 15–45, having taken 8–7 in the home team's second innings.

It has to be admitted that, in those days, South Africa were more or less what Bangladesh are today. Arguably worse – the matches between England and South Africa on this tour were only made into Test matches retrospectively. Yet Lohmann was no bad-track bully boy. His record against Australia proves it. The seventy-seven wickets he took against the old enemy cost less than thirteen runs apiece – cheaper even than those of S. F. Barnes. Nobody has a better record against Australia than George Lohmann.

And his record is all the more astonishing considering that for a large chunk of his career he was suffering from the debilitating lung disease that would kill him.

Lohmann was an easy-going man, but he was no mug. He may have looked like a Saxon aristocrat and batted like a gentleman, but he was a die-hard professional and knew his own worth. Like Alfred Shaw before him, Lohmann caused a furore when he went on strike. The Surrey man refused to play in the Oval Test of 1886 because the match fee for professionals had remained unchanged for several seasons at ten pounds, while the amateurs' expenses increased annually.

The patrician Warner would later claim that Lohmann – whom he praised, somewhat patronisingly, for his good manners and intelligence – had been 'ill-advised' by those around him over the strike. However, two seasons later the match fee for pros was doubled, which suggests that, badly conceived or not, Lohmann's protest had had some effect.

From 1892 onwards Lohmann was increasingly weakened by ill health. He was advised to emigrate to South Africa where the warmer, dryer climate would benefit his lungs. If it did so the benefits were transient: Lohmann died in Matjiesfontein in 1901. He was thirty-six.

By all accounts Lohmann loved cricket in general and bowling in particular. 'His bowling was a constant source of joy to him; he simply revelled in his art,' Warner wrote. A polite, intelligent man, the great trundler seems to have been popular with just about everybody who encountered him. When he died Surrey County Cricket Club, ignoring the difficulties created by the on-going Boer War, immediately had a marble memorial erected over his grave.

Lohmann was undoubtedly the best English medium-pacer of his generation. Indeed C. B. Fry, who took a dim view of the truculent Barnes and therefore ruled him out of consideration, as some of his predecessors had the over-arming Lillywhite, considered him the best such bowler England ever produced, superior even to Maurice Tate and Alec Bedser. I might add that Fry was rather free with this sort of compliment and also awarded the title of best ever medium-pacer to Charles Turner, adding that the only better English bowler he had seen was ... J. T. Hearne.

Since Pelham Warner described Hearne as the 'beau-ideal of a medium-paced right-hand bowler' we ought to take a look at him too.

Jack Hearne was the nephew of George and Tom Hearne (the latter one of the finest all-rounders of the 1870s), cousin of Alec Hearne and the brother of Walter Hearne, a fine bowler whose career was ended prematurely by injury. Old Jack sometimes also claimed that the later Middlesex leg-spinner J. W. 'Young Jack' Hearne was a distant nephew, but only when he was taking wickets.

Hearne was born in Chalfont St Giles in Buckinghamshire, and was twenty-three years old and working as a school groundsman when, in June 1890, he was summoned to Lord's to play against Nottinghamshire. Putting aside the mower, he raced down to London, took 6–62 in the first innings and his career was made.

Over the next twenty years Hearne took wickets with the same steady rhythm with which he bowled. He topped the averages five times, passed a hundred wickets on fifteen occasions and two hundred three times. In his best season, 1896, he dismissed 257 batsmen, the tenth highest number in history. That same year Hearne picked up 9–73 against the Australians playing for MCC and Ground, and further bamboozled the visitors later in the summer when selected for the South, taking 6 for 8. Three years later – when many felt Old Jack was burned out with exhaustion – he battered the Baggy Greens all over again, taking a hat-trick at Headingley in which he accounted for Monty Noble and Sid Gregory, caught in the slips off his faster 'arm' ball and then clean bowled Clem Hill with an off-cutter that apparently 'snapped like a crocodile'.

In all, Hearne took 3061 first-class wickets, the best performance ever by a non-spinner. Bowling at the same sort of slow-medium pace favoured by Lohmann, Old Jack came in at a leisurely trot. His sideways-on action was smooth and easy, his arm high. Like the great Lohmann his length was never less than perfect. He nipped the ball in to the batsman off the wicket, and occasionally ran one away from him with the arm. Like Turner he had a prodigious appetite for work, which was just as well as he was frequently the single professional in a rather aristocratic Middlesex team and thus was expected to shoulder the burden of manual labour – especially late on hot afternoons – rather more than would have been the case elsewhere. In the long dry summer of 1896 the uncomplaining Hearne sent down over ten thousand deliveries. Little wonder that in photos he sometimes looks a little hunched.

Unlike Turner and Lohmann, however, Hearne did not get dramatic movement with the ball (it was said that part of the reason for his success was that he never did enough to actually beat the bat, only to clip it – moderate in all things was Old Jack), nor was he particularly reliant on helpful surfaces, though he was probably at his most dangerous on the sort of parched and crumbling pitches usually favoured by spinners. On the hard, dry wickets that were so often the graveyard of the dobber, Hearne was masterful. Never as aggressive as Lohmann or Barnes, a backs-to-the-wall situation suited him well. Bowling to a defensive off-side field, with just long-on and mid-on to leg, torturously accurate, varying his line, length and pace minutely yet crucially, he pecked away at the batsmen for ball after ball, gradually bleeding the concentration from them. It was a simple method but it required craft, patience and stamina, and could only be thwarted by the sort of bloody-minded approach many late Victorian and Edwardian batsmen couldn't be bothered with.

'He was a great believer in slight variations of pace,' Warner later noted, and took many wickets with balls that were just fractionally slower or quicker than the one that preceded them. 'It is the little difference that often does so much,' Hearne wrote, adding: 'Change of pace is obtained at the moment of releasing the ball, a slower ball leaving the hand sooner than a faster ball, but much more upon the degree of spin imparted at the time of delivery.'

This is an intriguing passage, one of those that at first appears to unravel a mystery, but which – on closer inspection – actually does quite the opposite. After all, spin would have no effect on the ball's speed through the air, while letting the ball go earlier wouldn't make it move any slower, only land further down the pitch than the ball released later on. Hearne was a master of the disguised delivery and he seems to have sent down another one here: it looks like a wicket-taker, but is in fact a half-volley.

Like Lillywhite and Barnes, Old Jack had longevity. Apparently worn to a nubbin by 1899, he got his second wind as the century turned and, though his Test career was over, went on playing for Middlesex and taking wickets until the start of the Great War. He played his last first-class match in 1923. He became the first professional ever to be elected to the Middlesex committee, served on it for many years and was later awarded a bonus in lieu of benefit of five hundred pounds. Like Barkis, that good-hearted servant from Dickens, he was willing. Everybody liked him.

Chapter 3

Boys Start Swinging

When I was a boy, if somebody tried to prove a point by saying, 'All the scientists agree that it is true,' my father would often remark, 'Yes, but scientists also say that a cricket ball can't swing.' Leaving aside the fact that Hitler used to make a similar retort about scientists saying that it was impossible for a bumblebee to fly, my father was correct. The swinging of the cricket ball is such a great mystery that some scientists did indeed deny its very possibility until quite recently.

Nowadays quite the opposite is true. Scientists these days can't get enough of swing. On the internet there's a seemingly endless procession of physicists eager to explain how swing works or – more often – to chuckle at the utter ludicrousness of the last physicist's discourse on the topic. Whether any of it actually adds anything to what cricketers had already figured out is another matter entirely. As Bob Dylan observed, you don't need to be a weatherman to know which way the wind blows.

In the mythology of Yorkshire cricket the great gift of swing bowling is brought to humanity by a single, brilliant man, George Herbert Hirst, who in a moment that is the

Huddersfield and District equivalent to the time when Robert Johnson sold his soul to the devil in order to more or less invent Delta blues, went to Leeds for a few months in the winter of 1901 and came back with a sly grin on his jovial, round face and a delivery the like of which the world had never seen – the in-swinger.

Sadly the truth is not quite as mysterious or magical as that. Hirst did not invent swing bowling, he just popularised it, and for that he has reasonable grounds to claim, as *Wisden* once suggested, to be 'the father of all modern seam and swing bowling'. Like the steam locomotive at the start of the nineteenth century, swing was something cricketers all over the world had been tinkering with as Queen Victoria's reign entered its final years. Hirst is the George Stephenson of the style: he may not actually have invented it, but he was its public face. Without him it is unlikely it would have become quite so popular quite so quickly.

The left-handed under-armer Noah Mann of Hambledon was probably the first bowler whose ability to swing the ball was noted by observers. Mann, a short, swarthy and athletic chap who used to ride twenty miles just to get to the eighteenth-century equivalent of evening nets, began his first-class career in 1777. As a batsman he was noted for his big hitting (he ran a ten off one mighty straight drive), as a fielder for his speed across the ground. As for his bowling, well, John Nyren says of his team mate, 'his merit consisted in him giving a curve to the ball the whole way'.

Which way the ball curved – in or out – Nyren does not bother to say. We might guess that since Mann was left-handed he perhaps raised his hand from the vertical when he bowled and got some sort of movement in to the batsman 'with the arm'. Whatever, Mann's career was cut short when, at the age of thirty-three and after a heavy night of drinking, he fell asleep in front of the fire at the Half Moon Inn in Northchapel, Sussex, caught alight and burned to death. His son, Noah Mann junior, became an umpire and featured earlier in our story, no-balling the radical round-armer John Wiles.

Another man talked of as the originator of swing – at least by that great historian of cricket's early years, H. S. Altham – is the Kentishman Edmund Hinkly. Hinkly was born in 1817 and didn't begin his first-class career until nearly thirty. A round-armer, Hinkly, like many of the early swingers, delivered the ball with his left hand. Playing for Kent at Lord's in 1848 he became the first man ever to take ten wickets in an innings in a first-class eleven-a-side match, when he skittled out an England XI. After that triumph Hinkly's first-class appearances were sporadic, largely because he seems to have gone and played wherever and for whoever paid him most. Altham comments somewhat loftily that the bowler 'disappeared having taken professional terms up North', a phrase that suggests he disappeared into the Dark Age mist somewhere above the Watford Gap and was never heard from again. In fact, while Hinkly did play a season as a professional with 'the Northumberland Club' he also turned out for sides in South Wales, Cumbria, Lincolnshire, the East and West Midlands, Merseyside and Yorkshire as well as in Surrey and Wiltshire. Beyond Altham's comments about Hinkly being a master of the swerving ball, little more is known about his style.

Pelham Warner mentions three English bowlers whose mastery of swing pre-dated that of Hirst: John Rawlin of Middlesex, Walter Wright of Kent and William Collins of Middlesex. The latter two were, like Hirst and Mann, left-handed.

Rawlin was a Yorkshireman born in the splendidly named village of Greasbrough, near Rotherham, and after a couple of dozen games for his home county joined Middlesex, where he often bowled in tandem with Old Jack Hearne. A heavy-jowled man with a drooping moustache, Rawlin made over three hundred appearances for Middlesex, taking 811 wickets. His obituary in *Wisden* mentions his ability to move the ball off the wicket, but says nothing about swerve.

William Collins is an even more singular choice. Nick-named 'Colenso', possibly after a town in South Africa that would later be the scene of a Boer War battle, Collins played just seven games for Middlesex in the 1880s, but during his time at Oxford had sufficiently impressed various influential bluebloods, including 'Bun' Thornton, to ensure regular matches for the MCC and an assortment of invitation elevens such as that of Lord Londesborough, for whom he played against the Australians at Scarborough. Collins was a writer and apparently an agreeable and amusing chap, but about his bowling little is known beyond Warner's endorsement and the comment of Alexander Webbe, a Middlesex team mate, who said that Collins' deliveries were quick and 'came a lot with the arm'.

Walter Wright is worthy of more attention since W. G. Grace, for one, considered him the originator of swing bowling. Wright was born in Nottinghamshire and started out in life with an altogether more fitting name for a man of his profession: Walter Shooter. He began his career playing for the county of his birth, bowling left-arm round the wicket at a lively speed with appreciable in-swing to the right-hander. Like many seamers who were to follow him Wright was at his most effective with the new ball and once skittled out six Yorkshire batsmen for just ten runs with the fresh cherry at Trent Bridge.

In 1880 Wright was engaged to play for a touring team of Gentlemen of Canada after they had lost their star player in unusual circumstances – he had been arrested by military police as a deserter. In his first game as an honorary Canadian (and 'gentleman') Wright took fourteen wickets, but he left the tour shortly afterwards in a dispute over payments.

Six years later another wrangle over money saw the medium-pacer leave Nottinghamshire for Kent. Here he stayed for twelve productive years, taking 725 wickets at fewer than twenty each. He was especially effective when opening the bowling with another left-arm trundler, 'Nutty' Martin, and few visitors relished facing them, particularly at the Moat Ground in Maidstone, where the slope across the pitch would have delighted Lumpy Stevens and helped Wright's swing run 'down the hill'.

A fine all-round sportsman, Wright had been rated the second-fastest sprinter in the world at the start of the 1880s, played amateur football to a high level and went on to coach Reading FC. He retired from first-class cricket in 1899, aged forty-five. That Hirst would have encountered him on the county circuit seems beyond dispute.

It is often said that, prior to Hirst, bowlers had *swerved* the ball – movement through the air that was a gentle by-product either of spin or the angle of the bowler's arm. Hirst, however, actually swung the ball. More importantly, he swung it late, drawing the batsman into a stroke before the ball moved. It's possible that the bowlers mentioned above all fell into the swerver category. Three others who certainly didn't were an Australian (Monty Noble), an Australian-Englishman (Albert Trott) and an American (Bart King).

Trott and King had both grown up playing baseball (almost as popular as cricket in late-nineteenth-century Australia; Monty Noble played too) and their knowledge of how to swing the ball, or at the very least the possibility of swinging it, seems to have come from pitching. The influence of the United States on cricket is not widely heralded, but it ought to be in this case. In baseball the curveball – a pitch that dives as it approaches the batter – had first appeared around 1870, through the efforts of either Fred Goldsmith or Candy Cummings. Over the next decade its use became widespread, despite a predictable outcry from the guardians of good sportsmanship that it should be banned because it was deceitful, shifty and probably foreign.

The screwball, which swings (or 'fades') in to the right-handed batter, seems to have been introduced into the major leagues by Christy Mathewson in around 1900. While the curveball is held 'like a glass', the screwball is held in much the same way as a seam bowler grips the ball, with the index and second finger down the centre. Mathewson made his name playing in the National League for the New York Giants (later to become the San Francisco Giants), but he was a big-name pitcher in Pennsylvanian college baseball before he moved east. Pennsylvania was where Bart King played baseball and later cricket.

Did Mathewson's in-swinging delivery influence King? We shall, as they say, never know. What is for sure is that in baseball, as in cricket, there was a certain reluctance among the scientific community to believe that a ball really could swing in the air. Many physicists claimed that the apparent curve of the ball was merely an optical illusion created by it spinning as it travelled. While there is some evidence that a fraction of the curve may indeed be caused by some eye-to-brain shenanigans, most of it really does happen. Or, as one baseball pitcher put it, 'Get one of these guys to stand sixty feet away from me behind a tree and I'll slap him in the head with my optical illusion.' Such a pleasing scenario wasn't required, however, and in 1949 wind-tunnel tests carried out by aeronautic specialists from Sikorsky, the helicopter manufacturer, finally confirmed what the players had always known – that the ball did swing.

The dip of the curveball is created by top-spin (in cricket a similar dip seems to be the province of leg-spinners) and the technique was apparently appropriated by both King and Trott, each of whom could, if we are to believe contemporary accounts, bowl a ball that dipped late in its flight. According to Warner such deliveries 'dropped in the air just as the batsman was about to play it', leading to a number of lbw decisions against players who had gone to drive what they thought was a full toss, only to be struck on the foot as it suddenly turned into a yorker.

Is such a delivery possible? No cricket fan or cricketer I have talked to has ever witnessed such a thing. In baseball it occurs, but in that sport the pitcher delivers the ball in roughly a straight line and over a considerably longer distance, allowing room for it to dip. In cricket the bowler is aiming down at the ground rather than at the area between the batter's shoulder and waist. This seems to me to make it more or less impossible to get a cricket ball to dip in flight. And yet Warner and others attest to both Trott and King bowling such a delivery. Perhaps this *was* an optical illusion.

King toured England with the Philadelphians three times, in 1897, 1903 and 1908 (when he was captain). Over six feet tall and slim, with broad shoulders and narrow hips, the American bowled with a high, classical action and created a sensation on that first tour when he was instrumental in the visitors' eight-wicket victory over a full-strength Sussex team. In the first innings King took 7–13, his victims including the great K. S. Ranjitsinhji for a first-ball duck. In the second innings he finished with 6–102. The Sussex players were bamboozled by King's 'dipping' ball, but were largely undone by what the American considered his most devastating weapon, a well-disguised in-swinger (which King called 'the angler') used only sparingly to prevent opposition batsmen from working it out. His stock ball was one that went away 'with the arm'.

On his three tours of the British Isles King, whose deadpan sense of humour led to him being described as the Bob Hope of cricket, was never less than effective. In 1903 he took 9–62 against Lancashire and in his final tour enjoyed a fine day against Middlesex at Lord's, finishing with 6–30. He then travelled up to the Midlands, where atmospheric conditions evidently suited him as he took 12–116 against Derbyshire and 14–130 against Nottinghamshire. That season he finished with eighty-seven first-class wickets at eleven runs each, better figures than any English bowler. That King was playing in a team of amateurs with limited first-class experience adds to the value of the figures. Little wonder that C. B. Fry and Plum Warner among others regarded him as one of the greatest bowlers of his era. Warner in particular thought highly of the American, not only for his skill but for his fierce determination and charisma – 'He had that electric quality' – and said that had King been English or Australian he would have been tremendously famous.

King played his cricket in Philadelphia, where the club fixtures in the decades leading up to the start of the Great War were said to be of Minor Counties standard. During that period a representative eleven, the Gentlemen of Philadelphia with King very much to the fore, defeated the Australians twice and always did well against touring English sides. During his career the greatest of all US cricketers took 2088 wickets at an average of 10.47.

*

Albert Trott was a mercurial all-rounder who at his peak was arguably the best cricketer on the planet. Trott was born in Willesden, brought up in Australia and played Test cricket for both England and Australia. Nowadays he is perhaps best remembered for his extraordinary feat of hitting the ball over the roof of the pavilion at Lord's. (He also hit the ball clean out of Trent Bridge, damaging the wheels of a passing carriage.)

Trott bowled slow-medium pace with a slingy round-arm action. Like King, it is said he learned to swing the ball while playing baseball as a young man. Later he would practise moving the ball through the air by placing a box in front of the stumps and trying to swerve the ball around it. Like King his deliveries were reputed not only to swing laterally (in Trott's case, away from the right-hander) but also to dip in flight.

It was said of Trott that, 'If you could get him to bowl at the wicket on a bowler's pitch he was virtually unplayable.' The 'if' is indicative of his character. The great all-rounder was an eccentric and far more attracted to the impossible than the probable, or the likely. The drive over the pavilion was the apotheosis of his style: he spent the rest of his life attempting to do something similarly sensational, with increasingly disastrous consequences.

Trott was the star of the 1894–5 Australian Test team, but for some reason – perhaps relating to his personality – was not selected to tour England in 1896. Upset by the slight, he came to Britain anyway, got a place on the MCC ground staff, qualified by residency for Middlesex and, during the seasons of 1898, 1899 and 1900, was widely regarded as the best all-rounder in England.

As a bowler he was considered resourceful enough to be dangerous in any conditions. Indeed many felt that, true to his paradoxical nature, Trott was at his best when conditions most suited batting, varying his pace and length, and employing psychological tricks to unsettle opponents.

Whatever the conditions, captaining the mercurial Anglo-Aussie was never easy. As Warner noted: 'He was the sort of bowler who required supervision, for if he was left to himself he might work a theory to death and lose a match in four overs.' On sticky wickets he would often dispense with swerve and break, and instead loft up full tosses in an attempt to get the batsman caught in the deep.

S. F. Barnes, as we shall see, was a rebellious character, and so was Trott, though in a manner less stern and forbidding. At the height of his renown he put his name to a weekly newspaper column without bothering to write a word of it. One of these columns referred to the Middlesex team's fondness for drinking during matches, claiming that in one season 'the beer gave out before lunch on Whit Monday'. The committee were not amused by this slur on the club's reputation. Trott was brought before them at Lord's and asked to explain himself by Sir Francis Lacey, the secretary. In the style of a modern-day footballer Trott denied knowing anything about the words that had appeared under his byline, saying, 'I never wrote it. I know nothing about it, sir,' to which Sir Francis responded kindly, 'Then you must ask your friend, whoever he may be, to be more accurate in future.'

The more obvious tactics of the game may have failed to appeal to Trott, but he continued to do extraordinary things, including once taking four wickets in four balls and a hat-trick in the same innings. Even at his peak, though, Trott had the heavy-jowled, bulbous-nosed, bleary-eyed look of the seasoned boozer. After retiring from the game he became an umpire, but drinking took its toll physically and financially. In

1914 he wrote a note bequeathing four pounds in cash and his wardrobe to the landlady of his rooms in north London, then took a pistol and shot himself.

The bowler Trott hit over the pavilion at Lord's was Monty Noble, a man who, like Trott, was credited with introducing swing into Australian bowling. Noble's career had begun in the year after Trott migrated back to England, and he was soon considered by many the best exponent of right-arm medium-pace bowling in the country, swinging the ball through the air as well as cutting it nastily off the pitch. In the second Test against Archie MacLaren's England team in 1902, Noble took thirteen wickets and – as we shall see later – the style of some of his deliveries had a profound effect on the greatest of all trundlers.

Noble and George Hirst crossed paths for the first time when A. E. Stoddart's team toured Australia in 1897–8. It was not a happy tour for Hirst; he batted poorly and his bowling made little impact on the flat Australian pitches. In those days the Yorkshireman was a quickish left-armer whose pace had gradually slowed as his batting improved. Wilfred Rhodes, his Kirkheaton, Yorkshire and England team mate, said the Hirst of those early years was simply a 'straight up-and-downer'.

It has been said that until the epiphany of 1901 Hirst was little more than a bread-and-butter county bowler. Given that between 1891 and the close of the 1900 season he took 770 wickets (including a haul of 150 in 1895), we might reasonably say that if that is bread and butter, then we'd hate to see how rich the cake was. However, the truth was that on good batting wickets the simple approach of his early years was not enough. One of the shrewdest professionals of his or any other era, Hirst would surely have recognised that, and in

Wright, Noble, King and Trott he may have caught a glimpse of the way forward.

Quite what happened in the winter of 1901 is not recorded. Hirst's biographer, A. A. Thomson, says simply that over that close season he developed 'his remarkable ability to swerve the ball in the air' and leaves it at that. Presumably Hirst had been experimenting with swing as Trott – and later S. F. Barnes – did. Whatever way he went about perfecting this new skill, when he unleashed the booming in-swinger that would become his trademark it created the same sort of sensation that B. J. T. Bosanquet's googly would a few years later.

Hirst came in on a long, rhythmic run-up and, in the right atmospheric conditions – a heavy atmosphere coupled with a wind blowing diagonally across the wicket from behind the bowler – his deliveries, bowled over the wicket with a loose easy action, his arm at forty-five degrees, would appear to the right-hander to be angling straight across him and heading in the direction of gully, before suddenly swooping inexplicably in at him. Sammy Woods, the Australia and Somerset all-rounder, memorably summed up the feelings of batsmen across England in the summer of 1901 when he exclaimed, 'How the devil can you play a ball that comes at you like a hard throw-in from cover point?'

In his first season after mastering the mysterious art Hirst took 183 wickets at 16.38 each, with deliveries so extraordinary that *Wisden* described them as 'terrific'. (Hirst was not the only successful left-arm trundler that season. Lancashire's Jack Sharp, a fine all-round sportsman who played eleven seasons for Everton and won international caps for England at cricket and football, also took over a hundred wickets, as did Sam Hargreave, a Derek Underwood-style medium-paced spinner from Warwickshire, and the South African

Charlie Llewellyn of Hampshire, one of the first great over-seas exports to play in county cricket. Llewellyn bowled slow-medium pace, mixing up seam with spin and the occasional chinaman. He played fifteen Tests for his country, a singular feat since his mother was black. It would be eighty years until another non-white player was selected for South Africa.)

In the twelve seasons following the revelation Hirst only once took less than a hundred wickets (and that mainly because a thigh injury caused him to miss several matches), topping two hundred on one occasion and 150 three times.

According to Pelham Warner, 'on certain days Hirst's fast left-handers would curl so much that he could place five, and on occasion six fieldsmen on the on-side'. A typical Hirst field when conditions were in his favour would feature a leg slip, three short legs, mid-on and long leg. Surprisingly to modern eyes, he seems to have dispensed with conventional slip fielders altogether. Presumably because he tended to swing the ball in towards leg stump, wicketkeepers stood back to Hirst and Warner records that David Hunter at Yorkshire took many catches off him down the leg-side, a feat which would have been more or less impossible had he been standing up.

Warner declared that Hirst was most effective when bowling under the heavy, smoke-filled skies of Leeds and Sheffield. When the man himself was asked about it, however, he expressed a degree of bafflement about the whole thing. 'Sometimes it works,' he said simply, 'and sometimes it doesn't.' Such self-deprecation – not always a prominent feature in great Yorkshire cricketers – was part of the all-rounder's endearing charm, and, of course, it deflected further questions about his technique.

Hirst had ruddy cheeks and a moustache, and in later life

the roly-poly figure of a giant panda. His smile, the formidable Lord Hawke, his county captain, recalled, 'went right round his head and met at the back'. Despite the famous 'we'll get 'em in singles' incident against Australia in 1902 and the Edgbaston Test of the same year in which, alongside Rhodes, he helped dismiss Australia for 36, he was never as effective playing for England as he was for Yorkshire. He turned out for the Tykes from 1889 until 1929, and in those thirty years scored 36,203 runs and took 2727 wickets. Little wonder Lord Hawke described him as 'the greatest county cricketer of all time'.

After finishing with Yorkshire Hirst went to coach at Eton and carried on playing club cricket until he was seventy-two. He managed the singular feat of being tough, doughty and warm and friendly all at the same time. Certainly he was rarely critical of others, all the while brushing aside compliments about his own efforts. A. A. Thomson commented that he had 'to the highest degree, the virtue the Victorians called manliness, without a jot of Victorian sententiousness'. Little wonder that he was so hugely popular. 'It did you good to see him laugh', Pelham Warner wrote, which is as touching a tribute as you'd find, I reckon.

Chapter 4

A Slight Deviation off the Track

In the evolution of the summer game the ascendancy of William Lillywhite and the legalisation of first round-arm and later over-arm bowling might have been expected to have as dramatic an effect on the tribe of under-armers as the arrival of the Ice Age did on the dinosaurs. The original trundlers, however, proved to be tougher to do away with than the Tyrannosaurus Rex. Despite their obvious disadvantages, under-armers clung on and continued to play an important role in the first-class game. Some, such as Chris Tinley from Nottinghamshire, delivered the ball at a lively clip, racing and pinging it at the batsman from hip height. Others, like William Clarke – the leading bowler of his day despite having only one eye and playing virtually no county cricket until he was nearly forty – strolled in and bowled at a pace that was positively bovine.

Resilient though they were, the influence of the under-armers did gradually and inexorably fade as the nineteenth century neared its end. They were, however, to enjoy a late flowering as glorious as it was unexpected. It all started in 1891, several years after the Demon Spofforth had apparently ushered in the era of modern bowling.

*

Born in 1871, Digby Loder Armroid Jephson began life as a fast bowler and once took five wickets in eight balls for his club side. At Cambridge he won a blue for cricket while generally batting well down the order and rarely getting to bowl at all. Despite being more or less ignored in Varsity cricket, or possibly because he had been, Jephson was taken on as an amateur by Surrey. At the Oval he batted rather well, sharing a stand of 364 with Bobby Abel and hitting two thousand runs in a season. More arresting, however, was his bowling. In 1892 Jephson developed a case of the yips when it came to over-armers – a similar affliction would later blight the career of England spinner Nick Cook among others – and as a result gave up on the fast stuff and took to under-arm lobs instead.

Jephson's singular decision was inspired by watching a pair of lobsters who still plied their trade on the county circuit: the two Walters, Read and Humphreys.

Walter Read of Surrey was an accomplished amateur batsman (many considered him second only to WG) who bowled under-arm as a sideline, but did so well enough to get a hat-trick in a festival match at Scarborough in 1891. Despite his many successes with the ball Read's slow deliveries attracted a good deal of derision in the media. After he had dismissed Lancashire favourite Johnny Briggs with a daisy-cutter the *Manchester Guardian* fumed that it 'was the sort of ball a boy of eight or nine would send down' and denounced Briggs's failure to play the ball as 'absolutely ludicrous'.

Read also seems to have been the first bowler ever to suffer from a Kevin Pietersen-style attack of pinch-hitting, when Sir Timothy O'Brien of Middlesex switched stance against him during a game in 1893 and drove him to what ought to have been the fine leg boundary four times in a row. On the fifth attempt O'Brien, a forceful Irish aristocrat, apparently stood on his stumps, but when Surrey appealed he dismissed their cries as nonsense and carried on batting.

Walter Humphreys of Sussex (nicknamed Punter) is worthy of some attention, not least because he is one of many trundlers who have, down the years, been accused of sharp practice. Unlike some who would follow him, Humphreys (who made his debut in 1871) did not fiddle about with the seam or improve the shine with illegal unguents; instead he allegedly distracted the batsmen by bowling in a pink flannel shirt with flapping sleeves. Whether it was the sleeves or not, Humphreys was singularly successful for his county, taking 718 first-class wickets at 21.52 each – the record for an under-armer. He was selected to tour Australia with Stoddart's England team in 1894 but by then he was, in his mid-forties, past his best and failed dismally.

Humphreys was Sussex's best bowler for almost a decade. His success seems to have stemmed from an ability to deceive the batsman. With or without his pink flapping shirt, Punter was adept at disguising his deliveries; the Australian W. L. Murdoch, who batted against him in 1882, noted that: 'Even when I had made two hundred runs I could not tell from watching his hand which way he meant to turn the ball.' Admittedly, the fact that Murdoch made a double century does somewhat detract from the compliment.

Like many of the earlier under-armers, Humphreys's style was vigorous. He came in off a long run and his follow-through took him well down the wicket. 'It may seem easy, but it is not,' he once told an interviewer. 'I put out all my strength when I am bowling and a fast bowler could do no more.'

Jephson studied both Read and Humphreys. He practised

his lobs in club cricket, where they were surprisingly effective, and announced his arrival to the wider public with a devastating display of lobstering for the Gentlemen against the Players at Lord's in 1898. The professionals' batting line-up was formidable and the wicket perfect for batting yet, sauntering to the stumps and delivering his donkey-droppers, Jephson dismissed Tom Hayward, Harry Storer, Bill Brockwell, Albert Trott, George Hirst and Walter Mead at a cost of twenty-one runs. Asked to explain his secret Jephson praised the fielders, a self-deprecating touch that further endeared him to cricket followers around the country.

Like his county colleague Read, Jephson had his detractors in the press. Many cricket writers were affronted by his success, perhaps because to the casual observer it appeared comical and thus undermined cricket's credibility. When Jephson took three wickets against Essex in 1897 the *Essex County Chronicle* commented, 'As for Jephson's underhands. A little care and patience would soon have enabled the batsmen to deal with him', while the *Manchester Guardian* went on the attack once again after Jephson's rip-roaring display against the Players, snorting 'The failure of the leading professionals of the country against the lobs was truly ludicrous.'

Such attacks on his bowling didn't deter Jephson, and the Surrey committee were so impressed by his all-round performances and character that in 1900 they appointed him captain. His bowling action was captured in a Spy cartoon in *Vanity Fair*. It shows the tall, slender Jephson crouching in the act of delivery, his bowling hand about a foot above the ground (much lower than that of Humphreys). The fact that Jephson was sufficiently noteworthy to feature in *Vanity Fair* says something for the way his performance against the Players had caught the imagination of the British public, which traditionally delighted in the eccentric.

Sadly Jephson's involvement in cricket – like that of many Edwardian amateurs – seems never to have been entirely wholehearted, and in 1902 he determined to devote less time to sport and resigned the Surrey captaincy. He played only occasionally thereafter (still taking a hat-trick against Middlesex in 1904) and instead devoted his time to the stock exchange, journalism and the occasional burst of cricket poetry. In the course of his first-class career he took 297 wickets.

Like Digby Jephson, George Simpson-Hayward had gone off to university as a straight-ahead paceman. He played four times for Cambridge in that role, but took just a single wicket. And that might have been the end of his cricket career, had it not been for an evening spent messing around on a billiard table at his club. Simpson-Hayward was idly spinning the ball to left and right when it occurred to him that he might attempt something similar with a cricket ball.

In the privacy of his garden, against players from the local village side, Simpson-Hayward began to practise his new style. He started off bowling at the stumps from twelve yards before gradually retreating to the full twenty-two. In all it took him three years – and a lengthy conversation with Punter Humphreys – to get to the point where he felt ready to test himself in a competitive match. His chance came in 1897 when touring South Africa with the Corinthians. At Johannesburg on a matting-on-sand wicket, Simpson-Hayward (then just plain George Simpson – he would not adopt the grander hyphenated form until the following year) took the ball and, getting genuine fizz off the artificial surface, ran through the opposition to finish with 8–45.

After another summer in club cricket Simpson-Hayward was summoned for a trial by Worcestershire and took his first

first-class wickets in a match against Hampshire shortly afterwards. Due to business commitments Simpson-Hayward played first-class cricket infrequently until 1908, when he got sufficient matches to finish the season with sixty-eight wickets. The following year he took another fifty-seven, a return that was good enough to see him called up – at the advanced age of thirty-four – for England's 1909–10 tour of South Africa. The side was captained by H. D. G. Leveson-Gower and featured among the professionals a young opening batsman, Jack Hobbs.

On his previous visit to South Africa Simpson-Hayward had found the quick matting wickets to his liking and they hadn't altered much in the dozen years since. On his first appearance in the Test arena supporters in the stands apparently greeted him with hoots of mocking laughter. They soon shut up, however, as the lobster bamboozled the local batsmen with his peculiar tweakers. Simpson-Hayward took a total of twenty-three wickets in the three-match series at a strike rate of one every thirty-nine deliveries, his analyses including 6–43 in the first Test and 5–69 in the third.

How did a man bowling what most watchers clearly thought was the sort of stuff fit only to use against a nervous ten-year-old in the back garden achieve such success? Psychology certainly played a part. For batsmen, facing an under-armer was akin to a top-flight football team playing a village side in the FA Cup third round: they had everything to lose and nothing to gain. The fear of getting out to such stuff plainly paralysed some opponents and so contributed to their downfall.

Simpson-Hayward was also a skilled practitioner of his craft. He had practised long and hard, just as Barnes and Wilfred Rhodes had done with their more orthodox styles. Unlike other lobsters the Worcestershire trundler did not rely much on trajectory, though he did bowl an out-and-out donkey-drop that soared into the air before clipping the top of the stumps on the full. Altham noted that he bowled such deliveries 'with effrontery and aplomb'.

Simpson-Hayward's leg-break was also said to be poor. Instead he relied more or less completely on his ability to spin deliveries in to the right-hander using his powerful fingers and, even more so, his thumb, which he tucked under the ball and flicked at the point of delivery. According to Pelham Warner, Simpson-Hayward got these deliveries to genuinely rip off the pitch and varied the amount of spin he put on each: 'He bowled several different off-breaks, one turning a lot, another six inches and the third an inch or two.' The hard-spinning break was delivered with his fourth finger beneath the seam.

To add to the confusion of the batsman, according to the belligerent Gilbert Jessop when Simpson-Hayward delivered his straight ball he cunningly mimicked the flicking noise of his spinners by clicking the fingers of his left hand. Expecting one that turned in to them, batsmen played inside the line and edged the ball to the wicketkeeper.

Simpson-Hayward rarely bothered with slips. In fact, the field placement to his bowling was largely defensive. Aside from a leg slip (or fine draw, as the position was sometimes known) and a short-ish square leg he typically bowled with a cover point, deep cover, mid-off, long off, mid-on, deep mid-wicket and deep square leg – placements that seem designed to cut off boundaries from drives, the obvious stroke against a ball that by its nature was never likely to rise much above stump height.

More than any other type of bowler, the lobster required an iron nerve; not just against the attacks of the batsmen, but against the ridicule of the spectators too. Simpson-Hayward was imperturbable. His advice to anyone wanting to bowl underarm was simple: 'Keep your head, keep your temper, try to defeat your man.'

Simpson-Hayward's escapades in South Africa might have been expected to lead on to further glory, but unfortunately it had all come rather too late. Simmers, as he was known to his team mates, drifted away from the game following that glorious winter. He played less and less county cricket and took just two wickets in the 1913 and 1914 seasons. After that, world events rather intervened.

In a career that was spasmodic to say the least, Simmers took over five hundred first-class wickets including a best of 7–54 against Middlesex in 1909. While the assessment of many journalists remained caustic, opponents and team mates were more generous. Warner, for one, was full of admiration, writing, 'A cleverer bowler of his kind there never was.'

When cricket returned after the Great War under-armers had almost entirely disappeared from the first-class scene. Occasionally they would resurface as a joke in the fading light of a festival match, and once caused a serious diplomatic incident between New Zealand and Australia when Trevor Chappell ensured an Australian victory off the last ball of a one-dayer by bowling a 'grubber'.

The hostile attitude towards them continued, however. And not just when they were employed as a literally underhand stunt by the Aussies either. Back in the seventies the greatest of all cricket tacticians, Mike Brearley, made a study of under-arm bowling and felt certain it still had a place in the modern game. Impressed by the pace generated by Irish road bowlers (who play what is to some extent a cross between lawn bowls and the shot put – bowling cast-iron balls for distance), Brearley was determined to experiment with what many felt was an obsolete craft. Of his attempts to reintroduce the lost art to the first-class game he recalled, 'In 1980 I bowled a few lobs for Middlesex when we were stuck and trying to winkle somebody out. On the whole they were not approved of by our team, let alone the opposition (I was terrified that Brian Davidson was going to split my head open with his bat after the first lob I bowled to him).'

It appears that under-arm bowling faded from view not so much because it was ineffective, but because it lacked gravitas. It was not quite serious or manly enough to be allowed to survive. Professional sport has little use for whimsy, even – or perhaps especially – when practised by amateurs.

Chapter 5

The Gun-Swinger

When a teenage Cyril Washbrook was selected to play for the Lancashire Second XI against Staffordshire in the early thirties the captain came into the dressing room after the toss and said, 'We're batting. Washbrook, put your pads on.' 'But I thought I was in at seven?' Washbrook replied. 'You are,' the skipper said grimly, 'but Syd Barnes is bowling.'

S. F. Barnes was by then nearly sixty, but he was still playing as a league professional and was as much of a handful as ever. A few years earlier he'd turned out for Wales – he had a business in Colwyn Bay – against a touring West Indian team and taken twelve wickets, far outshining Learie Constantine and Manny Martindale.

S. F. Barnes was born in Smethwick in 1873. He was over six feet tall and rangy, with the gaunt cheekbones and deep-set, piercing eyes of a Wild West bounty hunter. He bowled medium pace with a high arm action, cut the ball off the pitch both ways and swung it through the air too. He extracted bounce from even placid wickets and the thought of facing him unnerved the bravest batsmen. Barnes was as accurate as the speaking clock. When one young batsman in the Bradford League announced that he would play Barnes by 'defending the good balls and waiting for the bad ones to hit', the reply was quick and solemn: 'You'll wait all year then, lad.'

Barnes had started out as a fast bowler, imitating his idol Tom Richardson, but he gradually cut his pace back to a military click. For a couple of seasons he played – sporadically – for Warwickshire, then in 1895 made his first appearance in league cricket, signing as a professional for Rishton, who eighty years later would cause a minor sensation by employing Viv Richards in the same capacity. Barnes was paid three pounds and ten shillings a week, with a bonus of seven shillings and sixpence every time he scored fifty or took six wickets in a match. In his first season with Rishton he took seventy wickets at less than ten apiece. The following season he took eighty-seven and the year after that ninety-seven, at a cost of just 8.46 each.

It was at Rishton that Barnes first deployed the leg-break and generally bowled in such devastating fashion that in five seasons he picked up 411 wickets at 9.10. The cash register rang regularly and the crowd dropped coins into his hat, which was how Barnes liked it.

While he was at Rishton Lancashire approached and offered Barnes professional terms. He turned them down flat. 'I could not see that it would benefit me,' he remarked later. He meant financially; that was how he saw things. Barnes had a regular job working as a clerk for a metal company, and his copper-plate script was as immaculate as his bowling. His salary, subsidised by his weekend work at Rishton, bonuses and collections from the crowd when he had pulled off a particularly astounding feat with the ball, was more than any county could pay him. And he didn't have to worry about what he would do in the winter either.

Barnes was suspicious of the world of first-class cricket,

scorning the typical county professionals who, 'after fleeting years as famous cricketers, fêted and fussed, dropped out, returned to the mine or the factory, or, at best took a fourth-rate beerhouse, trading as best they could on faded glories'. This was the fate that had befallen Tom Richardson, hero of all England who squandered his money and dropped dead of a heart attack at forty-one, and numerous others too.

Whatever his concerns, Barnes did play occasionally for Lancashire Second XI during that time and was eventually approached by them again about signing full-time. Once more he rejected the offer, apparently dissatisfied by the money. Lancashire's captain, A. W. Hornby, later said that Barnes wanted the wages of 'three men'. Rishton, mean-while, had also failed to satisfy Barnes so he jumped ship and went to their rivals Burnley instead. On the green-topped wicket at Turf Moor he was ridiculously successful, taking 225 wickets in two seasons at less than nine runs each.

Unsurprisingly, Lancashire came calling again. He played for them in the final game of the 1901 season and took 6–70 as Leicestershire were skittled out for 140. Archie MacLaren, the new Lancashire captain, was so impressed that a few days later he cabled Barnes and asked if he would be available for the England tour of Australia that he was leading. The money must have been reasonable because Barnes agreed.

Barnes had played just six first-class matches in his career, and the selection for an Ashes tour of a player who had made his reputation playing weekend cricket naturally created a bit of a stir. (In truth, MacLaren's hand had been forced some-what. Wilfred Rhodes and George Hirst were both unavailable for the simple reason that Yorkshire said so.) One newspaper ran the story under the headline 'Who is Barnes?' To which a Burnley paper retorted testily, 'They will soon find out!'

Barnes's reputation for truculence was already well

established. On the boat to Australia MacLaren told him, 'I would much rather have a man say what he thinks than be a "yes" man and then go away and grouse with the others.' 'I shall never do that,' Barnes assured him. 'If I do not agree with you I shall say so.'

Barnes was so little known outside the small world of the Lancashire League that the Australian press heralded him as a 'green youngster', though in fact he was already twenty-eight. Barnes played two Tests, taking nineteen wickets before a knee injury ended his tour.

His time in Australia with MacLaren changed Barnes from a very good bowler into a great one. And the key to the transformation was one of his opponents, Monty Noble. Noble – who would go on to captain his country on fifteen occasions – was perhaps best known as a dogged batsman in the Ken 'Slasher' Mackay mould (though unlike Mackay he doesn't seem to have picked up an ironic nickname), but he was also a very fine medium-paced bowler who took 132 Test wickets. *Wisden* noted, 'As a bowler [Noble] has plenty of spin and varies his pace well, though not with so little perceptible change of action as Howell. A good deal had been said about his ability to make the ball swerve in the flight, and there can be no doubt that this peculiarity in his bowling puzzled many of our batsmen, especially during the early part of the tour.' It was Noble's singular ability to combine spin with swerve that attracted the attention of Barnes.

Batting against Noble he noticed that the Australian had in his repertoire a ball that swung away in the air and then broke back in off the pitch. Barnes could swing and cut the ball both ways, but could not combine the two. Fascinated, at the close of play one evening he approached Noble and asked how it was done.

It is difficult to conceive of a situation in which Shane

Warne or Glenn McGrath would merrily have offered advice to an English Test rival, but Noble was, as Barnes later acknowledged in interviews, a good sportsman. In the course of half an hour the Australian happily explained his technique to the 'green youngster'. He told Barnes that the best way to perfect the delivery was to practise as he had done: placing two poles on the strip in the nets, one on a line of off stump approximately eleven or twelve yards down from the bowler and one on leg stump another five or six yards further on. Bowling over the wicket, he should then try to swing the ball inside the first stump and outside the second, with the ball pitching just outside off stump and breaking back in to hit middle or leg.

On his return to England Barnes worked on the new delivery and added a variation of his own: a delivery that swung in to the batsman and then broke away from him off the pitch. The latter would become his signature delivery, the great trundler's answer to the Bosie or the doosra. Neville Cardus, in a surprisingly prosaic moment, would dub it the 'Barnes Ball'.

Surprisingly, given his reputation for being taciturn and morose, Barnes took a similar attitude to Noble when it came to explaining his skills. The trouble was that, as the cricket writer Ian Peebles observed after spending an hour in the Long Room with the great man, 'even with all the "know how" so completely and thoroughly revealed, the execution was, of course, a very different matter'.

Barnes could bowl practically any ball imaginable, and he did: leg-breaks, off-breaks, in-swingers, out-swingers, top-spinners. Peebles points out that, unlike most medium-pacers since, Barnes did not bowl the 'cutter' of the medium-pacer; rather he 'gripped the ball firmly between his first and third fingers and *spun* it'.

The cutter involved the bowler running his fingers down the side of the ball. To alter the direction of the cut from off to leg he had to change the position of his wrist at the point of delivery, telegraphing his intention to the watchful striker. Barnes's method was at once more subtle and more vigorous.

A tall man for his time, he brought his arm over very high, hooking his hand across the ball and whipping it down the pitch. He had the powerful fingers of a chiropractor and it was these long digits, the knuckles gnarled and knotted like the roots of an ancient tree, that were the key to Barnes's majesty. He snapped them across the ball with such force that he could extract cut and bounce on even the most benign wickets without signalling in which direction the ball would move.

Barnes's power to spin the ball was such he could – and did – get turn from a ballroom floor. The spin on the ball was so vicious that on damp surfaces it ripped up the ground like a rotavator and spat off the surface. The England all-rounder Cec Parkin, who often came up against Barnes in the leagues, commented on 'the way he makes the ball "nip" from the turf. You would think an imp was inside the leather.' And Cardus recalled facing a couple of overs on a green wicket that left him with bruises all across his rib cage.

Like Lillywhite, Barnes was a deep thinker. 'Barnes brought brains to his natural capacity to bowl the [away-swinging] ball,' Parkin observed approvingly. 'He did not exploit it unconsciously but according to a deep plan. He was the most artistic, the most thoughtful bowler I have ever known – he was also the most richly endowed by nature. But he added craft and artifice to his superb natural powers.'

Warner noted that Barnes always bowled on or just outside off stump – the area Geoffrey Boycott would later dub 'the corridor of uncertainty'. He always made batsmen play at the ball and got a lot of wickets caught behind off the ball that swung away from the right-hander. A typical field to Barnes on a good track would feature two slips, point, cover, extra cover, mid-off and third man, with a short square leg and deepish midwicket. Though as Barnes himself once remarked with typical sharpness, 'Any field placing is right providing you bowl to it.' The wicketkeeper always stood up for him and rarely had to move much to take the ball.

Herbert Homer, who captained Barnes at Staffordshire, observed, 'His length and direction were so accurate that the batsman had to play the ball. I do not remember him ever bowling a full toss or long hop. He pitched the ball mostly about three yards from the crease, varying that according to the pace of the wicket. He bowled the ball leaving the batsman more than any other, but with the new ball the leg break that swung in to the batsman before pitching was most productive and many catches were taken at short leg.'

Another key position on damp strips was silly point. In a single season at Saltaire Barnes had twenty catches taken by the fielder in that position. One of them, George Parker, recalled: 'I caught many batsmen off purely defensive strokes. Barnes was very tall and his arm came over from a great height. When he put top-spin on the ball it came up quicker than expected off the wicket and often hit the batsman's glove, or high up on the splice of the bat.'

The astonishing thing was that whatever Barnes bowled, his grip remained exactly the same. The different types of spin were simply imparted with a different finger: the index finger to spin the ball in to the batsman and the third finger to make it break away from him. His middle finger was always held over the top of the ball. For a right-armer to bowl an off-break in such a manner is unremarkable. To bowl a leg-break 'at quick-medium pace with the wrist straight and the palm of the hand towards the batsman' is more or less miraculous. As Peebles observed, Barnes's was an easy method to demonstrate but a very, very hard one to copy (try doing it with a tennis ball). Nobody else could manage it at the time, nor since.

Having perfected his new swinging-spinners Barnes finally caved in and agreed terms with Lancashire for the 1902 season. He did not enjoy his experience that first year, calling it 'this melancholy season of bickering'. Nevertheless, he stuck with it and the following year took 131 wickets at 17.85. Despite his success, and the wickets he had taken on his previous visit, Plum Warner did not select him for that winter's MCC tour of Australia. When questioned, Warner said it was because Barnes could not bowl an off-break. This was patently untrue. Unfortunately for Warner, his Middlesex side had a game to play against Lancashire at Lord's shortly afterwards. Barnes tells us: 'I was bowling to Mr Warner from the Nursery End, which meant the off-break had to go slightly up hill. I had been bowling balls that went away from him, when I whipped one down just outside his off stump which broke in and knocked back the leg wicket.' The demonstration was not enough to earn Barnes a call-up, but it stuck in Warner's mind. Always willing to admit his mistakes, the Middlesex skipper selected Barnes at every opportunity thereafter.

At the close of the 1903 season Barnes announced that he had signed a contract to play for Church in the Lancashire League. He was to be paid eight pounds a week, plus collections and a benefit. He was no longer available for Lancashire, and lost to county cricket for ever.

The notion of a professional cricketer choosing the league game over the County Championship was hard for many –

particularly those who did not make a living from the game – to grasp. The widespread view was that the decision was another sign of Barnes's unfortunate attitude. That year's *Wisden* commented that 'Temperament is a great thing in a cricketer and in this respect Barnes has always been deficient. If he had possessed the enthusiasm for the game that characterised Barlow and Johnny Briggs he might have made a name for himself, his natural gifts as a bowler being so remarkable.' (A year later Barnes – who had continued to play for England despite it all – would be one of *Wisden*'s five Cricketers of the Year.)

Barnes's reasons for leaving Lancashire were purely economic: 'We were paid £5 for a home match and £6 for an away match and you had to pay for your own travelling expenses and lodgings out of that.' In the winter, meanwhile, the players received no money at all. Little wonder that Barnes would one day dismiss Lord Hawke's criticism that 'You only play when you like' with the words, 'And I intend to go on doing so. I have a berth besides cricket and I am looking after it. Cricket is a secondary consideration.'

Barnes's dislike of Lancashire also stemmed from what he regarded as the amount of work they expected him to do for his pay. 'I used to take the new ball at half past eleven and would still be bowling at six o'clock unless I'd bowled 'em out,' he grumbled. Barnes was no Jack Hearne, toiling uncomplainingly in the hot sun while the amateur fieldsmen strolled about in the cool shadows cast by the pavilion. Pelham Warner later suggested that Barnes had benefited from not playing day in and day out for a county, 'coming fresh and full of energy to Test matches when many other professional bowlers were starting to flag'. Certainly it is hard to imagine that he could have bowled any better for England than he did over the next decade.

The one batsman Barnes was prepared to acknowledge as if not quite his master then maybe his equal was Victor Trumper. Asked how he dealt with the great Australian strokemaker Barnes replied, 'I kept him quiet, which was as good as bowling many men out. You couldn't dictate to Trumper. With some, you could make them do what you wanted them to do, but not Trumper. He played as *he* liked, not as *you* liked.'

Yet Barnes got the better of Trumper on several occasions: most spectacularly at Sydney in 1907, when he bowled the great man with a delivery so brilliant Charlie Macartney, who was at the non-striker's end, later said: 'The ball was fast on the leg stump, but just before it pitched it swung suddenly to the off. Then it pitched, broke back and took Victor's leg stump. It was the sort of ball a man might see if he was dreaming, or drunk.'

South Africa's Aubrey Faulkner, a very fine defensive batsman, faced Barnes during the Triangular Tournament of 1912. At the Oval he got what he thought was a sound start, batting for an hour against Barnes (albeit for just ten runs). By then he imagined he had dealt with just about every variation Barnes could produce and was in confident shape when the great man suddenly let fly with what appeared to be a long hop. Faulkner began to move into position to hook, only to see his middle stump knocked out of the ground. Barnes had sent down a long hop all right, but it was top-spun and bowled at about twice the speed of anything he'd delivered before. It didn't matter how long a batsman had been facing Barnes, he always had another trick up his sleeve.

In the 1913–14 tour of South Africa Barnes, by now middle-aged, took forty-nine wickets in four Tests at less than eleven runs apiece. The First World War ended his international career – since he was already in his forties it is hard to say 'prematurely', but since he went on performing wonders in league cricket until well into his sixties that is probably the case. When the Great War ended, Percy Fender played against Barnes in a benefit match in Bradford and was baffled by the old man's brilliance: 'None of us knew what on earth to do against him.' In 1924 the touring South Africans came up against Barnes when they played Wales. He bowled sixteen overs and took 5–32. The tourists were stunned. Barnes had just turned fifty-one.

Doubtless there were many in the game's upper echelons who were pleased to see the back of Barnes. The Great One was not the deferential type. He was immune to charm in others, and possessed little himself. C. B. Fry was arguably the personification of the Corinthian gent – dashing stroke-maker, fast bowler, footballer for Southampton, holder of the long-jump world record and with such a regal air he was allegedly offered the throne of Albania.

Fry and Barnes did not see eye to eye. They were so different in their attitudes it is hard to imagine they were from the same century, never mind the same country.

'Barnes rarely said anything,' Fry noted after captaining him in 1912. 'He was not by nature an enthusiast.' Whenever he was asked to name the greatest bowlers he had played with or against, Fry never mentioned Barnes.

Fry was right that Barnes was not an enthusiast: he was a professional. He bowled purely to take wickets and make a living. When the owner of a construction company asked Barnes to play in a charity match he asked what his fee would be. When he was told that there was no fee, he responded curtly: 'Then I will play for nothing if you build me a house for free.'

No matter how long he spent with a club, Barnes remained

an enigma to his team mates. The great bowler was as laconic as Calvin Coolidge. When Saltaire had placed their advert for a new professional, Barnes had replied by telegram. His job application read simply, 'Will I do?'

The only known occasion that he made a joke was during a Lancashire League match when somebody shouted from the boundary the news that Australia were 400–2 at Lord's, and Barnes shouted back, 'Who's got all the wickets?'

Barnes played cricket with a remorseless, grim pugnacity. In a festival match he was bowling when a new batsman, a fashionable, dashing amateur, came out to the wicket. The great bowler's skipper drew him to one side and said, 'This chap was at a party last night. Didn't get to bed until four o'clock. Go easy on him for a few overs, will you?' Barnes scowled, went back to his mark, ran in and knocked the fashionable amateur's off stump out first ball. That was Barnes.

Yet despite all that the leagues welcomed Barnes back with open arms. When he left Castleton Moor, of the Central Lancashire League, the mayor of the town commented, 'He is a reticent man, and like all geniuses has his own way of doing things, but he is certainly not difficult to get on with; the boys adore him and will be sorry indeed when he goes elsewhere.'

Barnes's performances in the Bradford League were so remarkable that bookmakers stopped offering a bet that he would take five in a match and upped it to six. But as one happy punter later told the great man, 'That were the season you took 150 so I won a pot load of money.'

He kept on playing for Staffordshire and even at fifty-six would regularly bowl fifty overs in a game for them. His figures remained remarkable, though he never quite rose again to the heights achieved in 1908. Back then the Minor

Counties Championship was organised as many one-day competitions are now, with a group stage followed by a series of knock-out rounds. Staffordshire topped their four-county group and met Hertfordshire in the semi-final, and then Glamorgan in the final. In these latter two games Barnes took twenty-four wickets at 3.5 runs apiece, bowling sixty overs and conceding a paltry seventy-eight runs.

In the last match a singular incident occurred involving the Glamorgan batsman Harry Creber. Creber was ambidextrous, sometimes batting left-handed and sometimes right. In a bid to confuse Barnes he chose, during the course of the first over he received, to change his stance three times. Each time he did so the sightscreens had to be moved. Irritated, Barnes decided to put a stop to the nonsense. He ran in as usual, but instead of bowling the ball he trundled it underarm. The ball cut back in to the surprised Creber and struck him on the pad. The umpire raised his finger. Even Barnes's under-armers were lethal.

Barnes's style and attitude is recorded, perhaps unwittingly, by Herbert Homer, his captain at Staffordshire during that time: 'During the period I played with him all the captains agreed with his moving a fielder if necessary. I am sure it was right to do so.'

Barnes gave nobody any trouble, just so long as he was allowed to do as he pleased. In league and Minor Counties cricket, he was the kingpin and that was how he liked it. Late in life, when he was asked who his best captain had been Barnes replied simply, 'Me'. Invictus indeed.

In twenty-seven Test matches S. F. Barnes took 189 wickets at under seventeen apiece. Even more remarkable, he did it while hardly bothering with first-class cricket at all. As a professional in league cricket, for Rishton, Burnley, Church and Rawtenstall, Saltaire and Keighley and St Annes, as well as half a dozen other sides in the Midlands, his career ran from 1895 until 1940 and in that time he took over four thousand wickets at the meagre cost of 6.08 each.

Warner thought him the best bowler of them all, as did Arthur Gilligan (who placed his protégé Maurice Tate second) and just about every Australian who came up against him. When the great Yorkshire all-rounder Wilfred Rhodes was an old man he was asked who he thought the best bowler. He chatted for a while about various men he had played with and against and then, nodding, said, 'Aye, but I suppose on all types of wicket old Syd were the best.' Short of getting the nod from God, there can be no higher commendation in cricket.

Chapter 6

Dobbers in Excelsis

There are constant arguments between cricket buffs when it comes to naming the team with the best bowling attack in history. Some will favour the rip-snorting pace of the great West Indian sides of the eighties, while others will look to the greater balance of the Australians under Bradman or Waugh; a few spin-besotted romantics may even put in a plea for the seventies Indian side, or the Grimmett and O'Reilly axis. When it comes to an all-dobber attack, however, there is little room for disagreement, even among those of us with an irrational fondness for Paul Allott and Derek Pringle. The team that England sent to reclaim the Ashes under Pelham Warner in 1911–12 contained the greatest medium-pace bowler of all time, Sydney Barnes, backed up by Frank Foster and John Douglas, a pair of trundlers of such moderate brilliance that the genuinely quick Bill Hitch of Surrey, who once knocked a bail flying fifty-five yards, couldn't get a look in, while Wilfred Rhodes – the most successful spinner in history – was barely called on to bowl at all.

Foster of Warwickshire was an attacking all-rounder in the glowing Golden Age tradition, swooping gracefully about the field and straight-driving anything pitched up to him colossal distances ('like a golf ball from a tee', Warner said). A gentleman amateur whose family owned a successful chain of gentleman's outfitters, Foster had come close to quitting the game when barely out of his teens to concentrate on business but relented at the last moment and was made county captain aged just twenty-two. In his first season in charge, 1911, he led Warwickshire to the title with a series of brilliant performances (including a haul of 141 wickets) and some inspired bowling changes. 'There was about all his cricket an atmosphere of supreme confidence and inexhaustible vitality,' wrote H. S. Altham, 'that acted as a wonderful inspiration to his side', while *Wisden* was moved to compare Foster's impact to that of the young, exuberant W. G. Grace.

More than six feet tall, slim and agile, Foster bowled left-arm over the wicket from so far wide of the crease that right-handed batsmen had to crane over their shoulder to see his delivery stride. He angled the ball across the right-hander, swinging the ball in to him prodigiously and late even in the clear, hot sunlight of Australia. Tiger Smith, who kept wicket to Foster for county and country, claimed that his swing was so delayed the ball seemed to straighten up in the last few feet before the batsman played it. Shades of G. H. Hirst.

The young Warwickshire captain also had a well-concealed slower ball and occasionally broke one away from the right-hander off the pitch. Like Barnes he seemed to make his deliveries hurry on (*Wisden* claimed they 'doubled in speed after they hit the ground'). In-swing, however, was Foster's main weapon and he concentrated on a middle-and-leg-stump line to a field that featured six men on the on-side, three in close catching positions. He was so successful at this style of leg theory, in fact, that in the early thirties Douglas Jardine actively sought out his thoughts on it. The result was

Bodyline, which so disgusted Foster he went as far as to make a gramophone record on which he denounced England's tactics and apologised to the Australians that his 'experience and advice were put to such unworthy use'.

Foster is often described in contemporary accounts as fast-medium, but any idea that he was the Edwardian Wasim Akram should be put aside. Smith always stood up to him, and even got a leg-side stumping off him to dismiss Clem Hill. It seems that the term fast-medium was used only to distinguish his pace from that of Jack Hearne, Syd Barnes and George Lohmann. Foster was quicker than all of them, but he was a trundler sure enough.

Like many young amateur cricketers, Foster lived a fast life off the field. He once returned from a night out at seven in the morning and had no sooner got into bed than two Warwickshire team mates appeared and lifted him out again. They dumped the all-rounder in a cold bath, fed him steak and beer for breakfast and then shoved him, bleary-eyed and tipsy, out onto the field where his county were taking on Yorkshire. Remarkably, despite being barely able to keep his eyes open Foster caught Wilfred Rhodes in the first over. On other occasions he played cards through the night and turned up for breakfast at Edgbaston still in his tails.

J. W. H. T. Douglas, the third member of England's triumphant trundler triumvirate, was an anomaly – a wealthy southern gentleman who played like a hard-bitten northern professional. The Essex captain was a great all-rounder, but so lacking in the traditional amateur *joie de vivre* the wits commented that he was a medium-paced bowler and a slow-medium batsman.

Square-jawed, dark-haired, thick around the shoulders with the bristling masculinity of a Hollywood gangster, Douglas

batted in a mean, featureless manner that led Australian heck-
lers to claim his initials stood for Johnny Won't Hit Today
during a typically turgid 33 against Victoria early in the tour.
His bowling, like his batting, was not fancy: military medium,
on a length, gallingly accurate. He was the most successful
amateur bowler of his time, taking over a hundred wickets in
a season seven times, with a best of 147, and finished with a
total haul of 1879 – more than any other 'gentleman' aside
from WG. Jack Hobbs considered him the most difficult
bowler to play against in England.

Incredibly physically fit, Douglas bowled the sort of prodigiously long, niggling spells that were normally the province
only of the hired help. He had a free, springy run-up and a
powerful follow through, and bowled every ball as if he
expected to get a wicket, scowled when he didn't and strode
briskly back to his mark as if he resented the time it was wast-
ing. JWHT always rubbed the ball on his forearm rather than
his trousers or his shirt, maintaining that the natural oils from
the skin helped to retain the shine. Whether he coated himself in sunblock is not recorded, but I think we can regard it
as unlikely. Douglas was far too hard to worry about anything
as piffling as sunburn.

In the years after the Great War, Douglas had to carry an
Essex attack in which he was often not just the only opening
bowler, but the only quality bowler of any description. That
Essex were also a notoriously poor fielding side only added to
his workload. He was indefatigable, bowling on and on as the
ball got softer and more worn and the fielding increasingly
ragged. That Essex managed to win any games at all was
more or less entirely down to his spirit.

Douglas may not have been flamboyant, but he was
certainly tough. In 1905 he'd won the British amateur mid-
dleweight boxing title and, three years later, Olympic gold in

the same event. He was remorselessly hard and a fierce dis-
ciplinarian. As captain of Essex he had no time for shirkers
and whiners, and drove his men as hard as he did himself.
Pros who came to him complaining they had a temperature
of 103 were told to go in the nets until they'd sweated whatever was the cause of it out of their systems. One former
player, Charles Bray, wrote, 'You either liked and respected
John Douglas or you loathed him. There was no half-way
course.'

Those who didn't like him were plentiful, and came mainly
from his own class. As Sir Derek Birley noted, Douglas had
'aggression and a win-at-all-costs attitude that jarred on the
nobler minds at headquarters'. Unpleasant gossip had it that
JWHT had only been given the Essex captaincy because his
father – a wealthy timber merchant – owned the lease of the
county ground at Leyton, while the fruity Old Etonian cricket
writer Sir Home Gordon said that Johnny was 'not only bad
but brutal, almost incredible in his ruthlessness'. Perhaps he
had a point. In one infamous exchange the Essex skipper was
heard to remark to a young off-spinner, 'Joe, if you ever bowl
that sort of tripe again I shall punch your head.'

Yet like a good officer Douglas also took care of his team.
He always ensured, for example, that they stayed in good
hotels, made certain they were well served by their landladies
and even took young amateur players out on the town and
chatted up women on their behalf. He was equally solicitous
with the pros, though seems to have confined his attentions
to ensuring they had decent accommodation and a hearty
breakfast.

The year 1911 had been a good one for trundlers generally. Of the twenty bowlers who took over a hundred wickets
that season, ten were medium-pacers. This number included
Hirst, Old Jack Hearne and Foster, as well as George

Thompson, who was credited with gaining Northampton-shire first-class status in 1905 and was in the middle of a run that would see him pass the century mark of victims eight seasons in a row; Harry Dean of Lancashire, who mixed left-arm Hirstian swing with slower spinners, and Tom Rushby of Surrey, who a decade later would take all ten wickets in an innings against Somerset.

John Douglas was Pelham Warner's deputy in the MCC team that set off for Australia in 1911. The squad's ship took its time getting to the Antipodes, stopping briefly in Colombo for a one-day match against Ceylon. The MCC players took to the field in pith helmets but despite the unlikely headgear Barnes and Foster proved too much for the local batsmen on a damp wicket and bowled them out for 50.

In the first match of the tour, against South Australia, Barnes, Foster and Douglas took fifteen wickets between them as the state side were destroyed by an innings and 194 runs. Against Victoria, and with Barnes ill, Douglas picked up another eight. By then, though, the tour had taken an unexpected turn. Warner had struck an elegant hundred against South Australia but on the train to Melbourne he suffered a near total physical collapse, was rushed to hospital and later spent six weeks in a convalescent home. Douglas took over.

Despite the change in captaincy, the bowling continued much as before. Against Queensland, with Barnes restored, the trio took seventeen wickets, and in an up-country game against Toowomba Douglas bagged another five.

The new captain was – Warner noted – a man of character who possessed courage, determination and pertinacity to a marked degree. Douglas promptly added weight to this opinion by refusing to give Barnes the new ball in the first Test at Sydney. The plan backfired. Victor Trumper hit a century, the leg-spinner Herbert 'Ranji' Hordern (who had learned his cricket playing in the US with Bart King) took twelve wickets and, despite Foster picking up six wickets in the second innings on his Test debut, England were routed.

The second Test followed soon afterwards. Douglas, always at his best in adversity, rallied his men. At Melbourne Clem Hill won the toss and elected to bat. The sky was clear, the pitch as flat and lifeless as a night out in Eastbourne. Australia had a fine batting line-up that included, alongside Hill, Warren Bardsley, Warwick Armstrong and the ageing but still formidable Trumper. For the home supporters it seemed nothing could go wrong. Then Douglas threw the new ball to Barnes.

Peebles reckoned that because of the fierce spin he imparted on the ball Barnes was not reliant on the conditions in which he bowled, or on the state of the ball. He was the one who dictated what happened, not the grass, the shine or the atmosphere. This certainly seems to have been the prevailing opinion among those who played with and against him.

Proof beyond doubt came in the first hour at the MCG. With Foster bowling immaculately – if a little unluckily – at the other end, Barnes got Bardsley first ball with one that swung in, hit his toe and cannoned into the stumps. ('If it had not hit the wicket he would have been lbw,' Barnes snapped to anyone who suggested it was a bit lucky.) He trapped Kelleway in front of his stumps with an in-dipper, bamboozled Hill with one ball that cut in to him, one that swung in to him and one away swinger before putting him out of his misery with a delivery that pitched on leg stump and hit the off (Hill later said it was the best series of deliveries he ever faced). Warwick 'The Whale' Armstrong lumbered in, played back to one that fizzed and went away from him and was caught at the wicket for 1.

Straight after lunch Foster clean bowled Trumper with a ball Barnes was moved to describe simply as 'beautiful', and then the great man himself saw Roy Minnett drive desperately at one that looked inviting but wasn't, to be caught by Hobbs at cover. In a few hours, on a day made for runs, Australia were 38–6, Barnes had taken 5 for 6 and the whole balance of the series had tilted back in England's favour. More remarkable still, he was still so sick with the fever that had kept him out of the earlier state matches that at times he could barely see the stumps. Barnes later had to leave the field with dizziness and nausea. Australia struggled to 184 all out, but the damage was done. When England batted Australia's current left-arm swing bowler, Bill Whitty of New South Wales – who had been touted as 'the new Turner' after taking seventy-seven wickets on the 1909 tour of England, and thirty-seven in the subsequent Test series against South Africa – proved utterly innocuous. In Australia's second innings Foster took six wickets, Barnes three, and England won by eight wickets.

From that point on England's dobbers simply steam-rolled the Australian batters. Trumper's first-innings hundred in the first Test was the only one they posted and none of the batsmen averaged over thirty in the series.

In the third Test at Adelaide, on another perfect batting strip, Barnes struck first, getting Bardsley caught at the wicket for five, then Foster took over. Before lunch he bowled eleven overs, six of them maidens, and took one wicket for eight runs. After lunch, bowling to the leg-trap field and swinging the ball unmercifully he quite literally battered the Australians, hitting them constantly on the legs, thighs and hips, and took three wickets in seven balls as the home side slumped to 133 all out. England built a mountainous lead, with Foster striking a belligerent seventy-one. In their second innings

Australia knuckled down and the game became a grim slog. Barnes, bowling without much movement but with probing accuracy, sent down forty-six overs and took 5–105 (one of the few occasions in his career when a century of runs were taken off him) and Douglas – doubtless enjoying the attritional nature of things – chipped in with a couple. England battled home by three wickets.

It was back to Melbourne for the fourth Test. Douglas won the toss and, mindful of the psychological sway his dobbers held over the Australians, he put them in. Barnes and Foster took nine wickets, dismissing Australia for 191. Jack Hobbs and Wilfred Rhodes opened the batting for England and put on 323. Foster then hit another half-century and the England innings closed on 589. The pitch seemed benign, the first-day sting now a barely detectable tingle. Yet when Australia batted it apparently turned nasty again. The pugnacious Douglas, bowling with the kind of intense determination that was his signature, took 5–46. Barnes and Foster mopped up the rest and England ran out winners by an innings and 225 runs.

The Ashes had been regained and the MCC touring party celebrated with a magnificent dinner at which, alongside the oysters, red snapper and saddle of lamb, the waiters served a special soup named in honour of the captain. It was made from the slow-moving but hard-shelled turtle.

Australia made wholesale changes for the final Test of the series, but any hopes were undone by a thunderstorm midway through their first innings. Replying to England's total of 324, they had struggled to 133–5 when the downpour turned the uncovered wicket into a sticky mess and the remaining five wickets fell for just forty-one runs. England struggled too, against the persistent Hordern, and were all out for 214. By now the pitch had dried out and Australia needed 363 to win.

They progressed to 191–3 at the close of the fourth day and seemed to have the edge, but overnight it rained again. Foster and Barnes tore into the damp surface and Australia were dismissed for 292.

Hobbs and Rhodes had both batted well, Smith had kept wicket superbly and Frank Woolley caught anything that came near him, but there was little doubt that the series had been won by England's medium-pacers. In the five Tests the three bowlers took eighty-one wickets between them – Barnes thirty-four, Foster thirty-two and Douglas fifteen. In the other six first-class matches of the tour they picked up a further sixty-six. Hardly anyone else bowled at all.

For many, many years afterwards Australian pundits would say that Barnes and Foster were the best pair of bowlers ever sent to Australia. Douglas was the perfect first change. He was not as spectacular as either of the openers, but it was his 5–46 in the second innings of the fourth Test at Melbourne that secured England the Ashes.

Foster and Douglas were still young men, Barnes well into his thirties but apparently as ageless as the legendary Wilson of the *Wizard*, and so England supporters might well have expected this potent attack of moderate pace to prosper for years to come. Sadly it didn't. The summer of 1912 was – in the Yorkshire cricket writer A. A. Thompson's phrase – 'The wettest between Noah and 1958'. The much-anticipated Test cricket world championship, the Triangular Tournament, was badly affected by rain. Barnes was at his best, taking thirty-four wickets against the South Africans in three Tests, but though Foster did well in the first of those games he never rose to the heights of Adelaide. Batting on damp wickets, meanwhile, exposed faults in his technique that had not been evident in Australia during the hot summer of 1911. He continued to take wickets and score runs in the County

Championship but after that damp summer would never play for England again. Frank Foster played his last first-class match in 1914, aged just twenty-five. Had it not been for a motorcycle smash in 1915 he might have resumed his cricket career in 1918, as Douglas did. Instead his life went into a steady decline. The one-time golden boy of England found himself caught up in the Bodyline controversy, failed in the family business, separated from his wife and family, was declared bankrupt and charged with fraud. At the time of his death he was confined in a psychiatric hospital.

Barnes, as we have seen already, did not return to international cricket after the Armistice. Johnny Douglas did, but his captaincy of England was derailed by Warwick Armstrong's all-conquering Australians, the pace bowling of Gregory and McDonald and a rare old spat that ensued when he accused the opposition team of ball tampering (correctly, as it turned out) which further upset the already unimpressed mandarins at the MCC.

The rugged Essex skipper also met an unexpected end. On a business trip to Scandinavia he and his elderly father were both killed when the ship they were sailing on collided with another vessel in the North Sea and sank. It was reported that Douglas had died attempting to save the old man's life. Few who knew him doubted the truth of that.

Chapter 7

A Good Workman Improves His Tools

The basic requirements of the dobber's trade are simple: the wicket, the atmosphere, the ball and a small collection of sundry items to improve it.

From the twenties the state of cricket pitches gradually began to deteriorate, at least as far as the trundlers were concerned. New and much improved motorised lawnmowers replaced the primitive hand-pushed or horse-drawn varieties, leading to a closer and more evenly cropped playing surface. In the thirties groundsmen began to mix marl with clay to top dress the wickets for a harder, more consistent surface. In the same decade the use of heavier rollers (the one at the Oval was the size of a traction engine) became widespread. Strips were flattened, the life and moisture squeezed out of them. Shirt-front wickets became the norm.

The introduction of Law 11, allowing for the covering of pitches during games, was gradually phased into first-class and Test cricket during the sixties. The introduction of covered pitches – designed to make the game fairer – was met with predictable cries that such mollycoddling of the playing surface would inevitably lead to the extinction of spin, the irrevocable triumph of bat over ball and the stagnation and death of the game. Of course, none of these things actually happened, though spinners did take several decades to adjust to the new circumstances, and the sort of medium-paced twirlymen who thrived on rain-affected wickets and were once as prominent a feature of the English county circuit as men in white coats selling choc ices in the drizzle – Derek Underwood and Don Shepherd would be good examples – are no longer as prevalent as they once were. In the end it was the dobbers who, once again, suffered the most, but, as usual, nobody seemed much bothered by that. For while the cricket world feels about the wrist-spinner the way the normal world feels about the giant panda, nobody much cares about the medium-pacer. Spinners are dolphins, trundlers tuna.

When the covers are placed over a damp wicket, the surface tends to sweat (that is to say, surface moisture condenses under the covers and falls back onto the wicket). This will freshen up a surface for the trundler, but the advantage he gains is considerably less than it would have been if the rain had been allowed to fall directly on the strip and then dry. In thunderstorms in particular the combination of moisture and heat produces a soft, tacky surface on which the likes of Turner, Barnes and later Tate, Bedser and Shackleton would run riot. That Turner used to have the practice strip in his native Bathurst regularly soaked in water so he could practise bowling on 'gluepots' indicates how common such surfaces were back then. Not any more. Brisbane's infamous 'sticky dog' – like the one in the 1951 Ashes Test on which Bill Johnston ran amok – could reduce even the best batting side to an amorphous jelly. Normally benign, after a dousing it behaved, according to Lancastrian cricket writer John Kaye, as if it had 'thousands of demons prancing upon it'. Nowadays it is utterly and reliably bland, tamed by the ICC.

If the trundler can no longer look to the earth for help, he can at least still gaze up to the heavens for it. Well, until climate change takes its full and dramatic toll and turns Headingley into a northern Wanderers, at any rate. As we have already seen, meteorological changes in Australia in the latter part of the nineteenth century had a detrimental effect on the Australian dobber, a situation that man and nature have so far failed to rectify. (Although some people did blame the storm that created that 1951 Brisbane mud heap on the US nuclear tests at Bikini Atoll.)

Rain may no longer impinge on the trundler's art, but the conditions that bring it do. Low cloud and humidity, along with air pollution, have for centuries been seen as the medium-pacer's allies. Pelham Warner noted: 'Science has told us that when a ball is advancing rapidly through the air there is formed in front of it a small aggregation or cushion of compressed air which causes it to curl. The heavier the air the greater the cushion.' The one-time MCC president concluded that the grim, grey smoke-filled skies of Leeds, Sheffield and Manchester were therefore the ideal places for the swinger to ply his mysterious trade.

For those seeking a longer explanation we might say that the existence of swing bowling is down to the Bernoulli Effect. This simple rule states that the pressure in a moving fluid (the air in this case) is lower than in a static fluid. When the ball is bowled it creates a low-pressure area known as the boundary layer. If this boundary layer is the same on both sides of the ball there will be no swing. The bowler's job is therefore to make the boundary layers on either side of the cherry uneven. A rough surface generates turbulence (or chaos) in the boundary layer, and a chaotic boundary layer sticks to the ball longer than a smooth or laminar one. So, if the right-handed bowler delivers the ball with the polished side to leg, when the smooth boundary layer leaves the ball the tacky turbulent layer will suck it towards the off, producing an away swinger. At this point I should declare that I got a U in O-level physics, which is perhaps why I feel more comfortable with Plum Warner's more insubstantial and, in all probability nonsensical, explanation.

As to Warner's declaration that swing increases in heavier air, that seems to be beyond doubt, though the reasons why the humid atmosphere causes the ball to swing are once again complex and fiercely argued over. Recent studies by David James and John Hart of Sheffield Hallam University's Centre for Sport Engineering Research and Danielle MacDonald at AUT University in New Zealand have suggested that it is the stillness of the air that is the vital consideration. 'When the ground heats up, it creates convection currents which make the air rise off the cricket pitch, and that creates turbulence in the air on a sunny day,' Dr James told the BBC. 'On a cloudy day you get stiller air, because you don't get these convection currents coming off the ground. Stiller air does less to affect the imbalance of smooth and chaotic flow on either side of the ball, which is what leads to swing.'

For myself, I subscribe to another theory, one that involves a subject dear to many trundlers' hearts: ale. For over five centuries brewers in Belgium have made a type of beer called lambic. Lambic ale is made by placing uncovered tubs of barley mash in the open air and allowing the yeast in the atmosphere to bring about the transformation of the natural sugars in the mash into alcohol. The optimum time to brew lambic beer is during the thundery, clouded days of late summer, when the amount of yeast in the atmosphere is at its highest. If a hovering electrical storm can turn grain into ale, could it not also transform an innocuous straight one from Tony Nicholson or Peter Lee into something equally intoxicating?

At this stage I find myself recalling an interview with William Faulkner in which the inquisitor asked if the novelist had read Sigmund Freud. 'No I haven't,' Faulkner snapped back. 'I doubt Herman Melville had, and I'm damned sure Moby Dick didn't.' Or as George Hirst might have put it, 'Sometimes it works and sometimes it doesn't.'

When it comes to swing, the wind also plays its part. The Channel fret was a boon to Maurice Tate at Hove and Hastings, while the Fremantle Doctor ministered to the swing needs of Western Australian trundlers such as Terry Alderman. These coastal winds carried salty moisture and blew in directions (usually diagonally across the wicket) that helped the bowler swing the ball. Some trundlers liked the wind blowing across them diagonally from the rear; others felt they wobbled the ball more in the air if it was blowing in their face.

The ball, it goes without saying, has a vital role to play in the trundler's work. H. S. Altham tells us that this is the piece of cricket equipment that has changed the least over the centuries. While bats straightened and stumps multiplied, the ball remained largely unaltered.

That is true, to a certain extent. In 1770 – the same year that the appearance of Shock White with a bat as wide as the wicket led to the limiting of the width of the willow wand to four inches – the weight of the ball was regulated at between five-and-a-half and five-and-three-quarter ounces. The regulation seam made up of six rows of herringbone stitching was standardised a decade later.

Then, as now, the ball was made from a core – known as the 'quilt' – of cork, tightly wound with coarse worsted (in the past some makers added duck down. Possibly an ironic quip). Four quarters of 3.4mm-thick cowhide which had been soaked for a week in red alum dye were then stitched together and squeezed over the quilt with a high-pressure vice. The slightly puckered central seam was sewn shut with a six-thread, beeswax-impregnated twine (originally boar hair was also used) and then the regulation seam – eighty stitches per row on the best quality balls – was added. The ball was given its maker's mark in gold leaf (top-class dobber of the 1960s Tom Cartwright always believed that the swing of the ball was hindered by the gold lettering, and tried to wear it off as quickly as possible), finished with three coats of polish and sent off into the world.

Most of the globe's best known cricket-ball manufacturers still make the balls used in first-class and Test cricket by this time-honoured method. The process of hand-making cricket balls is – as you may imagine – laborious and very expensive. Hand sewing the seam can take a skilled leather worker up to an hour.

The Eden valley area around Tunbridge Wells has been the centre of the English cricket-ball industry since the mid-eighteenth century. At its peak just before the Great War the Kent cricket-ball manufacturers employed over two hundred people. However, by the seventies the number of manufacturers in the county had dwindled to just two, Readers at Teston and Tonbridge Sports Industries near Penshurst. Even these two venerable establishments had started to outsource work to the Indian subcontinent, where labour was cheaper.

Nowadays Jalandhar in India and Sialkot in Pakistan produce nearly all the balls used in club cricket. These balls are machine-made and while harder than top-quality balls they also lose their shape quicker. Generally the ball used in first-class cricket is still hand finished and hand stitched – bespoke Savile Row to the club cricketer's off-the-peg from Burton.

However, to say that the first-class ball today is exactly the same as the type used by Lumpy Stevens, William Lillywhite or even W. G. Grace and S. F. Barnes would be inaccurate. The core of the ball, for example, is these days generally round rather than the original square shape, and while cork is still used it's often mixed with rubber. Some veteran observers believe this has altered the way the ball moves, pointing to the fact that in recent years it has become increasingly common to see a delivery swing after pitching, something that occurred so infrequently in the past as to be positively freakish. The seam is also much more pronounced than it was in the days of S. F. Barnes.

Currently the Australian Kookaburra – which is machine-made – is used in Test matches in all countries except England and India, where the English Duke's ball is used. The Alfred Reader and the SG ball have also been used in Tests in recent times. Each has its distinct qualities.

The Duke's ball, being made in England to suit English conditions, tends to swing for a long period and has a pronounced seam. It is dark red and shines up well after the first coat of lacquer has worn off. Unsurprisingly trundlers love the Duke's. Unfortunately, in the more unyielding conditions of the southern hemisphere the Duke's ball tends to go to pieces rather quickly. You can insert your own Steve Harmison joke here, if you like.

Back when my friends and I were eager speed demons the Kookaburra was spoken of with awe. We had never seen one, naturally, but we knew from our reading that it was gaudier and harder than anything made in England – something that was also true of Australian cricketers, of course. Designed for Australian conditions the Kookaburra is indeed bright red, bouncy and keeps its shape even when pounded into the WACA by Jeff Thomson after a heavy night.

The seam of the Kookaburra is lower than that of the Duke's, and while it will swing early on that swing doesn't last for long. In fact you might think the Kookaburra had been designed specifically to thwart the sort of medium-pacers that have so often been the mainstay of the England Test attack. Then again, you might say the same thing about the Australian climate too.

Of the other top-class cricket balls the one made by Alfred Reader was a favourite of the Pakistan side of the nineties because they considered it the best when it came to reverse swing (we'll get to that topic later). The SG, meanwhile, has an even more pronounced seam than the Duke's and the ease of gripping it has made it popular with spinners, particularly on the subcontinent.

Pioneer swing bowler George Hirst was one of the first men to appreciate the value of the shine on the cricket ball. Prior to his perfection of the booming in-dipper, the majority of bowlers considered the polish more of a hindrance than a help, likely to make the ball slip from the hand. In the 1890s it was common to see dobbers and pacemen rubbing the ball on the ground to remove the polish. Hirst, in contrast, worked on it ceaselessly, becoming the first cricketer to leave the field with red stains down the front of his whites. As we now know, Hirst's efforts were all to do with chaotic and laminar flow.

The shine on the ball and the height of the seam is of such importance to the trundler that the second area of cricket in which his breed can truly be said to hold sway (the first being complex scientific explanations of what they are about) is in the matter of ball tampering. Yes, the odd paceman down the years may have chucked one, and the occasional spinner done the same, but when it comes to genuine skulduggery the dobber rules the roost, no question.

When exactly players began interfering with the ball is, strangely enough, not recorded, though given the generally dissolute nature of many of the early players and the amount of gambling money that was at stake it's hard to imagine the Georgians weren't in on the act. What is for sure is that raising the seam has gone on for the best part of a century. Arthur Mailey admitted doing it back in 1920 to help Gregory and McDonald, though he didn't volunteer that information until the fifties, by which time J. W. H. T. Douglas, the England skipper who'd complained about it, was long dead.

The thumbnail is the most common tool for prising up the stitching; it's said that some professionals are so subtle they can get away with using it even when standing having a chat with the umpire. Allegations of tampering are controversial.

During the second Test of India's tour of South Africa in 2001 film footage suggested that Sachin Tendulkar – who has been known to supplement his batting with a little trundling – was trying to lift the seam with his nails. Tendulkar denied raising the seam and said he was simply scraping some dirt out from it. Match referee Mike Denness was not convinced, and banned him for a match.

In an interview with his biographer Imran Khan admitted to ball tampering – using a bottle cap – during a County Championship match. 'When Sussex were playing Hampshire in 1981, the ball was not deviating at all,' he wrote. 'I got the twelfth man to bring out a bottle top and it started to move around a lot.' After a bit of work with it, the ball began to swerve about and Sussex ran out winners.

Of all tools, the bottle cap is probably the most versatile. It is used not only for raising the seam but also for scraping off the polish on what will become the, erm, chaotic side of the ball. During New Zealand's 1990 tour of Pakistan the traditional Kiwi military medium-pacer Chris Pringle – who was, like many of his team mates, convinced the prodigious swing of the Pakistani bowlers was created by not entirely legitimate means – cut a bottle top into quarters and covered the serrated edge with tape, leaving a sharp point exposed. It sounds like the sort of thing somebody might make to defend themselves in the prison showers. Pringle used the shiv to scratch the ball, creating chaos on one side of it and on the pitch too, as Pakistan collapsed from 35 for no wicket to 102. The miscreant trundler finished with his best Test figures of 7 for 52. In his later autobiography he expressed amazement that he got away with it: 'One side [of the ball] was shiny but there were lots of grooves and lines and deep gouges on the other side. It was so obvious. It was ripped to shreds.'

More primitive methods still can be used to scuff the surface. Kent captain Rob Key resorted to sandpaper in 2007, while others have – like the POWs in *The Great Escape* – carried soil in their trousers. Shahid Afridi even bit the ball 'like it was an apple'. In 2005 Gloucestershire fast-medium bustler Steve Kirby (who had famously abused Mike Atherton by telling him he could find 'better cricketers in my fridge') was given a suspended three-day ban and ordered to pay costs of £125 after Glamorgan complained that he had scuffed the polish off the ball on a concrete bollard in the Sophia Gardens car park.

Maintaining or improving the shine on the ball requires a markedly different approach. When I was a teenager in the seventies I often used to wonder why so many county medium-pacers affected the hairstyles of two decades earlier. Nowadays, of course, I realise that this was not because they lagged behind the times fashion-wise (although many of them did, obviously) but because Brylcreem and other types of pomade were a vital part of their job. Looking back to the Barbados Test of 1958, in which he batted for several days to score a match-saving triple hundred, Hanif Mohammad recalled that of a West Indies attack which included Roy Gilchrist and Alf Valentine, 'Eric Atkinson was the only one of the bowlers who really troubled me. He used to put a lot of cream in his hair. That may have had something to do with the fact that he managed to swing it both ways, and swing it late.'

Like many cricket fans of my generation, I was first alerted to the notion of ball tampering by the events in the first Test of England's tour to India in 1976–7. In Delhi India were reduced from 43 for no wicket to 49 for 4 late on the second day, thanks largely to the bowling of left-arm fast-medium John Lever. The Essex man swung the ball late, dipping it in to the right-handers from a Hirstian angle, and went on to finish with seven wickets in the innings, and ten in the match as England romped to victory. Nothing was said about Lever's bowling then, but in the third Test England's players took to the field with strips of Vaseline-impregnated gauze stuck to their foreheads, apparently to prevent sweat from running into their eyes. Lever found his more of an irritant than an aid and at some point took it off and threw it on the ground. The umpire picked it up and Bishan Bedi, the Indian captain, alleged that Lever had been using the Vaseline to help shine the ball: an illegal tactic, Bedi went on to say, that England had also deployed at Delhi.

John Lever had a very full head of long blond hair ('He looks more like a pop star than a county cricketer', *Wisden* gasped). Quite why he would have bothered sticking Vaseline to his forehead when he could easily have concealed it in his lustrous mane is open to conjecture. England admitted the gauze strips were a mistake and contravened the laws of the game, but offered the defence of naivety.

Tony Greig later admitted that Lever did mix sweat from his brow with the Vaseline and rub it on the ball, but said it was purely accidental. Lever meanwhile denied any such thing, but added another layer to the story by claiming that Ken Barrington, the England tour manager, had persuaded the Indian team to use a locally made ball that would favour England's swing bowlers by praising it to Indian administrators.

Whether Vaseline would help a ball swing or not is a matter of some debate. Not so the use of sugary saliva created by the sucking of a wide variety of sweets. This was first brought to our attention by predictably left-armed Australian fast-medium merchant Nathan Bracken, who alleged that during his time with Gloucestershire in 2003 the players used breath mints and lollipops to help shine the ball. '[A breath mint] makes your saliva very sugary. Every team has lollies and things like that. We had all our lollies checked before the first game to make sure there was nothing illegal. When I was playing at Gloucester as soon as we needed the ball to go "Irish" the captain would call and they would bring out some of these mints and it would work.'

Bracken then went on to suggest that England's Ashes-winning side of 2005 had also made use of sweets. England's pace bowlers immediately hit back. Simon Jones said Bracken's comments were 'silly': 'I can't believe that a guy who didn't even play in the series has come out with such a comment,' he said.

Bracken duly apologised and tried to pass the whole thing off as a joke that had misfired. A few years later England vice-captain Marcus Trescothick admitted to using sweets during the series.

Was the use of sugary saliva – even from Gloucestershire's legal lollies – actually illegal, though? Test match umpire Peter Willey didn't think so. According to Willey, if a player had sun-tan oil on his face and then rubbed it off mixed with sweat and onto the ball then that was fair enough. Likewise with the sugary spittle. In Willey's view, things would only shade into illegality if players were bringing bottles of sugar solution onto the field and spraying it on the ball. In cricket, it seems that if you apply styling gel to the ball via your hair that is fine, but to do it direct from the jar is against the law.

An example of the jam-in-a-hospital-sandwich thinness of the line came during a one-day international between India and Zimbabwe at the Gabba in 2004. TV cameras caught Indian skipper Rahul Dravid rubbing a cough lozenge on the shiny side of the ball. The Indians claimed that Dravid was not applying cough-sweet-tainted saliva to the ball, but attempting to remove some that had got on it earlier. Clive Lloyd, the match referee, was unimpressed, found Dravid guilty and he was fined half his match fees.

What players are allowed to polish the ball with is a murky area, and what they polish it on has also caused controversy. In the old days, of course, cricket whites were all made out of cotton or wool. That all changed in the seventies, when man-made fibres started to be introduced; these days a cricketer's kit is made out of all sorts of trademarked hi-tech fabrics that promise to keep players simultaneously cooler and warmer while dispersing sweat, preventing muscle strains, massaging their feet and doing myriad other things that stop just short of making them a chip butty and a cup of tea.

As we might expect, the polishing possibilities of the players' trousers were not overlooked. In 2008 New Zealand arrived in England carrying a new style of secret 'micro-light trousers' that had been developed under the supervision of Dipal Patel, a former engineering student at Loughborough University. The bowlers' version of the slacks – worn by typically solid Kiwi dobbers Jacob Oram and Iain O'Brien – included a patch of material resembling a window cleaner's chamois leather on which they could polish the ball. The trouser-maker had apparently also investigated the possibility of adding an alternate patch of some abrasive material to help scuff the ball as well, but the notion was abandoned over worries about its legality. As it was, the ICC cleared the pants as legal; New Zealand wore them in two Test matches and lost both of them. Clothes may make the man, but they don't make the trundler.

Chapter 8

The Yeoman Trundler

The Great War had a profound effect on the psychology of Britain. Perhaps understandably, people looked back to the years before 1914 as if it were some prelapsarian garden in which it was always summer and there were no wasps in the beer. For cricket lovers, the Edwardian era was perpetually bathed in the buttery light of late August, its protagonists chivalric upholders of manly Corinthian values who glided elegantly across the turf without grunt or sweat. The strikes, madness, drinking, suicides and cheating, the bloodstains on the train walls and the not entirely courageous behaviour of some of its greatest figures during the conflagration in France and Belgium, were all forgotten as a mixture of nostalgia and dread created the Golden Age.

If the First World War had shaped cricket's past, it would also shape its present and future. Cricket in England would now strive to live up to its sentimentalised past. The steely-eyed *High Noon* approach to the game adopted by the likes of John Douglas fell out of favour (Douglas Jardine – perceived as some harbinger of future doom by the MCC – was in reality a throwback to earlier, more brutal and ruthless days), while fear of the Bolshevik menace would mean that the likes of Shaw, Lohmann and Barnes, with their militant sense of their own worth, would no longer be tolerated.

Barnes, as we have seen, drifted off into the leagues where his remorseless destruction of opponents was still viewed with approval. The chirpy trundler Cec Parkin (who once had the temerity to write a newspaper article calling for England to appoint a professional as captain) would shortly follow him. Douglas carried on but was increasingly marginalised, his position as captain of the national side finally stripped from him after England had been hammered into the ground by Warwick Armstrong's team. The Australians had emerged from the war more self-confident and bristling with aggression than ever before – and given that Clem Hill had missed the 1912 tour after punching the chairman of selectors, that's saying something. England's wistful dreaming was no match for Gregory and McDonald.

With Foster's career finished, Barnes gone and Douglas far too belligerent for the Lord's oligarchs, England needed a fresh bowling hero: somebody who would reflect the attitudes of the new age, a decent, stout, uncomplicated, amiable fellow who would wheel away until his feet bled without complaint or a demand that the management pay for his ruined socks. In 1922 he appeared. His name was Maurice Tate and he came from the cradle of cricket, Sussex. To watch him bowling during his glory years was to see the very personification of everything England wanted so desperately to be.

Tate had the widest smile since George Hirst, a heart as big as a house and he bowled medium pace that was, in terms of swing, movement and accuracy, almost the equal of the glowering Great One. Not only that, Tate was so stubbornly modest that when he became a publican in later years he refused to let his wife hang any memorabilia on the walls because he didn't want folk to think he was showing off. No wonder the public and the cricket authorities loved him. Though in the latter case that love, as the curmudgeonly Barnes might have predicted, wasn't without conditions.

During my Spofforth years I filled the long winter months by reading the *Cricketer* and – when sufficient pocket money had accumulated – sending off for the vintage cigarette cards advertised in the magazine's classifieds. The first part-set I bought was Wills 1928; I still have it now, framed on my bedroom wall. M. W. Tate is there, of course, sandwiched between The Late R. Kilner and Mr J. C. White. In the drawing on the card Tate is standing by a set of stumps, a ball in his right hand and his arm raised in the standard bowling-but-not-really pose favoured at the time. His boots are the size of kipper boxes, his hips wider than his shoulders. It is not a caricature: Tate really was shaped like that. Fred Trueman was often heard on *Test Match Special*, discoursing on the importance of a broad backside in an opening bowler. If that was correct – and who would dare doubt it? – then buttocks-wise Tate was genetic perfection.

Maurice inherited the wide aft-beam from his father Fred. Fred Tate bowled slow-medium off-breaks for Sussex and late in his career played a single Test match for England, at Manchester in 1902. Tate senior was selected ahead of George Hirst and S. F. Barnes. Schofield Haig of Yorkshire might also have been picked. Haig was another solid medium-pacer, notable for his ability to cut the ball in to the right-hander on a helpful wicket and the fact that 58 per cent of all his victims were clean bowled. Unfortunately for Haig, his fellow Yorkshiremen Hirst, Rhodes and the Hon F. S. Jackson (himself a handy second-change trundler) were already in the thirteen selected for the game and Lord

Hawke – who viewed the County Championship as more important than Test cricket and therefore Yorkshire as more important than England – objected to losing any more. Tate it was.

Barnes was in the Old Trafford dressing room on the first morning of the game, and said that he had never seen a man so nervous as Fred Tate. Perhaps the veteran Sussex spinner sensed what fate had in store for him. He bowled just sixteen overs on the sort of rain-affected wicket that would have had Barnes grimacing with delight, dropped a crucial chance given by Darling in Australia's second innings and was last man out with England needing just four to win and Wilfred Rhodes at the other end. It is reported that afterwards Fred told his colleague Len Braund, 'I have got a boy at home who will put it all right for me.' If that's true it was a remarkable show of paternal faith: Maurice was just seven years old at the time, and so thin everybody called him 'Stalky'.

Young Tate's childhood lankiness was overcome by winters spent working on his grandfather's farm. Soon the beanpole boy had transformed so thoroughly into the sturdy if strangely proportioned man of later years that people stopped calling him Stalky and started calling him Chub instead.

By his late teens Chub was on the ground staff at Sussex, bowling the same trundly twirlers as his father. By his own account he was in those days 'a very late change, bowling my slow off-spinners and an occasional fast one'. If anything was going to redeem the family name, at that point it seemed more likely to be Maurice's dashing batting.

All that changed in the high summer of the 1922 season. The revelation came at Eastbourne against Hampshire on 26 July. Tate was bowling to Phil Mead, who was well set on 39 when, after a series of his usual slow spinners (delivered, Arthur Gilligan would recall, with a rather low arm), he suddenly produced a much faster ball that pitched on off stump and cut back viciously to hit the top of leg. Gilligan, the Sussex skipper and a fast bowler of infamous hostility, was so impressed he exhorted Tate to start bowling like that all the time. Almost by magic Chub was transformed. In the first thorough trial of his new style he opened the bowling against Middlesex and quickly reduced them to 26–5. In the last two months of the season he took fifty wickets.

That, at least, is the popular story of Tate's 'fluke ball' and how it changed the course of English cricket. Like Hirst's miraculous discovery of swing it is a good tale, but not an accurate one. The actuality is altogether blander and, Tate being a trundler, should we settle for anything more? Rather than stumbling across his breakthrough delivery it appears that Chub, after encouragement from the veteran Sussex pro Robert Relf and under the tutelage of Gilligan, had been practising for some time in the nets, where he had surprised his skipper with a couple of fizzing cutters earlier in the season. The first victim of Tate's new method was not Mead but more or less the entire batting line-up of Kent against whom, two weeks previously at Tunbridge Wells, Chub had taken 6–11 in an opening burst that *Wisden* found 'irresistible'. He finished with 8–67. From then on he seems to have taken the new ball, and by the Middlesex match was gaining enthusiastic notices, not least from the former Lancashire paceman Walter Brearley who told Gilligan, 'You've got an England bowler for the asking. He is absolutely international class.' Tate's ego meanwhile remained uninflatable. Asked about the Mead ball he explained, 'I accidentally cut a ball, which pitched on middle and off and hit the top of his leg stump.'

Tate's dramatic bowling had come too late to influence the England selectors, however, and he was not picked for the MCC's winter tour of South Africa. He did spend the winter there, though, coaching at a school in Kimberley (the trip arranged for him by John Douglas). In his spare time he continued to work on his new bowling. By the start of the 1923 season he would be ready.

Things did not get off to the rip-roaring start he might have anticipated, in part because Chub was still batting at number three. By June Gilligan was wondering if expecting Tate to come in first wicket down *and* open the bowling wasn't placing too much strain on him. In the final session of the second day of the match against Essex at Hove he got his answer. The visitors required 236 to win with forty-five minutes to close of play. By the time the umpires lifted off the bails they were 24–4 and Tate had all the wickets for just five runs. The following morning he wrapped up the innings, bowling out three more batsmen and finishing with 8–37. At Northampton a week later he scored 92 in Sussex's second innings and then helped skittle out the home side with 6–28. In the next match at Horsham he laid into Nottinghamshire, taking 6–22 and 7–46, and in the same week destroyed Glamorgan with eight wickets for 30, before bashing a whirlwind 76. Tate had bowled unchanged throughout three of the last four innings. He was at once a strike bowler and a stock bowler – apparently unquenchable either by batsmen or exhaustion. Indeed Gilligan's biggest fear was that Tate would simply work himself into the ground. Possibly quite literally, since the heavy pounding of Chub's giant front foot on the bowling crease often wore such a hole in it the skipper would joke that it looked like he was 'digging his own grave'.

On 30 July Tate became the first bowler to one hundred

wickets. That summer there were no Test matches, nor was there a winter tour. To fill the gap a couple of 'Test trials' were arranged. Tate was called up to play for the South in the first of them at Old Trafford. He took 7–51, largely thanks – he records –to the remarkable catching of Percy Fender. In the second Test trial (England *v* The Rest) at Lord's Chub, playing for England, exceeded even that performance. With The Rest's batsmen having reached two hundred for the loss of four wickets, Tate was handed the second new ball. Ten deliveries later and they were 207 all out. Chub had taken 5–0 in an extraordinary spell that featured one ball that whizzed through straight and true to bowl Percy Chapman, one that swung away and then cut back off the wicket to get rid of Arthur Carr, a vicious off-cutter to knock back Geary's middle peg, a straight one to trap a bamboozled Macaulay lbw and an in-swinger that ripped out Louden's leg stump before he had quite finished his shot.

After that performance all England hailed the unstoppable Chub. He was clearly a great bowler, but more than that he was always smiling, indefatigable and humble (asked about the secret of his success he responded, typically, that he had inherited all his ability from his dad), with an endearing gift for malapropisms that had him telling the *Evening Standard* an injury was 'a long-standing affection'. Most of all, he projected that quality of innocent, exuberant boyishness that many felt had sunk for ever in the mud of Flanders. The fact that Tate was actually twenty-eight did not detract from that image in the slightest.

After his exploits at Lord's a Sussex paper acclaimed their man as the 'Barnes of Brighton'. Barnes and Tate were very different men in temperament, but their bowling did indeed have similarities. Barnes himself outlined one: 'Like me he tries to take a wicket every ball and is surprised if he doesn't.'

Tate was never as great an analyst of the game as Barnes, but he was shrewd enough and was arguably the first bowler to truly make the most of the new, more pronounced seam. Chub rocked into the wicket off a run-up of just eight yards and swung the ball very late. His nip and swerve resulted largely from his action, which saw him swivelling his body so dramatically in the delivery phase he had to wear a corset to prevent injury.

Tate kept to his line and length, as one writer noted, as if it were 'a faith or an heirloom', and was one of the hardest bowlers to score off in the history of the game. His stock ball swung away from the right-hander, but he could also bowl an in-swinger and cut the ball both ways off the pitch. Like Barnes he seemed able to extract movement from even the most duvet-like featherbed pitch, and though his swingers were greatly aided by the sea breezes of the county grounds at Hove and Hastings, those who had denounced him in the early years of his career as 'a mere seaside bowler' were so wide of the target they were a danger to third slip.

When it came to extracting movement off the wicket the two men's methods were very different. Barnes, as we have seen, snapped the ball improbably hard with his fingers, giving it a vicious tweak. Tate, by contrast, bowled cutters, altering the position of his wrist according to which direction he wanted the ball to go and running his hand down the side of it at the point of delivery. This method imparted less genuine turn to the ball than Barnes's technique and also telegraphed the bowler's intention to the batsman. Tate's pace – he was several yards quicker than Barnes and, though wicketkeepers stood up to him, in Australia in particular the slips stood well back – at least partially compensated for that.

Speed off the wicket was common to both men and Tate

also seems to have made the ball slide or skip. Bill Ponsford described one delivery that defeated him: 'He was no express and I thought I saw the ball pretty well. I went to make my stroke. The ball swung a little, hit the pitch and fizzed through like a flat pebble off a mill-pond.' The skimming (I imagine here a slower, fuller length version of the sort of flat bouncers in which the late Malcolm Marshall specialised) made it unwise for batsmen to play back to Chub, even when the ball seemed short of a length. Many were caught halfway.

Tate was a simple man, but there was a subtlety to his methods that escaped many. Unlike most medium-pacers he did not use the width of the crease, always bowling from close to the stumps, but he did alter the position of his feet. When he wanted to bowl the out-swinger, for example, he banged his front foot slightly to the right of straight so that his action was more than side-on and he delivered the ball *across* his body.

By the end of the 1923 season Tate had taken two hundred wickets and was hailed in *Wisden* as 'by common consent the best bowler in England'.

In 1924 South Africa toured England and Tate finally got to make his Test debut, in the first Test at Edgbaston. On the eve of the match Chub was nervous, as his father had been on his only Test appearance, but he was soon set at ease by fellow trundler Cec Parkin, who took the debutant's mind off things with a series of pranks that included locking Mrs Parkin in a prison cell during a tour of Birmingham prison.

England batted first and made over four hundred on the first day. When South Africa came in England's captain, Gilligan, took a wicket in his first over and then tossed the ball to his Sussex team mate Tate to open at the other – a decision that rankled Parkin, who was at that time England's leading medium-pacer. Chub ran in and took a wicket with his first ball. Or as he put it, 'I sent a beautiful half-volley on leg stump to Fred Susskind and he hit it straight to Roy Kilner at short leg.' To hear Tate tell it, his whole life was just one lucky break after another.

In his next over Tate clean bowled South Africa's skipper Herbie Taylor. Gilligan, bowling fast yorkers at the other end, ran riot, finishing with 6–7, Chub got 4–12 and South Africa were all out for 30 in twelve and a bit overs. They did better in the second innings, but England won easily.

The second Test at Lord's was played without Cec Parkin. Following the Edgbaston Test he had – as was his habit – made a few sarcastic remarks to a reporter about Gilligan's decision to give Chub the new ball. The comments appeared in the newspaper the next day. Parkin never played for England again, joining Barnes in the leagues where his singular mix of medium-pacers, donkey-drops, tweakers, googlies and wisecracks kept him in gainful and profitable employment for many years.

The game at Lord's was harder fought and for Tate less fruitful, but in the first innings of the third Test at Headingley Chub – fortified by a large whisky and soda given to him by a monk at Ampleforth College the night before – took 6–42 as England cruised to another victory and wrapped up the series. The fourth Test at Old Trafford was washed out after Tate had taken 3–34 in South Africa's first innings and rain also terminated the final match at the Oval. Tate topped the bowling averages with twenty-seven wickets at 15.71 and had also hit his maiden Test fifty to finish with a batting average of 32.66.

After his performances that summer it would have taken a prejudice or perversity beyond even the capabilities of an England selection panel to leave him out of that winter's

Ashes tour. The England team for that series had a high quality batting line-up – Hobbs, Sutcliffe, Woolley, Hendren and Sandham were all there – but the bowling was on the waferish side of thin. Apart from Tate and Gilligan, who had missed large parts of the previous season due to injury, the only other specialists were the spinners Roy Kilner, Dick Tyldesley and Titch Freeman. John Douglas was there, admittedly, but though he had been bowling with his usual gumption for Essex he was forty-two. Apart from JWHT and Gilligan there was just Hobbs with his military medium to provide Chub with support.

As it turned out, Tate didn't need any help. He more or less bowled Australia out single-handed, completely eclipsing the great Jack Gregory (whose partner McDonald had gone off to play in the Lancashire Leagues too). The Australians were stunned by Chub's ability, particularly the legendary 'heavy ball'. 'Where did you get that new bowler?' Herbie Collins asked the England players at the close of play on the first day of the first Test. 'He nearly knocked the bat out of my hands.' Bill Ponsford, meanwhile, suffered the indignity of being sledged by England wicketkeeper Herbert Strudwick: after his first over from Tate the Australian batter turned to him and said, 'I've never played bowling like this before,' to which Strudwick responded, 'No, it doesn't look as if you have.'

In the five-match series Tate took thirty-eight Test wickets at just 23.18 each. He was penetrative, but he was also tireless, bowling nearly twice as many overs as anyone else in the England side. And all this despite a festering big toe – caused by the nail being driven back into the flesh by the hard Australian ground – that bled whenever he bowled and caused him such pain that 'I had tears in my eyes every time I delivered the ball'.

It was an heroic effort and, in the best tradition of English sporting achievement, all in a losing cause. Despite Chub's toiling brilliance England were crushed 4–1. Losing side or not, when he returned home Tate was – in the words of H. S. Altham – 'universally acclaimed as the greatest bowler in the world'. To Altham, Tate 'was not the equal of Barnes in ability to use a wicket', but still he praised his spirit, endurance and ability to swing the ball late. Moreover, Tate had often to carry the attack on his own in Test matches, a burden Barnes never shouldered.

In 1925 Tate had his best season ever, taking 228 first-class wickets. It was, in fact, a markedly fine season for trundlers across England. Twenty-three bowlers took more than one hundred wickets. Two of those bowlers, Ted McDonald and Harry Howell, were rated as genuinely fast, eight were spinners and eleven were medium-pacers. The two others, rotund Vallance Jupp and the Terry Thomas-esque Percy Fender, bowled both tweakers and dobbers.

Among the eleven medium-pacers were Abe Waddington, a tricky character from Yorkshire we'll meet again later; Jack Mercer of Glamorgan; Scots-born Alec Kennedy from Hampshire; Sussex's Bert Wensley; Nigel Haig, a tall, wafer-thin amateur all-rounder of Middlesex; and blond-haired Ewart Astill of Leicestershire who bowled medium-paced off-breaks, did the double nine times and was one of the few professionals to captain a county in the inter-war years.

Cec Parkin, bowling his medium-pace ragbag of Barnes-esque spinners interspersed with the occasional slow donkey-drop and other bizarre novelties the Durham-born all-rounder claimed to develop while bowling to his long-suffering wife in the back garden during the winter months, took 152 wickets, while George Macaulay of Yorkshire got 211 – not bad for a man who, five years earlier, had been dismissed by *Wisden* as having 'neither the pace nor the stamina to succeed'. Like his team mate Waddington, Macaulay was a tricky character, a trundler given to outbursts of vitriol who would often vent his fury at an opponent by pinging a beamer at his head.

The altogether more amiable Fred Root of Worcestershire took 219 wickets in that 1925 season. Root was a hardy professional – 'all kindness and in-swing', Denzil Batchelor said – who'd begun his career at Derbyshire, had a spell with Leicestershire and then been so badly wounded in the First World War that doctors told him he'd never play cricket again. Undeterred, Root went from hospital to pro in the Bradford League. In 1920 he signed for Worcestershire and, after a couple of nondescript seasons, hit on the tactic that would change his fortunes: leg theory. Bowling medium-paced swingers that dipped in at the right-hander late, to a field featuring five on-side catchers, Root broke a hundred wickets nine seasons in a row.

Root's branch, as it were, of leg theory – like that of Frank Foster a decade earlier – was not designed to intimidate the batsman but to frustrate him. His deliveries speared in to the pads, carrying a constant threat of lbw, while every attempt to flick them away for runs carried the risk of being caught. It was classic percentage cricket, and while the authorities and the paying public complained that it was boring to watch it perfectly suited Root's worldview, which was as down-to-earth as his name. Like Old Jack Hearne, the Worcestershire bowler was not one for anything fancy, adhering to the principle that 'the most dangerous ball is the one that moves a little'. He shared with Barnes a generally low opinion of the lot of the professional and in his autobiography, which is filled with advice to young bowlers on how to reduce chafing, treat heat rashes, limit the risk of blisters and other such unromantic stuff, comments wearily, 'It is popularly supposed that there is quite a lot of money in first-class cricket. If there is, I have not found it.'

For the next four years Tate continued to dominate batsmen from all across the cricket world. He took 147 wickets in 1926 and a further 116 during the MCC's tour of India in 1926–7; another 147 in 1927, 165 in 1928 and 44 when England again travelled to Australia in 1928–9, and this time returned triumphant.

On that tour Tate found himself in an attack that included the young Harold Larwood, and George Geary of Leicestershire, a man who shared his appetite for hard work. Geary had a decent out-swinger and could cut the ball in to the right-hander off the strip. His main attributes, however, were accuracy and doggedness. Geary simply bowled and bowled and bowled. In the Melbourne Test he sent down 486 deliveries. The following season he would bowl nearly nine thousand. His strike rate was not impressive by modern standards, but such was his volume of deliveries it hardly needed to be.

By the end of the Australia tour there were signs that Tate's powers were waning slightly. He had not become a frontline bowler until he was twenty-seven, and now he was edging towards his middle thirties. Like many trundlers he enjoyed relaxing after play with a pint or two, and though no one doubted his fitness there was certainly a little more to Chub than there had been.

Tate was one of those bowlers who are deemed unlucky. He frequently beat the bat with deliveries that were simply too good for the batsman to touch. His luck deserted him more severely late in his career because for the world's best bowlers something was drifting towards them as inexorably and dolefully as an ocean liner approaching an iceberg: Don Bradman.

During the 1928–9 Ashes series – Bradman's first – Tate had rather got the better of him and remarked to the youngster that he needed to play with a straighter bat. Given Tate's genial nature it is highly unlikely that he meant anything unpleasant by it – he was hardly a man for mind games. Bradman, however, was not amused. The batsman's future career would be marked by score-settling with those who offended him.

When he came to England in 1930 The Don made it one of his tasks to teach sweet, smiling Chub a serious lesson. The England captain Walter Hammond described what followed as a 'personal vendetta' against Tate. After a poor start in the first Test Bradman began ostentatiously farming the Sussex man's bowling as he flogged the England attack unmercifully throughout the rest of the summer, hitting double hundreds at Lord's and the Oval followed by a triple hundred in a day at Headingley – a ground where conditions notoriously favoured bowlers of Tate's type.

Though Tate claimed to have come within a coat of varnish of bowling Bradman at the start of that brutal innings at Leeds, The Don had sent his message. And he wasn't finished yet. When Bradman came to England in 1948 and was asked by the press who he considered the better of the two great English medium-pacers he had faced, Tate or Alec Bedser, without hesitation he nominated the latter. Jack Fingleton, who met Tate on that tour, thought he 'was very hurt' by Bradman's comments, and noted how the middle-aged Chub carried around a newspaper clipping in which the South African captain Alan Melville said completely the opposite.

The good and faithful Chub played in only two more Tests in England after 1930. As if that wasn't bad enough his selection to tour down under in 1932–3 was preceded by the

MCC publicly and humiliatingly admonishing him about perceived problems with his attitude. ('I was so taken aback by suggestions that there were matches in which I was considered not to have tried that I was tongue-tied,' Chub said of his reprimand.) That Tate, who had bowled for England until his boot filled with blood, should be treated in so high-handed a manner left him utterly bewildered and 'seething with righteous indignation'. Barnes, of course, would have seen it coming, expected nothing more.

In Australia with the ruthless Jardine, Tate was barely used even in the tour matches, a marginal and drifting figure as the mayhem unfolded in the middle. Worse was to follow. Towards the end of the 1937 season Sussex told him they would not require his services the following season and furthermore did not think they would need him for the remaining games of that season either. In a rare moment of bitter sarcasm Tate told his local newspaper that he would be missing from the county's next game at Hastings, but 'when you are an old man like me with a long beard, decrepit and haggard, one can't expect to play'.

As it turned out, Sussex lost several bowlers to injury and had to recall Tate for the game against Kent. Chub struck a blistering 73 in Sussex's first innings and then took 4–61 and 2–70 in a ten-wicket victory. With public and press opinion firmly behind him, the committee was forced to keep Tate in the team for the remainder of the season. If anyone thought that would earn him a new contract, however, they were wrong.

Tate, like Parkin and many other professionals before him, had been what was considered a little too vocal in his criticism of the ruling powers. That October he received a curt letter from the county committee, informing him that his services were no longer required but, as recognition of his service, he was to be given an ex-gratia payment of £250, 'a sum which in view of our financial situation is certainly generous'.

'It was not so much what was done, as the way they did it,' Tate would say later of the letter that broke his family's fifty-year association with Sussex. He had been made an Honorary Life Member by the county in 1934, but such was his disillu-sionment that he barely went to watch them ever again.

Adrift from the game he loved, Tate was forced to fall back on the profession Barnes had scornfully denounced as the last bastion of the faded cricketer: publican. Being a cheery sort, however, he did rather well at it.

The increasingly bland wickets of the inter-war years made the trundler's life more and more difficult. Many dobbers resorted to the sort of negative tactics that would culminate in Bodyline, bowling a leg-stump line to packed on-side fields, attempting to frustrate the batsmen into submission.

This breed of trundlers relied entirely on the swing of the new ball, or on favourable conditions, to get wickets. Thanks to the more pronounced seam they could now get move-ment off the strip not through spin or even cut, but simply by hitting it and hoping for the best. The result was stultify-ing. Warner, for one, was not impressed with the rising tide. In 1950 he attacked what he regarded as the county captains' over-reliance on medium-pacers and the stereotypical tactics that resulted. 'To-day the "seamer" – a horrid word! – is to my mind overdone.'

Tate exploited the seam, but he refused to be drawn into narrow thinking. Asked why he had not just tried to pin down Bradman during the disastrous 1930 series he responded in horror: 'Pin him down! Of course not! I bowled every ball to get the little devil out!'

His approach was highly successful. He took 2784 wickets in his first-class career and bowled over 150,000 deliveries – so many, it's said, that by the time he had finished he had lost all the spring from those enormous feet. 'He put his whole soul into every ball he bowled,' Pelham Warner said. Chub Tate died while working as a sports adviser at the Butlin's holiday camp at Clacton in 1956. For the first and only time in his life his heart gave out.

Chapter 9

Eau de Trundle

'Here was a scene so dreadfully hideous, so intolerably bleak that it reduced the whole aspiration of men to a macabre and depressing joke.' H. L. Mencken was describing Pittsburgh during the Great War, but he might well have been looking at English cricket in the mid-seventies. Smashed by Ian Chappell's hairy Australians; crushed by the cool West Indies of Richards and Holding; apparently obsessed with recalling any former great who wasn't already retired and working in insurance.

As a teenage cricket fan there was one man I held responsible for the fiasco, the man who had been chairman of the selectors since 1969: Alec Bedser. I loathed Bedser with the bitter, self-righteous door-slamming fury that is the province of the young, the mad and Jeremy Clarkson. I hated everything about him, this big, lumpy man with his broad face and mighty teeth, like some polite, club-tie-wearing Little England version of Ernest Borgnine. I had never met him, never been close to him, never even seen him in the flesh, but I knew what he smelled like, because the minute he appeared on the TV screen the whole living room seemed to fill with a ration-book era scent of overcooked cabbage, damp gabardine, outdoor toilets and that hair lotion that left a pickled-egg coloured stain on antimacassars. My nose wrinkled as I caught the niff and I scowled at the screen. If Bedser had a bag of sweets in his blazer pocket I knew they'd be those medicated lozenges that tasted of mustard gas.

I hated Bedser for what I perceived as his anti-northern bias (Jack Hampshire, Frank Hayes, Barry Wood and Richard Lumb all ignored yet again in favour of Keith bloody Fletcher!), his stolid adherence to the establishment line and his steadfast unfashionability. Most of all I hated the fact that cricket buffs of my father's generation just went on and on and on about how brilliant Alec Bedser was as a bowler, apparently oblivious to the fact that everything they told you about his immaculate line, his perfect length, his hard work and his remorselessly moderate speed just made him sound like the most boring individual in the history of the game.

To me, the fulsome acclaim for Bedser seemed utterly perverse. If they were going to get excited about some old, bald bowler, why didn't they get excited about somebody, well, exciting, like the man who replaced him, Frank Tyson? It was like rejecting King Arthur, Robin Hood, Sir Francis Drake and Admiral Nelson and hero-worshipping Harold Macmillan instead. It seemed to me this whole attitude, this Bedser Syndrome, was at the core of everything that was luke-warm and stodgy about English cricket. He was the essence of medium pace; he gave off the odour of dobber.

Looking back, I can see my dislike wasn't entirely irra-tional. Sir Alec Bedser was conservative with both a lower-case and a capital C. He didn't like change, long hair or jeans and, I imagine, had dim views on men who didn't shave first thing every morning, women who smoked in public and boys who didn't eat their Brussels sprouts. A founder member of the right-wing Freedom Association, he was one of the selectors who decided to leave Basil D'Oliveira out of the England side in 1968, after the South African government had indicated that a 'non-white' man would not be acceptable to them. (Strange that somebody who believed so strongly in liberty should willingly acquiesce to the demands of a foreign regime – but then freedom is a perverse mistress.)

My contempt for his bowling was, I now recognise, totally misplaced. Bedser was no Tate or Barnes, that's for certain: he didn't go in gung-ho, looking for wickets no matter what the surface and conditions like they did. He was as conservative in his approach to bowling as he was to life in general. Bedser knew how to bowl an out-swinger, but by his own admission he never used it because the out-swinger is a high-risk ball. An out-swinger needs to be aimed at off stump and pitched well up. It needs to wink at the batsman and give him the come-on. It must make him lick his lips, smile and think, Oh ho, I'm in here. There is not much margin for error with an out-swinger; a few inches either way and potential caught-at-the-wicket turns into a wide half-volley that gets smacked to the boundary. Tate and Barnes were prepared to take the risk. Bedser didn't like the odds, so he binned it. His strategies to get wickets were more long-term. He was attritional. At least at first.

Conditions for Bedser were, however, very different from those that confronted Barnes and Tate. Wickets, as we have seen, had gradually improved as far as the batsmen were concerned. By the late thirties most pitches were like billiard tables. The one at the Oval, where Bedser played most of his county cricket, was a batting paradise. In 1938 England scored 903–7 on it. It was the sort of total that would have been unimaginable in Barnes's heyday, and in Lohmann's the stuff of the wildest fantasy. After the war Alf Gover, the Surrey fast bowler who had laboured on that pace-sapping strip throughout the thirties, would tell Bedser that he had spent the Blitz praying the Luftwaffe would drop a bomb on it.

The greatest batsman of the Victorian age, W. G. Grace had a career Test average of 32.29. The Doctor's Edwardian equivalent, Victor Trumper, averaged 39.04. Jack Hobbs, the best batsman of the twenties, finished with 56.94. In the thirties Walter Hammond averaged 58.45 and he was only the second best batsman of that era; the greatest, Don Bradman, was so far out of sight if you'd told WG about his achievements back in the 1880s he'd have thought you were drunk or insane. By the time Bedser arrived on the scene the balance of power had shifted, and in the age-old contest between bat and ball, bat had ball in a headlock and was hammering it against the ringpost, laughing. When Bedser met Tate in 1947, Chub – who had been playing in a few veterans' matches – told him he was glad to be retired, given the shirt-front state of modern English wickets: 'There used to be some spring in them, but nowadays all the life seems to have gone out of the turf.'

Fearful that the game was going to fizzle out in a series of tedious draws, the authorities in England at least attempted to do something about it, asking groundsmen to doctor the pitches to make them more bowler friendly and introducing a law that allowed the new ball to be taken so often it never got old – in fact, it hardly got past puberty. Things were slow to change, however, and Bedser found that at grounds like Trent Bridge, even if you found an outside edge there was a fair chance the ball wouldn't carry to the slips. On such wickets, the medium-pacer lamented, 'A second rate batsman can, in cricket terminology, play down the line and make runs in his own time.'

Barnes was part of an England attack so good that Wilfred Rhodes was surplus to requirements, and while it is said that Tate often lacked support when he bowled for his country he did frequently open with Arthur Gilligan, whom the Australian cricket writer Ray Robinson reckoned was as quick as Bill Voce. On other occasions he took the new ball with Voce's Nottinghamshire partner Harold Larwood – hardly a mediocrity.

Bedser had no such luck. Since Larwood had been flushed away in the guilt over Bodyline, England's faster bowling had been moribund. Voce was decent but tainted by association, Bill Bowes not quite good enough and Ted Clarke of Northampton had a kink in his action that many thought looked a bit like throwing (he only played for England in one series, far away in India where nobody was really looking). Even the nation's once-rich vein of trundlers seemed to have been worked out. The best of a sorry bunch was probably the persistent, ginger-haired Dick Pollard of Lancashire, whose 1119 wickets at 22 each in county cricket seemed to matter less to the England selectors than his action, a sprawling, slingy fandango that made him look like a man trying to stay upright on a rolling log. When he did get a turn for the national side he distinguished himself at Old Trafford in 1948, partly by trapping Bradman lbw and partly by hitting the ball into the body of the irritatingly cocky 'Bagger' Barnes at short leg with such power the dapper little chap whose foul mouth had had him banned from the Lancashire League for life had to be carried from the field by his team mates.

The bareness of England's pace cupboard is reflected in the unsettled nature of England's opening attack immediately after the war. Between 1946 and 1950, eleven different players opened the England bowling with Bedser: Bowes, Voce, Pollard, Gover, Bill Edrich, Jack Martin, Alec Coxon, Allan Watkins, Cliff Gladwin, Trevor Bailey and Derek Shackleton. With the exception of the ageing Voce, none was ever an established frontline Test bowler (though, as we shall see, maybe Shackleton might have been). Of the two who became regulars in the England side, Bailey was a solid all-rounder from Essex who, in the manner of John Douglas, played as an amateur but like a professional, bowling successful medium pace off a melodramatically long run. Edrich was a batsman who bowled not all that often (but quickly enough when he did, admittedly). During his nine-year England career Bedser would share the new ball with seventeen other men. Even by English standards that was wildly promiscuous.

Given the disadvantages it's perhaps unsurprising that Bedser chose a more cautious path than his predecessors. That it suited his character – an outlook that had been formed during childhood – was clearly a bonus.

Alec Bedser was born at Reading in 1918, ten minutes after his twin brother Eric. The boys were initially brought up in two rooms belonging to an aunt on Horsell Common, and later moved to Knaphill, Surrey.

Their father was a bricklayer, money was tight and there was little room in the Bedser household for anything fancy. An attitude of prudence prevailed. 'We were brought up with nothing,' he would later recall. 'The years of the Depression were terrible. Every Friday my father would come back home out of a job.'

The Bedser twins – they were identical and remained pretty much inseparable as adults, not only living together in a house they helped build, but also sharing a bank account –

were diligent at school and outside it: they played football to a good standard, sang in the church choir and played cricket for a team run by the local vicar. At fourteen they left formal education and took work as solicitor's clerks in London.

Shortly afterwards a former Surrey cricketer, Alan Peach – an all-rounder who'd bowled right-arm medium pace – opened a cricket school in Woking, near the Bedser home. The twins went to it at every opportunity, bowling long spells in the nets under the tutelage of Peach. The teenagers were both tall and strappingly built, and both bowled medium pace. Judging that this would inevitably mean competing against each other in the future, they tossed a coin to decide which should change his style. Eric lost and took up off-spin. If he'd won I would in all likelihood be writing about him instead. As it was, he did pretty well: in 1949 he scored 1740 runs and took eighty-nine wickets for Surrey.

Peach recommended the Bedsers to Surrey, and in 1938 they abandoned their clerical jobs to join the Oval ground staff. In the summer they were paid two pounds a week plus minimum-rate match fees; in the winter a pound per week as a retainer. A rigid hierarchy existed in the Surrey squad. The gentleman amateurs – always called Mister – had their own dressing rooms, and the senior professionals changed in a separate room from the juniors, who were not allowed to speak unless spoken to. Far from resenting this situation (as many did), Alec Bedser seems rather to have relished it. That first close season he and his brother used their time sensibly, taking a correspondence course in accountancy. 'Our candid advice to the young pro,' the twins opined in an early joint autobiography, 'is not to idle the winter away.'

Within weeks of signing on the Bedsers were playing alongside the elderly Jack Hobbs in a charity match, and in June 1939 they made their Surrey debuts against Oxford

University, though Alec failed to take a first-class wicket before Hitler brought play to a close.

The Bedsers joined the RAF, escaped from the Germans at Dunkirk and subsequently served in North Africa and Italy. Formal cricket was rarely available, but they kept in practice anywhere they could find twenty-two yards of even ground, pegging out one stump and laying a handkerchief on the ground as a target so they could work on their line and length. When county cricket resumed in 1946 Alec immediately caught the selectors' eye, and after only seven Championship games was selected for the first Test against India at Lord's.

The war had bitten a big chunk out of Bedser's cricket years. He was now twenty-eight and his style well-established. He came in from about twelve yards with galloping strides and the labouring tread of a man running up a sand dune. His action was much smoother: left arm flung up high, body in the classical sideways-on position, left leg braced, right arm swinging through high and after delivery whirling round almost in a full circle. If there was a certain stiff muscularity about Bedser's delivery, Neville Cardus was not alone in viewing it as 'proof of compressed and concentrated power'.

Bedser was not quick, but like Tate he bowled that mysterious thing, the 'heavy ball'. Trevor Bailey commented of batting against him that 'he just kept on hitting the bat. Alec jarred my hand more than any other bowler I faced.' And while he may have held off on the out-swinger he did have plenty of other weapons at his disposal. He swung the ball in to the right-handed batsman late, and since his action tended to suggest the out-swinger that on its own was often enough to trap the unwary. Like Barnes, Bedser had massive hands and used his powerful fingers to actually spin the ball that broke from leg rather than cutting it as Tate had done.

The Great One himself acknowledged that 'Bedser came nearest to me in bowling a leg break like mine'.

He could also combine swerve through the air with movement off the track. Certainly it was all too much for the Indians. Bedser ran through them like a virus, taking twenty-two wickets in two Test matches to establish himself as the best opening bowler in England. A cartoonist in the *London Evening News* called him the 'biggest cricket discovery since Maurice Tate's feet'. Not that anyone in the Bedser household was getting carried away. When a journalist rang the family home and asked his mother for her reaction to her son's wicket-taking exploits, she replied simply, 'Well, isn't that what he's supposed to do as a bowler?'

That winter the Surrey trundler travelled to Australia with Wally Hammond's team. His skill and determination found favour with both the Australian public and players. At Adelaide he bowled Bradman for a duck with a ball – swinging in then cutting away in the Barnes style – that the great man later nominated as the best he ever faced. But it was a doomed cause. The Don, 'Bagger' Barnes (who at Sydney batted for 624 minutes), Arthur Morris and Lindsay Hassett were all in imperious form; the rest of the English bowling, with the exception of Doug Wright, was so weak it was less an attack than a mild rebuke.

Wright was a leg-spinner, but he is worth a mention here because he bowled at military medium pace (according to Bedser, 'His fast ball is really fast and devastating'). This hybrid style was much more common in the days of uncovered wickets than it is today. Bill O'Reilly, who was, until the arrival of Shane Warne, generally regarded as the finest leg-spin bowler of all time, also delivered the ball at a pace similar if not equal to that of men like Barnes, Lohmann and Turner. Indeed, Tiger was often compared to Barnes by the Australian press.

Other members of this fraternity of trundly-twirlers included Roy Tattersall, a beanpole Lancastrian off-spinner whose deliveries, Denzil Batchelor noted, 'travel with some speed through the air, and rise sharply from the wicket'. Tattersall also bowled a very effective 'seam-up' away swinger and in 1950 took 193 wickets at 13.59 each. A year later he destroyed the South Africans on a rain-affected wicket at Lord's, taking 12–101. My father recalls watching him bowl to Neil Harvey on a rain-affected pitch at Old Trafford; the Australian left-hander was concentrating so fiercely 'you could see the sweat dripping off his nose'. Unfortunately for Tattersall there was another rather good off-spinner around at the time – Jim Laker.

Wright's rapid googlies were highly successful – among other things he took a record seven hat-tricks in his career – but he was not to everyone's taste. Purists were forever claiming, as they would later of that other trundly-twirler, Derek Underwood, that he ought to 'slow down and give it more air'. Wright's cause was hardly helped by his bowling action, of which a marvelling Bill O'Reilly commented, 'He waves his arms widely, and rocks on his legs like a small ship pitching and tossing in a fairly heavy sea.' Batchelor likened his approach to the wicket to that of a ping-pong ball wearing diving boots. The Kent man gave the ball a big tweak, but was one of those bowlers who almost did too much with it, beating the bat often but finding the edge rarely. His was the opposite of Old Jack Hearne's less-is-more approach.

With no real pace support, Bedser bowled and bowled until his feet bled, sending down over three thousand deliveries on the tour, but so unyielding were the native pitches that broiling summer he took just twenty-eight wickets. At Brisbane he bowled forty-one eight-ball overs in Australia's only innings, at Sydney during Barnes's marathon forty-six. In the fourth

Test at Adelaide temperatures on the field reached 134 degrees. Bedser lost six pounds in weight in a single day and had to leave the field to throw up. His sixteen wickets in the series cost him 54.75 apiece. (It is hard to read the accounts of Bedser's labours in the sweltering heat without thinking of another big slab of a seamer, Angus Fraser, and his prodigious endeavours in the Caribbean in 1997–8. Fraser was even larger than Bedser, and his feet may have rivalled Tate's in scale. Just watching him wearily tramping back to his mark in Kingston and Port of Spain was enough to induce a sympathetic mop of the brow even in those of us watching in freezing Northumberland.)

Bedser may have grumbled but he never gave up, and successive captains piled more and more work on his broad shoulders. In 1947 he bowled 1220 overs in first-class matches and the workload continued to rise. He never bowled fewer than a thousand overs a season for Surrey, while for England he was strike bowler and stock bowler just as Tate had been. By 1950 the best medium-pacer of his generation seemed finally to have buckled under the weight. Against the West Indies that summer he appeared heavy-limbed and his bowling limp, his once high arm seemed to have dipped. He was dropped for the final Test. At thirty-two it looked like his international career might be over.

Instead, something rather mysterious and remarkable happened. Over the autumn Bedser rejuvenated, much as Old Jack Hearne had done back when he had been deemed fit only for the knacker's yard. Cardus believed that something clicked in Bedser's mind, that a bowler who previously had been content to rely on natural strength and instinct suddenly began to apply his intellect to the task, for 'nothing distinguished can be done in this world without some amount of hard thinking thrown in'.

Maybe that was it. Or perhaps it was simply the elation
that came from the knowledge that England were about to
embark on an Ashes tour which for the first time in twenty
years wouldn't involve staring down the wicket at Don
Bradman for hour upon hour upon hour (Bedser had a
good record against the Don, but all things are relative. The
Australian skipper still averaged over ninety in Tests against
him). Whatever it was, Bedser came back better than ever
before. Under Freddie Brown – his favourite captain – the
Surrey seamer was used purely as a strike bowler and his
workload, especially in the tour matches, was kept within
sensible limits. Even though England were heavily beaten
in the series, the management of Bedser paid off. In the
second Test at Melbourne he moved the ball all over the
place. The great Neil Harvey played and missed at him five
times in two overs, before finally managing to touch one and
be caught at the wicket. The Australian opener Ken Archer
declared afterwards that it was the best bowling he had ever
come across.

Bedser's first hundred Test wickets had cost over thirty-
three runs each. In Australia that winter he took thirty at
16.06, ten of them in a remarkable display at the final Test
in Melbourne, where the English recorded their first win over
the old foe in thirteen years.

By now Bedser was getting more support from other pace
bowlers, Brian Statham among them. The Lancastrian had
begun life as a medium-pacer in the Chub Tate mould,
but in his early twenties remodelled his action and became
genuinely quick. Despite his pace, something of the old
moderate mindset remained. Statham was noted for his
immaculate line, his dogged adherence to a good, full length
(he rarely if ever bowled a bouncer), his uncomplaining
attitude when ordered to bowl uphill and into the wind, and

a manner that was generally as mild as camomile lotion. Statham was a trundler trapped in a fast bowler's body, the quickest dobber in history.

The following summer against South Africa Bedser proved that his revival that winter was no final flourish, taking another thirty wickets at 17.23. Then, against the visiting Indians in 1952, he picked up another twenty at 13.95, and when the Australians came in 1953 he took thirty-nine at 17.48, beating the record for wickets in the series that Maurice Tate had set in 1924–5 and doing more than anyone to ensure England won the Ashes for the first time since the Bodyline tour. The other nine bowlers used in the series managed just fifty-two between them.

Bedser's best performance of that glorious summer came in the first Test at Nottingham. The Trent Bridge wicket was traditionally benign and this one was no exception, yet on the featherbed surface he took 14–99 – overhauling along the way Barnes's England record of 189 Test wickets that had stood since 1914 – and performed with such excellence many doubted anyone could ever have bowled better. The ball that did for Lindsay Hassett, who had batted flawlessly over six and a half hours to reach 115, in particular stood out. It started outside the off stump, dipped in sharply at the end of its flight, pitched on leg stump and then whipped across him to clip the top of off stump. Hassett observed wryly, 'I tried to play three shots at one ball and almost made contact with it the third time it moved.'

Later that summer Bedser established a world record for Test bowling when he surpassed Clarrie Grimmett's total of 216 Test wickets. He also became the first England bowler since Barnes to take one hundred wickets against Australia. Bedser opted out of that winter's tour of the Caribbean, and the following summer there were no Tests in England. The rest ought to have done the medium-pacer good: he was now in his late thirties, after all. Unfortunately, in his absence the England captain Len Hutton had started to formulate plans for a faster, more hostile attack. He already had Brian Statham. Fred Trueman had misbehaved in the West Indies and temporarily been ushered away from the international scene, but the captain had his eye on another genuinely quick bowler to take Fiery Fred's place, Frank Tyson.

The Ashes series of 1954–5 was to be a glorious one for England, but a bitterly unhappy one for the man who had been the mainstay of his country's bowling for the previous five years. Things got off to a bad start for Bedser when he was struck down by shingles on the voyage out. Not yet fully recovered, he still played in the first Test at Brisbane. Australia, sent in to bat on a perfect wicket, declared at 601 for eight, with Bedser getting a single wicket for 131 runs – though seven catches were dropped off his bowling.

Before the start of the next Test, at Sydney, Hutton and Bedser, as vice-captain, went out to inspect the pitch. It looked ideal for seamers. But when Bedser returned to the pavilion he found he had been dropped. Feeling better recovered from his illness by the third Test at Melbourne, he anticipated being recalled and only learned that he hadn't been when he saw his name crossed out on the team sheet pinned up on the dressing-room noticeboard. With Tyson and Statham on top form Bedser played only once more for England, against South Africa in 1955.

Alec Bedser finished his fifty-one Test matches with 236 wickets at 24.90 each. This total stood as a world record until 1963, when it was overtaken by Brian Statham. Bedser continued to turn out for Surrey until the early sixties, and in all played in 485 first-class matches and claimed 1924 wickets at 20.42 apiece.

Though the end of his Test career somewhat mirrored that of Maurice Tate, who was also ditched in favour of two much quicker men, Alec Bedser's post-cricket career didn't see him cast in the role of genial mine host. As well as being the chairman of the England selectors (a job in which his record was actually pretty good), he was also a successful businessman. He and Eric had set up an office-equipment business in the fifties and by the time they sold out to Ryman in the late seventies it was turning over £1.8 million a year. Office equipment. Never mind publican, that's a job for a retired trundler if ever there was one.

Chapter 10

The Nabobs of Dob

In England the success of trundling was based on the climate. Damp wickets and moist air favoured the medium-pacer. Meteorology would also play its part in the proliferation of the dobber in another very different part of the cricketing planet, India. It was not that pitches and atmosphere on the subcontinent were particularly favourable to medium-pacers, more that they were even less favourable to the genuinely quick. The heat and the dry, dusty wickets seemed to suck all speed and bounce from a delivery: the more energy the bowler put in, the less he got out. Fast bowlers collapsed with nervous exhaustion; those who saved their strength, bowled a length and let nature take its course might not prosper, but at least they survived.

When Maurice Tate went to India with Arthur Gilligan's MCC side in 1926–7 the tour was organised in such an ad hoc manner that the team were not given their itinerary until they docked at Port Said on the way out. When they discovered they were scheduled to play thirty-four games many of the players let out a whistle of disbelief. Yet if it seemed their hosts were squeezing every last drop out of the tour, perhaps that wasn't so surprising. Gilligan's was the first English team of any kind to tour the subcontinent since 1902–3. The last official contact between the two countries had come when the Indians had visited England in 1911.

I say official contact because over the intervening years a strong trade in cricket services had been established between some English professionals and the wealthy, cricket-mad princes of India. In the late Victorian period a few extraordinarily wealthy potentates had taken to hiring English and Australian professionals to coach and play for their private teams during the European winter.

Rajinder Singh, the Maharajah of Patiala, educated at Cambridge and said to be second only to Ranjitsinhji among Indian cricketers, was the pioneer. A fine polo player, a crack shot, an expert at billiards, the first man in India to own a motor car and the husband to over three hundred women (at least one of whom – the *New York Times* reported in his obituary – was Irish), Rajinder Singh had built a cricket ground and needed a team to play on it. To that end he secured the services of J. T. Hearne and Bill Brockwell, a useful medium-pacer whose opportunities at Surrey were limited by the presence of Lohmann, Richardson and Lockwood, and brought them over to his vast estates surrounding the Moti Bagh Palace in the Punjab.

When Rajinder Singh was killed in a riding accident in 1900, he was succeeded by his son Bhupinder. The new maharajah was even more extravagant than his father – he would proceed about the country in a motorcade of twenty Rolls-Royce cars, and often batted wearing pearl earrings valued at several thousand pounds – and just as committed to cricket. He hired George Hirst for nine consecutive winters and also brought George Brown, Roy Kilner and Abe Waddington to India. The first was a rough-hewn Hampshire all-rounder who, despite spells keeping wicket in motor-cycling gauntlets, took 624 first-class wickets with his robust trundlers. Waddington, a controversial Yorkshire seamer, had been roundly rebuked by the MCC after a poisonous encounter against Middlesex in 1924 in which he displayed contempt for every umpiring decision that went against him and, allegedly, deliberately tripped and injured Jack Hearne.

The Maharajah's most successful import was Frank Tarrant, an Australian who was Hearne's team mate at Middlesex. Tarrant, who came from Victoria, bowled medium-pace left-arm spinners that were lethal on any sort of damp wicket, though *Wisden* declared that he needed to bowl with a bit more zip if he was to be considered genuinely top class. Tarrant was particularly successful in India. He bowled an immaculate length at a military pace that made him hard to jump out to and took bundles of wickets, his most notable performance coming in 1917 when he took 5–9 and 7–36 as the Maharajah of Cooch Behar's XI defeated the Bengal Governor's XI by an innings in front of packed stands at Eden Gardens. The Australian seems to have taken to life in India; as well as playing and coaching he also umpired matches and took his share of groundsman's duties, laying one of the country's first grass wickets at the Maharajah's ground at Amritsar.

Rajinder Singh's main rivals among the cricket-sponsoring Indian nobility were the Nawab Moin-ud-Dowlah in Hyderabad, who brought the West Indian all-rounder Learie Constantine to play for him. (For Constantine the trip was revelatory. When playing for Nelson in the Lancashire Leagues he had encountered for the first time white people who weren't wealthy; now he met wealthy people who weren't white.); Sir Nripendra Narayan, the Maharajah of Cooch Behar, who imported two spinners, George Cox and

Joe Vine, from Sussex to Bengal and – in an impudent piece of business – lured Tarrant away from Patiala; and the Maharajkumar of Vizianagram who, in a coup worthy of an IPL franchise, secured the services of Jack Hobbs and Herbert Sutcliffe.

The professionals lived in the cricket pavilions, self-catered from the local bazaar and in between playing and coaching did the odd bit of tiger shooting. For a man like George Hirst, who had grown up poor among the woollen mills of West Yorkshire, the opulence and splendour (not to say the erotic excess, for as well as having almost as many wives as his father, Bhupinder also kept a troupe of dancing girls) of life in the Patiala household must have been quite an eye-opener.

It would be nice to think that Hearne, Brockwell, Brown, Waddington, Hirst and Tarrant had some kind of influence, paving the way for the great legion of Indian trundlers who were to come. Sadly there's little evidence to support the theory that a direct line runs from Old Jack's arrival in Delhi to the dibbly-dobbers of Praveen Kumar.

The best Indian bowler of these early days, Mehellasha Pavri, was actually pretty quick. A round-armer in the manner of a youthful W. G. Grace, Pavri bowled with sufficient vigour to uproot stumps and send bails flying to the boundary. In 1890, playing for the Parsees against the first English team to tour the subcontinent he took 7–34 in the second innings as the Parsees ran out victors by four wickets. On the Parsee tour of England that followed, Pavri took 170 wickets at 11.66 apiece, though WG was rather sniffy about the quality of the tourists and Lord Hawke scoffed at the amount of time they spent over the drinks intervals.

Bhupinder Singh was a decent cricketer himself and played for the MCC. (His son Yuvraj, benefiting from all that professional coaching, played Test cricket.) It was the

Maharajah who organised and led the 1911 tour. In playing terms it wasn't a great success: the team took a fearful pounding, notably against Staffordshire, for whom Barnes was in imperious form, finishing with 14–29 in the match. Strangely Bhupinder Singh never signed Barnes for a winter, though it is pleasant to speculate as to how the wealthy playboy and the Great One would have got along. And how many wickets Barnes would have taken on the matting strips.

When Maurice Tate toured, the wickets were still mainly matting and the outfields 'as brown as Demerara sugar'. Despite playing in a sola topi, Chub bamboozled the locals with his swing and cut, and when he came up against the Maharajah of Patiala – who that winter had hired three Yorkshiremen, Wilfred Rhodes, Maurice Leyland and Arthur Dolphin – bowled him for 17. That night, according to Tate, the players were taken to see a ram fight, but one of the rams got loose and chased the Maharajah, 'who, in his excitement, almost fell into a well'.

During the tour skipper Arthur Gilligan had been much taken with the all-round displays of a youngster named Nazir Ali, an attacking batsman and purveyor of military medium pace much in the manner, I imagine, of his half-namesake of the seventies, the great Abid Ali (of whom much more later). Gilligan suggested to Nazir that he might make a fist of it in England and proposed a trial at Sussex. Somewhat to his surprise the young Indian took him at his word and, having secured funding from his patron the Maharajah of Patiala, came to England the following May. He turned up on the Sussex CCC secretary's doorstep at one in the morning, apparently expecting dinner and a bed for the night. Nazir Ali played a bit of club cricket and was then called up for the Sussex first eleven when they took on Cambridge University at Hove. The Indian all-rounder batted at number six and opened the bowling with Tate. Unfortunately scores of 9 and 0 and match figures of 1–91 were not enough, and he never played a first-class game for the county again.

In many ways, the first really great Indian bowler was a lot like Tate. Amar Singh was a tall man with shoulders like a buffalo, a broad round face and the easy-going, simple manner of the rustic. He bowled sprightly medium pace (wicketkeepers stood up to him) off a shambling run of about twelve yards. He could – *Wisden* noted – 'curl the ball in the air from leg or off' and did so late in flight. Amar used his height and arm speed to extract extra bounce and pace from the wicket. Wally Hammond, for one, was impressed, saying that the Indian's deliveries 'came off the pitch like the crack of doom'.

Amar Singh was from Rajkot in Gujarat but grew up in the town of Jamnagar, where the princely ruler, the Jamsaheb of Nawanagar, K. S. Ranjitsinhji, spotted him. With Ranji pulling the strings, Amar Singh got a place in a trial match in Delhi before the 1932 tour of England and did enough to earn selection. English conditions were ideally suited to the burly trundler's style, and on what was India's first official tour to England he took 111 first-class wickets at 20.78 runs each.

Amar was partnered with the new ball by Nissar Moham-mad, who was described as a 'youthful heavyweight with a long bounding run' by the almost breathless Altham. Nissar seems to have been genuinely quick so we shall pass over him here. Not so the third member of a pace attack that may well have been the best India ever had. Jahangir Khan, father of Majid and uncle of Imran, bowled at the quicker end of medium and is probably best remembered for the delivery at Lord's – aimed at T. N. Pearce – that killed a sparrow. Jahangir came on first change during the 1932 tour and in the second innings of the only Test at Lord's took 4–60, his victims being the distinctly high-class quartet of Percy Holmes, Frank Woolley, Wally Hammond and Eddie Paynter. He played three more Tests but never took another wicket. At Cambridge he opened the bowling with the fearsome Ken Farnes, and in 1933 the pair decided to deploy Bodyline against Oxford in the Varsity Match. Farnes was menacing and dangerous, and drove sections of the crowd into a frenzy of rage, but visiting pressmen thought Jahangir way too slow for such nonsense, with one even claiming that he was 'merely an off-spinner'.

Backed up by Nazir Ali who, despite the rebuff by Sussex, was still a useful performer who would return best Test figures of 4–60 during the 1933–4 series, the pace attack should have made India a formidable proposition for years to come. Sadly the sort of rifts that would come to be a feature of Indian cricket teams had already surfaced. A constant power struggle between the Indian cricket authorities and the Maharajah of Patiala (whose dissolute lifestyle didn't endear him to colonial administrators) infected the squad. The 1932 tour of England was captained by the Maharajah of Porbandar. When he withdrew from duties on the field due to ill health the role fell to his vice-captain, the Ghanshyamsinhji of Limbdi, and when he too was struck down Colonel C. K. Nayudu took over.

Nayudu was a splendid cricketer who, playing for the Hindus against Gilligan's side, had astounded everybody at Bombay Gymkhana by striking 156 in 116 minutes, including eleven massive sixes. The visitors were so impressed they presented him with a silver bat as a souvenir. As well as batting with cyclonic fury Nayudu also bowled trundly light spin at a pace befitting a senior military figure.

Colonel Nayudu, a tall, elegant man who took to the field

with a silk handkerchief tied around his neck, was a member of the ruling elite. Like many of the British administrators in India he believed the majority of his fellow countrymen were unruly children who needed firm discipline. As far as Nayudu was concerned, Amar Singh, who had turned up for some of his early matches wearing makeshift kit consisting of a black fur cap, white shirt, khaki breeches and black leather shoes, fell firmly into this category. He treated the great bowler as he might a dim-witted servant, and Amar Singh did not take kindly to the high-handedness. The atmosphere between the two men was so poisonous that even Jack Hobbs, who normally shied away from controversy like an elephant from a mouse, commented on it. The result of the feud was that at times Amar Singh – affronted by some instruction from his captain – took to sulking. Others – including Nazir Ali, who had done well on the 1932 tour scoring one thousand runs and taking twenty-three wickets at 21.78 – declared themselves unavailable whenever they felt they could take no more of Nayudu's draconian leadership.

Amar Singh was particularly good with the new ball, mixing swing with a devastating break-back. Unlike some of his contemporaries in the trundling fraternity, he took the Barnes/Tate attitude and always attacked the stumps. It is reported that he never bowled a negative line or went on the defensive and that his field placings invariably consisted of two or three slips, a gully, a cover point and third man on the off-side. On the leg-side a short fine leg, a forward short leg, a silly mid-on and a long leg. Hammond was so impressed by Amar Singh's cleverness that he told the press he believed he was the best user of the new ball in the game. Given that England's attack included Harold Larwood and Bill Voce, that was high praise indeed. Warner also thought Amar Singh uncommonly good, writing that 'he would be a strong candidate for a world XI', while Len Hutton, who'd come up against him in a tour match, reckoned 'there is no better bowler in the world than Amar Singh'.

The Indian was also a powerful hitter of the ball with a first-class hundred to his name, as well as an excellent slip fielder. Unsurprisingly given these qualities, he soon found himself being visited by emissaries of various Lancashire League clubs and eventually signed for Colne in 1935. Singh played at the Horsefield for three seasons. He was the club's first overseas professional and his arrival doubled gate receipts. He was highly successful and hugely popular, and at times his performances even eclipsed those of his legendary rival up the road at Nelson, Learie Constantine. The first meeting of the two men, when Colne travelled to Seedhill, drew a crowd of fourteen thousand.

Amar Singh's best Test figures came at Madras in 1933–4 against an England team led by Jardine and fresh from its triumph over Australia in the Bodyline series. Without Nissar, his regular bowling partner, Amar – who had spent the early part of the series in a bit of a mood – bowled a marathon 44.4 overs in sweltering heat and finished with 7 for 86. It wasn't the only example of his stamina: later in the same series he bowled 54.5 overs in an innings in Calcutta.

The 1936 tour of England under the Maharajkumar of Vizianagram was not without controversy. The best player, Lala Amarnath – who delivered medium pace in a singular manner, shuffling up to the wicket off a three-pace run and then bowling off the wrong foot – had been sent home after shouting abuse at his upper-class skipper in a dispute about the batting order. Amar Singh, meanwhile, appeared for India straight out of the Lancashire League. He grabbed 6–35 at Lord's to skittle out the home side for 134, the first time in Test cricket that India led on first innings.

Back home Amar took ten wickets at nineteen runs each against Jack Ryder's Australians in two unofficial 'Tests' in 1935–6, while missing the other two due to an illness that might have owed something to the captaincy. In 1937–8 he bagged thirty-six wickets at sixteen runs apiece in five unofficial 'Tests' against Lord Tennyson's visiting MCC side. Joe Hardstaff, who played against him on that tour, rated Amar as the best bowler in the world, ahead of Bill O'Reilly.

In 1938, while playing for Colne, Amar Singh was picked to represent an England XI against the visiting Australians at Blackpool. He captured six Australian wickets including Stan McCabe, Lindsey Hassett and Bill Brown (Bradman was having a rest).

In 1939 Amar left Colne for Burnley, and his performances at Turf Moor proved to be even more spectacular than those at the Horsefield. He hit two centuries, six fifties and took 101 wickets at 12.11. It was to be the burly medium-pacer's last great hurrah. That winter he contracted pneumonia and died. He was just twenty-nine. With the possible exception of Kapil Dev, India has not produced a better opening bowler.

Part of the reason that the Indian attack of those early years was so pace heavy was, of course, that the country had not yet been partitioned. Had they been born a decade or so later Nissar Mohammad and Jahangir Khan would both have played for Pakistan.

Separated from the more pace-oriented provinces of the north-east, India fell increasingly under spin's guileful spell. The first great bowler of the newly independent nation was Vinoo Mankad, who had begun life as a medium-pacer only to be coaxed into becoming a slow left-armer by an old Sussex pro named Bert Wensley (who should really have known better, since he was a high-class military medium man himself, and had opened with Chub Tate).

In Pakistan, by contrast, the leading wicket-taker in the first decade of self-rule was Fazal Mahmood, one of the greatest trundlers of the Atom Age. Born in Lahore in 1927, Fazal was tall with a broad chest, a mass of dark wavy hair, blue eyes set in a handsome, studious face and when not on the field usually had an unfiltered cigarette elegantly posi- tioned between the first and index finger of his right hand. In his native land he was treated like a film star and featured in adverts for Brylcreem. John Arlott, not a man much swayed by glamour, wrote: 'His action was not prepossessing; but he was strong, immensely fit, built like [a] policeman.'

The fitness and sturdy physique Fazal owed partly to his father, a professor of economics who had put the teenage trundler on a strict fitness regime that involved him getting out of bed at half-past four each morning, walking five miles from his house and then running back. The diligent young- ster kept up this punishing schedule for seven years. Little wonder he had so much stamina as an adult that he was capable of feats of endurance worthy of Chub Tate, such as bowling 250 overs in the first three Tests of Pakistan's series against the West Indies in 1957–8.

Fazal learned his cricket playing on the coir-matting- on-concrete pitches of what was then still northern India. Matting, whether it was made from coir, jute (as it was at Karachi) or coconut fibre had a deadening effect on pace, limiting the effectiveness of the truly quick, but the ball gripped on the rough surface, making it the ideal strip for wrist spin or the sort of powerful leg-cutters that were Fazal's stock ball. It was on matting in South Africa that Lohmann and Barnes had ripped through the opposition and on that same surface the powerful spun lobs of Simpson-Hayward had given under-armers their final days in the sun. Fazal had had more practice on the surface than any of that trio and, encouraged by the way matting rewarded the input, gave the ball a powerful rip.

According to England fast bowler Frank 'Typhoon' Tyson, Fazal's leg-cutter pitched on leg stump then jumped across the right-hander in the direction of first slip. Australian googly merchant Richie Benaud, amazed by the amount of movement the Pakistani obtained, said that he turned the ball more than most spinners. As if that wasn't enough, Fazal could also move the new ball both ways in the air, and occasionally jag one in like an off-break.

Fazal was often termed 'The Pakistani Bedser', but though the two men were similar in some ways – big, strong, accurate, tireless – there were a number of major differences. Brought up in the damp of England, Bedser relied on swing and seam, and only occasionally cut the ball. Fazal had started out as a leg-spin bowler and he retained a lot of that breed's attacking flair. He was a dashing cavalier to Bedser's meticulous roundhead.

The great trundler made his first-class debut for North Zone in 1944, aged just seventeen, and narrowly missed out on selection for India's tour of England in 1946. After partition Fazal was selected to play for Punjab against Sind in the new nation's first ever first-class match. He celebrated the occasion by taking six wickets in the first innings.

Fazal was duly selected for Pakistan's first Test series, away to India in 1952–3, and distinguished himself in the victory at Lucknow where, on a jute matting strip, he took 12–94. Watching Indians might well have felt rueful: Fazal had been selected to go on India's tour of Australia in 1947–8 and had withdrawn at the last minute. He could very easily have been playing for them.

In 1954 Pakistan travelled to England. Conditions were
very different from those in Fazal's homeland and had been
the undoing of a number of trundlers who had learned
their trade on man-made surfaces. Jimmy Blanckenberg and
Eiulf 'Buster' Nupen of South Africa, for example, were both
hugely effective on woven strips but struggled on natural surfaces. Blanckenberg, a right-arm medium-pacer who was said
to make up for his lack of speed with unflagging accuracy,
took sixty wickets in eighteen Tests between 1913 and 1924,
but by his own admission found adapting to the very different demands of grass highly problematic and on South
Africa's tour of England in 1924 rarely troubled the better
batsmen. He later spent four seasons with Nelson in the
Lancashire League. There were rumours of Nazi sympathies
and Blanckenberg died in West Berlin in 1955, though
nobody seems to know exactly when. Unusually, *Wisden*
did not publish an obituary.

Nupen, a tall right-armer, was less controversial. The son
of two Norwegian immigrants, Buster had been blind in one
eye since childhood, which compromised his ability to bat
and field. He bowled a leg-cutter as his stock ball, mixing it
with the occasional ball that broke the other way. Both were
bowled from round the wicket. Nupen earned a place on his
nation's tour to England in 1924 after taking 184 wickets for
Transvaal in the Currie Cup at just 12.75 each. On matting
Nupen's cutters fizzed and jumped; on grass they simply
lumbered. Like Blanckenberg he was neutered, finishing the
trip with just twenty-nine wickets at a cost of a little under
thirty. Back on jute and coir in South Africa he continued to
be a menace, however, and proved it against Lord Tennyson's
touring team the following South African summer, taking
thirty-seven wickets against them in four representative
matches. From 1930 onwards the South African cricket

authorities replaced artificial surfaces, but Nupen was still picked for his country for matches played on his beloved matting – he took eleven wickets in the first Test against England in 1930–1 – but was left out when they weren't. As grass wickets spread, Nupen's opportunities to shine became fewer and fewer until by the mid-thirties his career had been brought to a premature end.

Fazal proved more adaptable than either of these men. The sort of soft, green wickets that had delighted that earlier trundling tourist 'Terror' Turner proved to be almost as helpful to him as coir and jute. In the traditional opening match against Worcestershire in early May he ripped the ball off the fresh surface, taking 4–54 and 7–48.

The first Test at Lord's was badly rain-affected and didn't start until the afternoon of the fourth day. Pakistan batted with what was then their usual deadly slowness and were all out for 87 the next morning. England were then reduced to 117–9 – Fazal and his opening partner, the right-arm fast-medium Khan Mohammad, bowling throughout – at which point Len Hutton declared and put a stop to the proceedings. Fazal had taken 4–54. In the next meeting at Trent Bridge England won easily and they were on top again at Old Trafford when rain brought a premature end to things.

Rain again delayed the start of the fourth Test at the Oval. Pakistan captain A. H. Kardar won the toss and despite the wet wicket elected to bat. His side's innings lasted barely three hours. They were all out for 133. The rain returned before England could start their reply. The wicket had the making of a real gluepot and Fazal and Mahmood Hussain, another right-arm fast-medium bowler, exploited it superbly. An England batting line-up that included Hutton, Peter May, Tom Graveney and Denis Compton struggled to a total of 130. Fazal, bowling unchanged once again, had taken 6–53

including most of the top order. With the pitch now drying
out England's spinners went to work and dismissed Pakistan
for another low total. With a day and a half remaining the
home side needed 168 to win. Fazal took the wicket of
Hutton (reckoned the best bad-wicket batsman on the planet,
possibly of all time) early, but then Peter May struck a half-
century as various partners came and went. On the final
morning England needed 43 with four wickets standing.
They fell twenty-four runs short. Fazal had taken 6–46. The
Oval was Alec Bedser's home ground and this was his era;
unfortunately he'd been rested for the game (Frank Tyson
was his replacement) so we can only speculate on whether
he'd have exploited the conditions as well as Fazal Mahmood
did, or not.

Many observers feel that after the series in England Fazal
lost some of his edge. Like Tate and Bedser he was a bowler
whose big heart and tireless limbs often led to him being over-
bowled. If that was the case then Australia may have been
glad he was no longer quite as spry as he'd once been, because
when they visited Pakistan in 1956 he ripped into them like
a child into a Christmas present. On the jute at Karachi he
took 6–34 in a first innings in which Australia were dismissed
for 80 and followed that up by taking 7–80 in a marathon
forty-eight overs in the second. The trip to the West Indies
was altogether harder work, with both sides' batsmen piling
up the runs on wickets that seemed designed to drive bowlers
to drink or suicide. Fazal bowled 320 overs, giving away a
meagre 764 runs. His twenty wickets seemed a poor return
for all the sweat and blisters.

With Kardar retired, Fazal now added the captaincy of his
country to his workload. In the last Test ever played on a matting wicket – against Australia at Karachi in 1959 – he bade
farewell to his favourite surface with another five-wicket haul.

His final overseas tour was as captain on an ill-starred visit to India the following year. Both sides were concerned only with avoiding defeat and the Tests were played out in an atmosphere of mounting tedium and distrust. Fazal was noted for his quietness on the field and his gentlemanly conduct. If he made any sort of remark to an opposition batsman it was likely to be a compliment or a comment on the weather. At the gala dinner to celebrate the end of the series in Calcutta, however, he couldn't contain his rage and delivered a fiery speech in which he roundly condemned the umpiring (in those days the home nation still supplied the match officials for the Test series). Fazal had been particularly upset when he'd had the Indian skipper Nari Contractor caught behind, only to have the umpire call 'No ball' when the batsman was halfway back to the pavilion. When asked why it had taken him so long to make his intervention the umpire explained feebly that a piece of chewing gum had got stuck in his teeth. Fazal's scorn proved to be just as effective as his bowling and the two countries didn't play another series against each other until 1978.

John Arlott had said that Fazal Mahmood was built like a policeman, which was lucky because he was one, rising to the rank of Deputy Inspector General in his home city of Lahore. He took 466 first-class wickets at less than nineteen runs each, and 132 Test wickets at 24.70. He bagged ten wickets in a match against England, Australia, India and the West Indies. If he'd ever played against South Africa and New Zealand you can bet he'd have done the same against them too. He was, Arlott wrote, 'in many ways ... the ideal fast-medium bowler'.

Chapter 11

Left-Wing Moderates

During my years as a teenage cricket geek I adopted a fundamentalist approach to averages. As far I was concerned, everything they told me was true. I had no truck with those people who insisted on interpreting *Wisden* according to their own wishy-washy liberal worldview. The ones who were always telling me that, 'Well, you know, in a very real sense a fifty against Lindwall and Miller on a rough strip can be worth two hundred against the New Zealand of Dick Collinge and Ewen Chatfield on a featherbed', or that the bowler I was hailing as the best on the planet because his average was 7.56 had only actually taken five wickets all season, and 'those were against Jammu and Kashmir, which hardly counts'. No, as far as I was concerned the averages never lied. They were the way, the truth and the life. That is why, when I was thirteen, if you asked me to name the three greatest batsmen in the history of the game I answered without hesitation, 'Don Bradman, Geoffrey Boycott and . . . Bill Johnston.'

My reasoning was very simple – in 1974 these three were the only men who had ever averaged over one hundred in an English first-class season. Bradman (115.66) had done it in

1938; Boycott (100.12) in 1971; Bill Johnston (102.00) in 1952. Bradman had scored 2429 runs, Boycott 2503 and Johnston 102 (highest score 28*).

People told me that Johnston's effort didn't really signify anything. They said it wasn't good batting, just a weird statistical anomaly. I dismissed such Church of England waffle for the cowardly revisionist rubbish it was. The Australian Johnston had gone out to bat seventeen times on that tour and given up his wicket only once. If that wasn't genius batting, then what was? If Hammond, Hobbs and Hutton were better batsmen than Bill Johnston, as many people assured me, then how come they got out so often? Obvious, really.

Strangely, beyond one small house in North Yorkshire during the Edward Heath years, Bill Johnston's batting feat has gone largely uncelebrated. When the Australian died in 2007 the obituaries passed quickly over it, pausing only to record the Australian's dry quip to his team mates, 'Class always tells.' Instead the obituarists concentrated on Johnston's more obvious talent, his bowling.

Big Bill Johnston was one of that breed of bowler of which Australia alone seems to have an inexhaustible supply, the left-arm seamer. Pelham Warner believed that the left-arm bowler imparted a natural swerve to the ball that often eluded his right-handed counterpart. If that was true, it may have been because men like George Hirst bowled with their arms at forty-five degrees. When bowling round the wicket this angle has a tendency to encourage the ball to 'go on' and swing in towards the stumps. Left-handers who bowl with a more classically high action and attack from over the wicket push the ball across right-handed batsmen, so that a ball pitching on middle stump will carry on to miss off. This natural angle exacerbates any away swing the lefty may generate and gives his in-swing a dangerous potency. Despite this, the left-arm medium-pacer is something of a rarity in England (Hirst, John Lever and Bill Voce are the only ones that spring easily to mind) as, for some reason, left-handed English bowlers tend to focus on spin. Pakistan has produced a few left-arm opening bowlers (too quick to bother us here); South Africa's frill-free bits-and-pieces man Trevor Goddard bowled uncannily accurate left-arm trundlers between 1955 and 1966, and back in the early seventies the West Indies could call on Bernard Julien and Garry Sobers. But no nation has shown quite such commitment to unearthing left-arm seamers as Australia. At the last count they had four such bowlers with international experience or the potential to get it: Mitchell Johnson, Mitchell Starc, Aaron Finch and James Faulkner. Another one, Nathan Bracken, has just retired.

We have already met Charlie Turner's partner in terror, the left-arm wobblyman J. J. Ferris. He was followed in the lefty line by Jack Massie, a debonair six foot, four inch left-arm medium-fast man with a matinée-idol moustache. Massie was an excellent all-round sportsman – rower, rugby union star and heavyweight boxing champ. He came into the New South Wales team in 1912–13 and took fifty-nine wickets at 18.66 apiece, impressing everyone with his ability – unusual in a cadgie-hander – to swing the ball away from the right-handed batsman. The following season he took thirty-seven more at 16.32. Great things were predicted, but with war on the horizon Jack Massie joined the army. At Gallipoli he tied a red rag to his right arm to make it a more obvious target for Turkish snipers than his bowling hand, but his luck was out. He was caught in a grenade blast that wrecked his left shoulder and never played cricket again.

Charlie Macartney, a mainstay of Australian sides in the decades before and after the conflict that ended Jack Massie's career, is best remembered as a rather dour right-handed batsman, but he also bowled left-arm in the trundle-twirly style of Derek Underwood. Cardus reckoned he was the best medium-paced left-armer of his day. At Edgbaston in 1909 he clean bowled MacLaren, Fry and Hobbs for a total of five runs. Later in the series at Leeds he finished with match figures of 11–85. Macartney varied his pace nicely and his quicker ball was said to be fast enough to take any batsman by surprise.

Macartney retired in 1926. In 1929, seeking a similar angle of attack, the Australians turned to the tall, slender figure of Percival 'Perc' Hornibrook. Hornibrook bowled his left-handers at a sedate medium pace, swung the new ball prodigiously and once the shine had gone could give it a hefty tweak as well. He'd first come to public attention nine years earlier when he'd gone on a tour of New Zealand – not then a Test-playing nation – and taken over eighty wickets at nine apiece. Unfortunately Perc played for Queensland, which was in those days the Aussie equivalent of a minor county, and that counted against him when it came to Test selection. Now, at the age of thirty, he finally got his chance. At the final Ashes Test at the Oval in 1930, on a pitch decent enough for England to have posted a first-innings total of over 400, Perc bewitched the batsmen during their second knock to take 7–92. Hornibrook had all the talent to be one of the truly great trundlers; unfortunately, by the time he got his break he was already on the downward slope. His arm had begun to dip and his accuracy was failing him. Deciding to go out on a high, Perc retired at the end of the tour.

Preceding Bill Johnston into the Australian Test line-up was another left-arm trundler, Ernie Toshack. A country boy from the New South Wales bush town of Cobar, who moved to Lyndhurst when he was orphaned, he had turned thirty before he first set foot in the state capital, Sydney. Toshack was tall, broad shouldered, with dark wavy hair, craggy features, a big grin and the physique of the boxer he'd once been. The rest of the Australian team plainly considered Ernie a bit of a hunk and nicknamed him 'The Black Prince'. 'Bagger' Barnes, who prided himself on being a dapper chappy, was so overawed by Toshack's good looks he called him 'The Film Star'.

Success didn't come easily. Rejected by his local club in Lyndhurst, Toshack played grade cricket for Marrickville before his appendix ruptured with such force it left him in a wheelchair. Unfit for military service, he spent the Second World War working in a munitions factory. His health never fully recovered.

Toshack bowled at moderate medium pace (Batchelor calls him 'slow', which is a bit harsh) and, unusually for a left-armer, could make the ball cut in to the right-handed batsman off the wicket. He could move it away off the pitch, too, and wobble the ball both ways in the air. Like all the great trundlers through the ages he was accurate to the point of pedantry and possibly the most difficult bowler to get a run off that Australia has ever produced.

Toshack was chosen for New South Wales as soon as the war ended, and found his rhythm almost immediately. In March 1946, after seven first-class matches, he was opening the bowling for Australia against New Zealand in Wellington. The match was only given Test status retrospectively, so the Black Prince won his first international cap without actually knowing it. The pitch in Wellington was damp, which perfectly suited Toshack's style of medium-paced cutters and Bill O'Reilly's trundly-twirly leg-spin. New Zealand were routed in two days, and Ernie came away with a match bag of 6 for 18.

In the first Test against England in 1946–7 Toshack was lucky enough to find himself on a typical Brisbane sticky dog. Cutting his pace to exploit more fully the conditions he finished with a match analysis of 9 for 99. During the rest of the series the pitches were not nearly so helpful but, while not taking wickets, Toshack demonstrated that he had plenty of that great dobbing virtue: stamina. At Adelaide, in the same paralysing heat that made Alec Bedser vomit, the Black Prince bowled an extraordinary sixty-six eight-ball overs of naggingly accurate medium pace. Over the wicket, aiming at leg stump to a predominantly on-side field, he jabbed away at the batters, setting them for the knock-out blow from Lindwall or Miller. Despite his burly prizefighter physique, or perhaps because of it, Toshack was dogged by a range of injuries – including to the cartilage of one knee and to the muscles of his lower back – that made his endurance all the more remarkable.

Next season, the Indians toured Australia. In the first Test the Gabba again offered up its signature gluepot and Toshack took five wickets for two runs – in twenty-one deliveries – in the first innings, and six for twenty-nine in the second.

Even with doubts about his fitness the Black Prince travelled to England in 1948 with the group of players that would become known as the Invincibles. It was a happy time: a big, genial man with a clownish sense of humour and a fondness for beer and Scotch, Toshack was so massively popular with the British public he had to employ a friend to help him sign all the autographs that were demanded.

He took over fifty wickets in first-class matches, and – shades of Johnston four years later – ended the Test series with an average of fifty-one, below only Morris, Barnes, Bradman and Harvey. Toshack's role in England was very much a defensive one. The new ball was now being taken

every fifty-five overs, so after Miller and Lindwall's initial
assault Toshack was expected to tie up one end while the
fearsome pace duo and Bill Johnston took turns from the
other. His astonishing ability to straitjacket batsmen was
demonstrated in the tour match against Sussex, where Ernie
so suffocated the opposition they managed just three scoring
shots off him in seventeen overs.

Toshack's dodgy knee finally gave out in the fourth Test.
He underwent a cartilage operation in London, and by the
start of the 1949–50 season was back in action, taking nine
wickets in a Sheffield Shield match at Brisbane. But the knee
and his back wouldn't take the strain any longer and the
Black Prince was forced to retire shortly afterwards.

As a consequence of war and injury, Toshack's Test career
was jammed into just twenty-nine months. In his twelve
matches he took forty-seven wickets at 21.04 each.

Toshack's place as the leading lefty in the Australian team
was taken by Johnston. If the Black Prince was the Ronald
Colman of the side, then Johnston was its George Formby.
Standing six feet two, Big Bill had a gangly frame and the
sloping shoulders and balding head of an office drudge. In
the field he was notoriously galumphing; one spectator yelled
that he looked like 'a galloping hatstand', while Ray
Robinson compared his attempts to field the ball to 'Walt
Disney's Pluto in pursuit of Donald Duck'.

His bowling action did little to dispel the impression of
impending slapstick. Head down, Johnston lolloped to the
wicket, elbows jutting and pumping like the pistons of some
misfiring engine, twisted sideways, arched his back and
whipped his arm over in a high windmilling arc. The whole
thing was so leisurely that his follow-through came to a halt
more or less the second he'd let go of the ball. It wasn't elegant, but it was durable and it remained unchanged from the

first ball to the three hundredth. Which was just as well, because like the early Alec Bedser and his own team mate Ernie Toshack, Bill Johnston was called on to bowl an enormous amount, usually while Ray Lindwall had a breather and Keith Miller attempted to shake off his hangover. Johnston indeed was two trundlers in one, equally happy bowling medium-fast with a hard, shiny ball or medium-slow spin with a soft, dull one. At the higher speed, which he preferred when playing for Australia, he swung the ball late in both directions and made it fizz and jump off the strip in a manner that put older watchers in mind of the unfortunate Massie.

Johnston was born in 1922 at Beeac in Victoria, and learned to bowl with his brother on pitches mowed in the pastures of their father's dairy farm. At seventeen Big Bill moved to Melbourne and played grade cricket. In late 1941 he was selected by Victoria for the game against Queensland (by now a first-class state, cricketwise). Unfortunately for him – and many others – the Japanese intervened by attacking Pearl Harbor, the game was called off and Johnston's debut postponed by four years.

When he did finally make his bow, Big Bill met with little success. In his first two seasons he took just twenty-four wickets at a cost of thirty-three each. The experts were not put off, however. The Australian selectors were already looking for the right type of bowlers to take to England in 1948, men who could exploit the very different conditions that would prevail there just as Turner had done in the 1880s, and Terry Alderman would do in years to come. With Britain in mind, Johnston was selected to play for Australia in the 1947–8 series against India. He did well enough to make the Ashes trip.

In 1948 the left-arm trundler's stamina seemed an inexhaustible resource. In the second innings of the first Test at

Nottingham Big Bill had already sent down twenty-five overs when Lindwall suffered a groin strain and was unable to continue. Undaunted, Johnston ploughed on, bowling another fifty-nine overs to finish with 4 for 147 and – along with Miller – setting up Australia's eight-wicket win.

History views Johnston as a stock bowler, a distinct second fiddle to the romantic, explosive talents of Lindwall and the glamorous former fighter pilot Miller. The figures suggest a slightly different story. In the 1948 Ashes series Big Bill took twenty-seven wickets: the same number as Lindwall, fourteen more than Miller. And he took 102 wickets on the tour, the only one of the Australian bowlers to reach three figures. It is, of course, the medium-pacer's fate to live for ever in the shadow cast by others.

And to be truthful, that was probably the way Johnston wanted it. He was a droll man who didn't take cricket, or himself, too seriously. Bill O'Reilly said the only thing that stopped Big Bill from being a truly great bowler was his lack of a hot temper. If it made him a poorer cricketer it made him a better man. The shambling appearance was slightly deceptive too. Johnston could throw a cricket ball over 130 yards and you can't do that if you're uncoordinated.

By the end of 1948 Johnston had established himself as a vital member of the side – all the more so since Ernie Toshack was on his way out. Johnston confirmed his status with a successful tour of South Africa in 1949–50. The first Test, at Johannesburg, yielded the best analysis of his international career: 6 for 40 in South Africa's second innings.

In 1950 Brisbane (with, as we have seen, a little help from a nuclear explosion) delivered yet another sticky dog. Bill exploited the conditions just as Toshack, O'Reilly or Barnes would have, finishing with 5 for 35 as England were reduced to 68 for 7. He continued as the perfect foil for Lindwall and Miller in Australia's home victory against the West Indies in 1951–2 and in the tied series against South Africa a year later.

Back in England for the 1953 Ashes, Johnston – whose fitness, like his line and length, never seemed less than perfect – strained his right knee during a practice match at East Moseley at the very start of the tour. In constant pain, he was forced to modify his well-grooved action and was nowhere near as effective as he'd been five years earlier. In the final Test he dropped his pace and bowled spin.

When England visited Australia in 1954–5 Johnston's nineteen wickets made him easily Australia's leading wicket-taker, even though he missed the last Test. But his career ended shortly afterwards, when the troublesome knee went again in the Caribbean.

In his forty Test matches Johnston took 160 wickets at 23.91 each. In all his first-class matches, 554 wickets at 23.35 each. His career batting average was 12.68.

Bill Johnston wasn't quite done, however. Just as his career was coming to a close that of another Australian lefty was beginning. Twenty-one-year-old Alan Davidson came into the national side for the 1953 Ashes tour and Johnston became his mentor. 'Bill was terrific to me on my first tour of England in 1953,' Davidson recalled. 'I fielded mid-on to him in the county matches.' And fielding to Johnston was an education in itself. Big Bill showed the youngster how to bowl a well-disguised slower ball by tucking the cherry in the palm and spinning it so that it looped and dropped. He taught him how to regulate the amount of swing by using different angles in the finger or thumb. Not that the effects were immediately obvious, because while Davidson was an efficient performer with ball and bat in the Sheffield Shield, he initially struggled to make a mark on the international scene. A combination of injuries and a tendency to bowl too many bad balls stymied his progress. Between 1953 and 1956 he played in twelve Test matches spread over four countries and didn't once finish on a winning side.

Like Toshack and Johnson, Davidson grew up in rural Australia. His family were poor and their smallholding didn't have electricity. Just as Chub Tate had done, the adolescent Davidson built up his physique with farm work, chopping wood and lugging two-hundred-pound bags of chicken feed around the barn. Since there was no cricket pitch in the neighbourhood Davidson made his own, flattening an area of hillside near his house. If he could find someone to bat he'd bowl to them, and if he couldn't he'd bowl anyway.

Initially, like Big Bill, Davidson bowled orthodox slow left-arm spin, converting to fast-medium only when the team he was playing for found they didn't have anyone to open the attack. If Johnston was one positive influence on Davidson, the other was a lad he came up against regularly in schools cricket: Richie Benaud.

In 1956 Australian cricket was in a period of transition. Bill Johnston had retired, so too had Keith Miller, while Ray Lindwall was coming to the end of his career. Ian Johnson, the team's captain and main spinner, had also decided to call it a day. Mindful that places were up for grabs, Benaud – who had also struggled in Tests – and Davidson became training partners, bowling three-hour sessions in the nets and spurring each other on in state matches. No touring teams visited Australia during the 1956–7 season and Davidson was able to focus completely on his game, correcting the minor kinks in his action and approach that had limited his effectiveness at the top level. That season in eight matches he hit 374 runs at 34.00, including three fifties, and took thirty wickets at 27.50. In what was effectively a Test trial between Neil Harvey's XI and that of Ray Lindwall, Davidson lined up with his mate Harvey and took 5 for 65 in the second innings to help secure a seven-wicket win. Over that Australian winter Benaud and Davidson stuck to the daily marathons in the nets. It was a level of dedication rarely found in an era when most cricketers practised largely by playing.

The sessions improved Davidson's control and accuracy. Ray Lindwall was the benchmark. The great fast bowler was noted for being able to run up and hit any nominated stump; now Davidson could do exactly the same. In 1961 he even did it on the deck of a ship while wearing sandals and swimming trunks, just to show BBC commentator Brian Johnston that England's Brian Statham wasn't going to be the only deadly accurate bowler in the forthcoming Ashes series.

Benaud and Davidson were selected for Australia's tour of South Africa in 1957–8 and this time both played to their full potential. Davidson scored four centuries and took seventy-two wickets on the trip. His fielding had always been exceptional; his slip catching was so astonishing Keith Miller nicknamed him 'The Claw'. On his previous tour, the disas-trous Ashes series of 1955 in which Laker and Lock had destroyed the visitors, Davidson had ended up bowling spin-ners again, but now he was back doing what he did best, running in smoothly off fifteen yards and delivering the ball with a catapulting pivot of the hips and a classical sideways action that helped him swing the ball both ways. At times he even made it 'go Irish', an early term for what would later become the ultra-fashionable 'reverse swing'.

For the next five years Davidson was one of the best new-ball bowlers in the world and probably the best non-spinning left-armer of all time too – though that's a title that would now be contested by Wasim Akram (and Geoff Dymock, obviously). Another famous Australian left-armer, Ian Meckiff, partnered him over several of those years. Suffice it to say here that Meckiff's action was not as easy on the eye as his opening partner's.

In forty-four Tests Davidson took 186 wickets at an average of 20.53. One of his greatest performances was against the West Indies in 1960–1. In that famous series five West Indies batsmen scored more than 350 runs, yet Davidson still managed to pick up thirty-three wickets at a cost of eighteen runs apiece (the next best Australian bowler averaged over thirty). Davidson was a strike bowler, but like the Black Prince was as parsimonious as a Presbyterian parson at Lent, conceding fewer than two runs per over in international cricket.

Davidson did not have much luck with a certain number of imaginary injuries (not an unusual trait in a trundler, though The Claw was no 'Chilly' Old, admittedly), and was also dogged by some genuine ones. He chipped a bone in his ankle on one of his early tours of England; pulled a muscle and went down with a stomach bug during the 1956 visit to India; played in the Tied Test with a broken finger; and laboured with a damaged back on his final trip to England. He played his last Test match at Nottingham in 1963 and, in a piece of business that might have been scripted for Ian Botham, took a wicket with his final ball.

Down the years there have been nearly as many 'new Bradmans' (Doug Walters was probably the best) and 'new Len Huttons' (step forward Bill Athey) in cricket as 'new George Bests' in football. There has, I think, been only one 'new Alan Davidson', and that was Gary 'Gus' Gilmour.

Even those who view celebratory nostalgia as the first step

on the stairway to senility will find it hard to watch footage of Gilmour in his stubby, jutting-bellied prime without chuckling happily and muttering, 'Oh yes, they don't make 'em like that any more.'

Gilmour was short and broad-beamed with a coach-driver's haircut and the sort of bucolic face that might have earned him a place in the Wurzels. He bowled left-arm over the wicket from very wide of the crease, angling the ball dramatically across right-hand batsmen. He produced the in-swinger naturally and occasionally got some out-swing, though with his angle of attack even a straight one seemed to move away. His length was full and he hit the seam hard enough to get the odd one to move off the pitch. When he took a wicket his celebration, following a small arms-raised leap, consisted mainly of a forlorn attempt to hitch his trousers up over his stomach. Even at his peak, Gus had the look of a man plucked straight from the pub. As he later observed, 'I couldn't play under today's conditions, what with the travelling and training and scientific aspects. It's not a sport any more, it's like going to work. You know how some mornings you get up and don't want to go to work – that's how I'd feel playing cricket these days. I'd clock on for a sickie.'

The world was first alerted to Gus Gilmour's jolly presence in 1972, when on his debut for New South Wales he smacked 122. Two years later, and called up to play for Australia against New Zealand, he was similarly inspired, hitting a half-century and taking 4–75. When the Australians came to England in 1975 Gus found Yorkshire to be his natural home, taking 6 for 14 at Leeds in the World Cup semi-final as England floundered to 93 all out, and following that with a match analysis of 9 for 157 in the Headingley Test. In those days Yorkshire did not employ anyone who had not been born in the county, which was a pity as Gus would have proved an amusing foil to Geoffrey Boycott.

On his return to his native land Gilmour – who had also taken five wickets in the World Cup final – performed brilliantly against the West Indies, topping the bowling averages ahead of Dennis Lillee and Jeff Thomson and thrashing 95 in the Test at Adelaide. In the 1976–7 season Thomson was injured and Gilmour found himself opening the attack with Lillee, first at home to Pakistan and then on a brief tour of New Zealand. He thrashed a rapid century in the first Test at Christchurch but suffered a leg strain that impaired his bowling. After that a misdiagnosed foot injury – he had floating bone in his heel but doctors failed to spot it – combined with an approach to training that might best be described as light-hearted (allegedly, during his days playing in Kerry Packer's World Series Gilmour did some of his training runs in a taxi) took such a sudden and dramatic toll on his abilities that in the Centenary Test that followed the return from New Zealand he bowled just nine overs and never played for his country again. He was twenty-five. There have been other Australian left-armers since, the bearded Dymock, curly-haired sprite Mike Whitney who was plucked out of league cricket in Lancashire to bowl at the belligerent Botham in 1981 and crazy beanpole Bruce Reid among them, but there will never be another Gus Gilmour.

Chapter 12

They Also Serve who Only Dob and Wait

Down the years there have been many dobbers who might have played more Test matches – even *a* Test match – but for one reason or another have been strenuously ignored by the selectors. Fred Root of Worcestershire, for example, who in the twenties not only bowled immaculate in-swinging trundlers but did so with his cap still on, and whose 1512 first-class wickets converted to just three England caps. Or the late and sorely lamented Tony Nicholson of Yorkshire, with his Swiss Toni pompadour and Gilmouresque stature, who took 879 first-class wickets at 19.76 but never got the call at home and missed out on a place on the 1964–5 tour to South Africa through injury (despite the fact that few imagined he ever did enough exercise to hurt himself). Or perhaps your thoughts might turn to Peter Lee of Lanky-lanky-lanky-lanky-Lancashire during the Jackie Bond-inspired glory days of the seventies, for would it be possible in the current age for an English seamer to take a hundred wickets in a season – as the Zapata-moustachioed maestro did in 1973 and 1975 – and not even get picked for a ODI against New Zealand?

Even these unlucky trundlers can consider themselves decently served by the England selection panel, however,

when compared to Don Shepherd of Glamorgan. A purveyor of brisk off-cutters, the Welshman took 2174 first-class
wickets, yet never won an England cap. In terms of wickets
to non-international appearances that's a world-record ratio,
and one that's unlikely ever to be beaten.

Shepherd was a bowler in the trundle-twirly style. He not
only cut and sometimes spun the ball, but he swung it too.
Shepherd had come into the Glamorgan second eleven in the
late forties as a youngster who bowled medium pace with a
high arm; he was neat and tidy and hard to score off, but too
straight-up-and-down to take many wickets. Over the next
few years, while his line and length remained flawless he
gradually learned to cut the ball, adding subtle changes of
pace without ever becoming a standard slow bowler. By 1952
he was penetrative enough to finish the season with his first
hundred-wicket haul, a feat he would repeat ten times during
his lengthy career; in 1956 – his best season – he took 177.
On damp or crumbling wickets Shepherd's style was as
effective as that of Underwood and the medium-paced off-
spinning incarnation of Tony Greig would be later. And on
good wickets he could accurately peg away, daring the batters
to come after him.

According to *Wisden*, Shepherd 'struck a balance between
seam and spin which gave him the best of both worlds'. In
the Edwardian era that might have served the Welshman
well; after all, it's pretty much what Barnes did. Unfortunately, as Plum Warner lamented, by the forties tactics in
cricket had become much more fixed than they had been
previously, especially when it came to bowlers. When he was
captaining sides, Warner complained, opening bowlers had
been chosen according to the conditions, or because the
skipper felt that variety of pace or style would confuse the
batsman. At Yorkshire Hirst tended to open alongside the

slow left-armer Wilfred Rhodes, while at Kent right-arm away swing bowler Arthur Fielder and the leg-spinner Colin Blythe invariably took the new ball. At Middlesex it was trundler deluxe Old Jack Hearne and the Maharajah's favourite spinner, Frank Tarrant, who generally opened up. In those more flexible times a hard-to-categorise bowler such as Shepherd might have found a berth with England, at least on tour, but in the post-war years in which he emerged the authorities preferred cricketers who were more easily pigeon-holed and nobody quite seemed certain whether the Welshman was a spin rival to Laker and Lock, or a first-change medium-paced stock bowler who might stop up one end like a Celtic Ernie Toshack. He might, in truth, have done the latter job rather well: most experts considered him the hardest bowler to score off on the county circuit.

Other things counted against the Welshman too. Unlike his more orthodox contemporaries Ray Illingworth and Fred Titmus he wasn't much of a batsman, and he tended to be at his best on the sort of damp seaside pitches – such as his home patch at Swansea – that Tate had so enjoyed. He rarely performed well at Lord's and the Oval which, as far as many of the selectors were concerned, were the only places that really counted. And then there was Glamorgan. The county had been awarded first-class status in 1921 but you'd be forgiven for thinking some people at HQ hadn't noticed. Shepherd wasn't the only player from the Welsh county who was entitled to feel hard done by. Opening batsman Alan Jones scored a thousand runs in every season from 1961 until 1983, hitting fifty-six first-class hundreds along the way. By the end of his career he had accumulated 36,049 runs yet Jones got just one England cap, and since that was against the Rest of the World it has since been taken off him. Jones is the highest run-scorer never to play Test cricket, which gives Glamorgan top slot in both categories. Coincidence?

If Shepherd's team mate Malcolm Nash had played for one of the Home Counties he might have got a tour too. Nash is mainly remembered for being the man Garry Sobers (purveyor of medium pace, among much else) smashed for six sixes in an over. 'We are in the record books now and you couldn't have done it without me,' Nash quipped to the West Indian as they walked off the field at close. But he was a more than useful all-rounder. A big-hitting batsman who had himself once smacked four sixes in a row off Somerset's Dennis Breakwell, and one of the most skilful and attack-minded left-arm medium-pace tweakers on the county circuit. In his seventeen seasons with Glamorgan Nash scored 7129 runs, held 148 catches and took 993 wickets.

Shepherd wheeled down well over a thousand overs for season after season, the wickets clicking up as he did so. He was an intelligent, shrewd bowler and the sort of tough competitor who never allowed his will to win to spill over into nastiness. Richie Benaud commented that if he had 'been Australian' Shepherd would 'have played for his country many, many, many times', and one first-class umpire felt the injustice of his never being selected was so grievous that Shepherd should sue the ECB. Instead, like the true trundler he was, the Welshman simply shrugged and got on with it.

One of the threads that ran through my primary school days was the constant search by the world's naturalists to find a mate for Chi Chi, the female giant panda at London Zoo. At least once a year, it seems, some prospective black-and-white furry suitor would be flown in from a far-flung corner of the globe and placed in Chi Chi's compound at Regent's Park. The hours passed, the media waited, and then, inevitably, the announcement would come through that, yes, Chi Chi had rejected him.

As we have already seen, a similar process was carried out in London in the years following the Second World War as the selection committee at Lord's cast around for a compatible partner for Alec Bedser. Among those tried, tested and found wanting were some of the most redoubtable trundlers the world has ever known, men who not only bowled medium pace but seemed almost to embody it.

One of them was Cliff Gladwin of Derbyshire, a county that is to fast-medium what Cliff Richard is to pop music (not necessarily the best producer of it, but undoubtedly the most persistent). Derbyshire's run of really-quite-decent big, strong dobbers of the lively persuasion probably began with the fabulous Billy Bestwick, a pitman, who galloped into the county side in the Edwardian era and mixed broad-shouldered spells of medium pace with ferocious boozing. True to the less gilded traditions of the Golden Age, in 1907 Bestwick – whose wife had recently died, leaving him with a small child to bring up – was involved in a fracas in a pub that ended with a man stabbed to death. Bestwick was charged and tried but found not guilty on the grounds of self-defence. His drinking was not diminished by the experience and Derbyshire fired him in 1909. He was forgiven a decade later and in 1921 famously took 10 for 40 before lunch at Cardiff, when aged forty-six and allegedly still drunk from the night before.

Gladwin was a good deal more temperate than Bestwick but his bowling was in the same Peak District tradition. At Chesterfield, where the wicket always seemed to be the colour of Connemara marble and the sawdust piles were in perpetual need of replenishment, Gladwin came tiptoeing to the wicket off a short run and bowled feisty in-swing that

ninety-nine times out of a hundred pitched on the traditional Derbyshire spot – middle-and-off just back of a
length. Gladwin used the full width of the crease to vary his
angle of attack and occasionally ran the ball away. He'd first
appeared for Derbyshire in 1938 and honed his skills during
the war years by playing at weekends in the Bradford League
(which, controversially, refused to allow Hitler to stop play).
He went straight into the Derbyshire team for the 1946
season and snaffled 109 wickets at 18.36. Called up to face
South Africa at Old Trafford the following summer he was
given the traditional trundler's role of bowling a marathon
spell into a headwind stiff enough to upend a sightscreen.
He sent down fifty overs for fifty-eight runs. At the Oval in
the fifth Test the weather was so hot that members in the
pavilion were given permission to remove their jackets. With
no help from the pitch and even less from the atmosphere,
Gladwin bowled thirty-two overs but failed to get a wicket.
Already the selectors were starting to feel they didn't much
fancy him after all. He was brought back a couple of times –
for the winter tour of South Africa in 1948–9 and a single
Test against New Zealand in 1949 – but by then it was obvious that, as far as the people who mattered were concerned,
the chemistry just wasn't there. Free to concentrate his efforts
on the emerald wickets of his native county he seamed his
way to a hundred wickets in twelve of his thirteen first-class
seasons. In the other one he got ninety-four. Gladwin's new-
ball partner at Derbyshire was Les Jackson, also cruelly
ignored by England but, on balance, a bit too fast for us to
worry about.

Cliff Gladwin made eight Test appearances for England,
which was one more than another of the Chi Chi trundlers,
Derek Shackleton, managed. Tall, immaculately turned out,
numbingly accurate, minimal of fuss, devoid of fanciness,

rolling in remorseless as the waves for day after day, summer upon summer, Shackleton was the sine qua non of trundlers. The unshining star of the medium breed. Its acme. Its quintessence. He was every dobber. It was all in him.

Shackleton, the son of two Lancastrian weavers, was born in Todmorden, that tipping point between Yorkshire and Lancashire that also spawned Peter Lever. Luckily he was born on the right side of the border. As is traditional with the trundler Shack's entry into the ranks of medium pace was reluctant. He started out playing as a batsman for Todmorden in the Lancashire League. One day, a bowler short, the captain asked him to turn his arm over. Shackleton obliged with some wibbly-wobbly bits and pieces and took four wickets for nine. He was given the new ball against Nelson and took five more. Yet he was unconvinced that dobbing was the route to happiness, and so gave it up in favour of the more erudite leg-spin.

At eighteen Shackleton joined the army. He was based in the south for much of the war and was spotted by Hampshire when playing for a representative team at Didcot. He had a trial with the county in 1947 and was promptly signed on professional terms, as a batsman.

At his new county Shackleton continued to experiment with his leg-breaks, but one day when he was bowling them in the nets his captain Desmond Eagar and one of the Hampshire committee suggested he might try mixing them up with a few quicker deliveries. Perhaps they were hoping for another Doug Wright. In matches the leg-breaks failed to trouble anyone, but the quicker deliveries did. Soon Shackleton was bowling them exclusively. In his first season he took twenty-one wickets and in 1949 a hundred. That season he also scored 914 runs with batting that had all the flamboyance his bowling lacked. However, his days as a genuine all-rounder didn't last long. Like George Hirst he found that as one skill sharpened the other dulled. His batting fell away, but his bowling became more and more potent and in every season from 1949 to 1958 he took at least one hundred wickets.

That Shack managed such a feat is a testament to his skill, because the fifties in England were not the happiest time for medium-pacers. By 1955 England had finally unearthed fast bowlers quick and good enough to bring down the curtain on Bedser's international career. In county cricket, meanwhile, spinners were having a fine old time. In the 1955 season sixteen twirlymen took more than a hundred wickets (seventeen if you include the Australian Vic Jackson, who varied between spin and seam depending on conditions). Only half as many trundlers broke that barrier, among them Alan Moss and Alan Watkins of Middlesex and Ian Thomson of Sussex, all of whom got Test caps. Future TV commentator Jack Bannister was also on the list, along with Bedser, Gladwin and, top of the tree average-wise, Shackleton.

Hampshire had already had one great trundler, Alec Kennedy, who had been born in Edinburgh in 1891 and moved with his family to Southampton when he was five. He made his county debut as a sixteen-year-old in 1907 and was still bowling his medium-pace in-swingers and leg-cutters, 'his right arm as high and straight as a hop-pole', three decades later. During that period Kennedy took 2874 first-class wickets. It would have been well over three thousand if the First World War hadn't intervened. Despite the deluge of wickets he played just five Test matches, all on the 1922–3 tour of South Africa, but though he took thirty-one wickets he was never called on again. The reason was simple: Chub Tate.

Kennedy was praised for his 'machine-like regularity' and

Shackleton's approach was similarly metronomic. His run-up was so smooth and emollient it was almost as if he was deliberately setting the batsman at his ease. His head was absolutely still, and tilted slightly back so he appeared to be looking down his nose at his opponent. His action was pleasingly sideways on. His left elbow pointed directly at the batsman while his right wrist was cocked at ninety degrees to his bowling arm, snapping forward at the point of delivery. All this was done with so little apparent effort or obvious menace that spectators frequently went away shaking their heads, amazed not that Shackleton took so many wickets but that somebody who appeared so innocuous took any at all.

In truth, this smooth gliding action, as easy as a golfer's swing, was the key to Shackleton's success and longevity. It was from this that all his trickery flowed. At first he relied mainly on the late out-swing that came naturally; later he perfected an equally late in-swinger. He hit the seam with every delivery and his stock ball was one that went straight, pitched on middle stump and moved a couple of inches to the off. His accuracy was also a key factor. John Arlott wrote of Shackleton 'beating down as unremittingly as February rain', the nagging length that always left the batsman feeling that maybe, no, yes he should play forward, the sudden subtle change of pace or line, sometimes even the less than subtle and therefore totally unexpected beamer. It was mesmerising. The runs were reduced to a trickle. In his early years Shackleton conceded, on average, 2.13 runs per over, and as the seasons rolled by it would drop below two. It was said he didn't even know what a long hop was.

Often Shackleton worked attritionally, weaving a web around the batsman. He had to. In the fifties Hampshire really only had two bowlers, Shackleton and his new-ball partner and fellow trundler Vic Cannings. The pair were expected to take wickets early and then carry on. If they could get sides out quickly, then so much to the good. If not, they were expected to keep the scoring to a minimum and grind the opposition down. 'Shack was allowed to bowl one half volley a season,' Cannings later explained, 'and I was allowed two.' Eagar, the Hampshire captain – mindful that his team was not as talented as many others – set defensive fields and expected them to be bowled to. Loose deliveries were not tolerated. Anyone who was hit for four was immediately given the hook. It made it hard for spinners and few stayed long. Instead, Shackleton wheeled his arm over through session after session. He sent down over a thousand overs every season from 1951 to 1968. In 1962 he bowled 10,303 balls in first-class matches, the last bowler ever to break five figures in a county season.

Often his long spells and accuracy brought an added bonus: on dry wickets he hit the same spot with such unerring regularity he wore and dented it, causing the ball to jump or shoot. In a game against Don Shepherd's Glamorgan at Newport in 1953 Shack's deliveries created a shallow pothole six inches in diameter in the first innings. In the second he hit it repeatedly and finished with nine wickets.

Shackleton had the family-friendly good looks of a gameshow host and was so polite on the field that umpire Syd Buller reported 'when Derek handed you his sweater it was always neatly folded'. And no matter how many overs Shack had bowled, he never, as *Wisden* noted approvingly, 'had a hair out of place'. It was something another great trundler made note of. Asked what he thought was the key aspect of bowling, Tom Cartwright replied, 'To keep your head still throughout the cartwheel of the arm-swing. All great bowlers keep their heads still. Derek Shackleton was a good example.

His hair was exactly the same after forty overs as it was when he started.' Of course Shack could have been using product, but the point is well made.

Despite the nice, sensible hair, the decency, the accumulation of wickets and the admiration of those who played with and against him, the England selectors were oddly reluctant to give Shackleton a run in the side. Perhaps they considered him too similar to Bedser, whose career had begun at more or less the same time. Shack's seven Tests came in two short bursts separated by almost twelve years. He played once in 1950, again in 1951 and then toured India in 1951–2, where he took plenty of wickets in the tour matches but was given only one chance in the Tests. He had to wait until 1963 for a recall, taking fourteen wickets at 34.53 against the West Indies, including a best 4 for 92 at Lord's.

Shackleton finally retired from first-class cricket in 1969, aged forty-five. He took a hundred wickets in a season twenty times (only Wilfred Rhodes managed it more often) and his career total of 2857 is the highest by any bowler who began his career after the Second World War. In total he sent down 159,001 deliveries in first-class cricket. Shack drank and ate modestly and was barely injured, despite taking a less-than-strenuous approach to training. His pre-match warm-up for county matches is said to have involved little more than smoking a cigarette and – what else – combing his hair.

Tom Cartwright was eleven years younger than Shackleton, but because of the war and Shack's longevity their careers ran in parallel for almost two decades. Cartwright made his first-class debut for Warwickshire in 1952 aged seventeen, and from the late fifties through the sixties the pair seemed to stage an almost annual contest for the title of the Best Trundler England Has Chosen to Ignore.

If Shackleton's action was good, Cartwright's was better: so technically perfect – many said – it should have been filmed and shown to every young bowler in Britain. A dip of the head then seven bouncing strides to the crease, left arm high, leading shoulder facing the batsman, front leg braced, head still, eyes looking over the shoulder towards the target area, the delivery arm brushing the right ear as it wheeled loosely over. The pace of the two men was much the same, as were their weapons of attack. Initially the Warwickshire man could bowl only in-swingers, but during National Service his physique thickened, changing his action almost imperceptibly – but just enough to add the out-swinger to his armoury. He hit the seam too, though arguably his most potent threat to the batsman's well-being was his brain. Like Lillywhite and Barnes, Cartwright was a thinker. He had an awareness of the strengths and weaknesses of all the great batsmen of his era: Geoffrey Boycott sometimes misjudged length, Tom Graveney often gave bat-and-pad catches off an in-swinger early in his innings, Roy Marshall would murder any out-swinger. Nowadays it's the sort of information that is easily compiled for bowlers from videotapes and the internet, but in those days it was knowledge that took years to accumulate. Little wonder Mike Brearley described Cartwright as the nearest thing he knew to an ideal craftsman.

By his own admission, Cartwright did not run up and try to get a wicket with every ball. Instead he bowled with a plan in mind, thinking ahead 'in two- or three-over permutations'. Like a boxer Cartwright did not simply rush in flailing in the hope of landing a knock-out blow; rather he manoeuvred his opponent until he had set him up for one.

Cartwright's view – and it was one Barnes shared – was that the key to taking wickets was to get the batsman moving his feet. In Cartwright's case he would bowl several identical deliveries on the trot, say an out-swinger bowled from wide of the crease, so that the batsman became accustomed to moving his feet into the same position, then he'd throw in a slightly different delivery – the same out-swinger but this time from closer to the stumps. 'There's a good chance,' Cartwright observed, 'that his feet will go into the same position from which he played the previous deliveries but now the angle of the ball is different' and the batsman would have to move the bat away from his body to meet it, often a fatal error. Like Old Jack Hearne, Cartwright was a man who succeeded through small changes. It was a question of degrees.

Cartwright was born in the West Midlands into a working-class household with a background of iron foundries and coal-mining. Like Bedser he suffered childhood poverty and witnessed life in the dole queue, though his reaction to the experience was totally different. Cartwright became a committed socialist, tough, obstinate, highly principled and, like S. F. Barnes, with a keen sense of his own worth as a craftsman and a habit of upsetting those in charge. He had strong views about the way players should behave both on and off the field and set high standards. For Cartwright, being professional didn't just mean getting paid. As John Arlott wrote of the Wolves manager Stan Cullis, he was a passionate puritan.

While S. F. Barnes seemed to relish his job and Tate was happy in it, Cartwright at times exuded a kind of wary sombreness about the difficulty of it all. Trundling was to him – as poetry was to Dylan Thomas – a craft or sullen art.

In an illuminating chat with the BBC's Peter Walker (himself a medium-pacer of some renown) that at times reads like one of the author interviews from the *Paris Review*, Cartwright explains the difficulty of the dobber's trade: 'A

genuinely quick bowler or a finger spinner can get away with
the odd really loose ball, but at medium pace, a slight wandering away from length or line almost certainly means four
runs. It's a hell of a strain to bowl accurately for a long spell.
I nearly always bowl with a short square leg, and I know
above all else that his physical safety depends on my accuracy ... after a long day in the field I often come off feeling
as limp as a rag through the accumulated anxiety.'

At Warwickshire Cartwright was – a familiar story – signed
on as a batsman. His bowling was considered useful for net
practice and maybe as fourth change on a hot day. But when,
towards the end of the fifties, three of Warwickshire's frontline seamers all retired in the space of a season and Cartwright's
bowling went from occasional to regular, his batting remained
obstinate and he did the double of a thousand runs and a
hundred wickets in 1962. On the county circuit his bowling
was much admired. Like Shackleton he was a model of accuracy and dauntingly hard to score off. Unfortunately the
England selectors took rather the same view of Cartwright as
they did of Shepherd – that he was a man who could only
take wickets when conditions were in his favour. As if to
prove themselves correct they finally called him up for the
fourth Test against Australia in 1964. The match was played
at Old Trafford on a track so lacking in malice it might have
been played by Doris Day. Both teams hit totals of over six
hundred in their first innings and Australia's Bobby Simpson
scored a triple century. On the shirt-front strip Cartwright
laboured heroically, sending down seventy-seven overs and
taking 2–118. As if that wasn't punishment enough he
was retained for the final Test at the Oval, where the wicket
remained such a paradise for batsmen it often seemed that
the best form of attack for the fielding side would involve a
snake and an apple. In south London Cartwright bowled

sixty-two overs in Australia's marathon first innings, finishing with 3–110. It was enough to earn him a place on that winter's tour of South Africa. The trip was not a great success for the Warwickshire seamer – he broke a bone in his foot early on – but what he saw of the apartheid system as he moved around the country was to have a profound effect on cricket.

Back in England Cartwright was picked to play against New Zealand, but was then injured again (a persistent shoulder complaint that despite several operations would dog him for a decade). He returned for the Test with South Africa but broke his thumb trying to take a catch in the first innings and could not bowl in the second. It was the last time he played for his country.

After three years in the international wilderness Cartwright's selection for the tour of South Africa in 1968–9 was a surprise. When he withdrew, citing his troublesome shoulder – others suggest it was a matter of conscience – it paved the way for the selection of Basil D'Oliveira. D'Oliveira was a useful medium-pace swing bowler, having switched to trundling from leg-spin after coming to England to play in the Central Lancashire League. It was not D'Oliveira's bowling that concerned the Pretoria regime, however. It was the colour of his skin. The political furore that surrounded the affair, in which Bedser played a central role, led to the cancellation of the tour and the sporting isolation of South Africa.

Like many cricketers of his generation Cartwright was worried about his future. He left Warwickshire in 1969 and took a coaching job at Millfield School. A year later he signed for Somerset. Cartwright's spell in the West Country ended after a stand-up row over his fitness with the county chairman in a toilet at Weston-super-Mare. He went to

Glamorgan as coach, playing a handful of games during the 1976 season.

During his career Cartwright took 1536 wickets at 19.11. Some criticised him for negativity and for masterminding skull-numbing sessions in county games in which runs were squeezed out as easily as water from rock. But complaining that a medium-pacer was accurate was to miss the point. As Cartwright himself observed, 'At my pace you have to bowl accurately to survive.'

Cartwright's influence could be seen in the sideways-on action and mastery of swing of his protégé Ian Botham. The Somerset all-rounder might have followed in his well-worn footsteps and become another Tate or Bedser but, as I said earlier, Botham was a very different character from Cartwright – who may have had a profound effect on his cricket but seems to have had none whatsoever on his politics. Botham was at once more right-wing and paradoxically less conservative than his mentor. If Cartwright was a barrack-room lawyer, Botham was a saloon-bar non-conformist. The attitude influenced his approach to bowling. Arguably his best performances came when he abandoned attempts to shock or startle opponents with speed and bounce and concentrated instead on his craft. At Edgbaston in 1981, for example, when he swung the ball both ways at a pace only slightly above military medium, used the width of the crease intelligently and plotted the downfall of the Australian batsmen in the chess-like way Cartwright had done. He might have stuck to that approach. He didn't. How could he? When Botham batted or bowled the crowd expected something dramatic, a highlights package for their memories. When he strode to the crease or took off his sweater a hush descended. Cartwright was a professional, Botham was a star. He had a love of the spotlight that distracted him from the steady focus of line, length and frugality. If he hadn't, perhaps his career would have lasted longer and he'd have taken five hundred Test wickets. On the other hand, maybe, like Cartwright, he'd have laboured away productively on the county circuit, earned the admiration of his peers and passed unrecognised in public: the traditional career path of the trundler.

Chapter 13

A Nation of Pie-Chuckers

By the mid-sixties, when Cartwright and Shackleton were nagging away taking wickets and frustrating batsmen with an infuriating mastery of their craft, a rising tide of anti-trundler feeling began to sweep through the cricket establishment. The 1968 edition of *Wisden* carried an impassioned article by the great strokemaker Denis Compton, in which the former Brylcreem boy did what none of the current crop of batsmen seemed willing or able to do – hit out at the medium-pacers.

According to Compton, men like Shackleton and Cartwright were, pure and simple, strangling the life out of the summer game. On wickets that suited them, their style of bowling was apparently so difficult to play against it was markedly unfair to the middle order, while on wickets ideal for batting their confounded accuracy prevented the willow-wavers from entertaining spectators with their gallant stroke play. Trundling, in Compton's view, was literally murdering the game, not only denying the public the chance to watch cover drives, late cuts and the other pretty adornments of the batter's art, but threatening the very existence of more exotic bowling types such as the capricious wrist-spinner and the steam-snorting paceman.

We had been here before, of course. Back in the days of Alfred Shaw there had been dark mutterings about the damage a plethora of dogged dobbers was doing to the national pastime (though the fact that W. G. Grace had, by common consent, almost killed off genuine fast bowling by bashing its practitioners' deliveries all around the ground was treated as rather a splendid thing, proof of his talent and mastery). When Hirst had popularised swing bowling there had been an even greater clamour. Packed leg-side fields waiting for the in-swinger to do its work were – it appeared – going to sound the death knell of all that was good and noble in the sport. Though off-spinners had been bowling in a similar manner since the glory days of Australia's George Giffen way back in the 1880s, it was the humble seamer who was held responsible.

Nobody seems to have found the metronomic batting of Don Bradman particularly thrilling ('It was like watching a machine,' an old Yorkie who'd sat through his three hundred at Leeds once told me) but his massive accumulation of runs excited the public in the way the hoarding of dot balls plainly didn't. Well, not when a medium-pacer did it anyway.

When a spinner such as South Africa's 'Toey' Tayfield bowled maiden after maiden it was tense and thrilling. When a trundler did it, well, it was just plain old boring. The fact that the run-ups of the genuine fast bowlers were getting longer and longer, slowing over rates to a tortoise-like crawl, was yet to become an issue. Never mind that Wes Hall took almost as long to walk back to his mark as Cartwright took to bowl an entire over. Hall was dramatic, exciting. Cartwright wasn't.

Few who weren't medium-pacers themselves were prepared to step in and fight their corner. As Peter Walker observed, medium-pace bowling, 'with its lack of visual aggression or artful flight, finds few sympathisers either in the press box or from the supporters on the boundary'.

That seems about right. In most books that name the hundred greatest cricketers of all time – Christopher Martin-Jenkins's from 2009 is the most recent – the only medium-pacers likely to find a place are Turner, Lohmann, Barnes, Tate and Bedser. Spinners and pacemen fare much better. In fact, if you are planning to become a famous bowler it seems you are twice as likely to succeed if you pick spin over seam and three times as likely if you can wang it down at around 90mph. This can only mean one of two things. Either trundling is the hardest of all types of bowling to do really, really well; or it's a bit like running a fish and chip shop – always popular but never likely to get the person standing at the fryer a Michelin star or their own TV cookery show.

Despite the grumbling, and the introduction of covered wickets in the late sixties – a move designed to limit the effectiveness of men like Don Shepherd – the trend towards trundling in England continued moderately and inexorably onwards.

And this is where I came in. By the time I started to attend County Championship cricket it had become almost the antithesis of sport. When people went to football or rugby, boxing or tennis or all-in wrestling, they did so to be thrilled, to be lifted momentarily out of their humdrum lives. When you went to an out ground like Harrogate or Tring to watch a Championship match it was for quite the opposite reason. It was to escape the excitement of the domestic scene, with its roller-coaster of emotions and arguments over whether sitting watching *Farmhouse Kitchen* was really the best way to spend your afternoons. To visit Acklam Park or Amersham was to retreat to a quiet and contemplative place where you could relax and read Dicky Rutnagur's account of the latest round of Ranji Trophy matches without your mother disturbing you by Hoovering the stair carpet, while out on the field John Spencer, Graham Burgess, Paul Pridgeon or Bob Ratcliffe put up what was the athletic equivalent of a Do Not Disturb sign with their dobbers.

It is hard to imagine now, but in the mid-seventies the very notion of an English fast bowler was so far-fetched it might have made an episode of *Arthur C. Clarke's Mysterious World*. Yes, we knew there had been such a thing in the past, and some even claimed to have seen one – John Snow. Things were so desperate that Ted Dexter started a Find a Fast Bowler competition, a kind of cricketing version of *The X Factor* in which javelin-throwers and the like would be picked up, taken to a secret location and trained by experts to fill the gaping hole where Frank Tyson and Harold Larwood had once stood. The winner was a lad named Junior Clifford. Like Steve Brookstein, nobody much recalls him now.

Occasionally a rumour would begin to circulate. At Scarborough one Sunday afternoon, as we sat beneath watery skies watching Arthur 'Rocker' Robinson tripping to the wicket, tongue protruding from the corner of his mouth, chest puffed out like that of a stroppy robin, we heard a whisper. Somebody, it was said, had heard that in the Bradford League there was a young bowler, really, really fast – the new Fred Trueman. If only Yorkshire would give this lad a try. Then we'd see. We'd wipe the grin off the smug faces down south. One look at this lad and those Surrey and Middlesex boys'll cack themselves, you watch, the whisper said. Eventually the great day came. It was a Roses match, televised live in those distant days. The excitement was so great I could barely sleep. Here at last was the man we needed. Soon Yorkshire would win the Championship again and England the Ashes and everybody would sing the name of ... Steve Silvester. You cannot possibly imagine the disappointment.

And so it went on. The trouble was, or so it seemed, the weather in England. Even players who came here from overseas were changed by it. Basil D'Oliveira was not the only one to change his style of bowling to suit his new environment. The Australian all-rounder Bill Alley (possibly the best cricketer never to play a Test) came to England a leg-spinner but quickly swapped to niggardly military medium seam-up. When his compatriot Greg Chappell joined Somerset he too was a leggie, but switched to trundling swervers. Garry Sobers already bowled quick (his bouncer was said to be as fast as Hall's) and slow when he joined Radcliffe in the Central Lancashire League. After a few months in the damp of Greater Manchester he'd added swinging left-arm dobbers to his repertoire. If even West Indians and Australians succumbed after a few months, what chance did bowlers who grew up here have? No, complaining about the seamers in English cricket was like moaning about the lack of sunshine. If Denis Compton didn't like it he should bugger off and live in the West Indies.

And so it went on. That day at Scarborough Robinson – a local man, and the announcement of his name drew applause – bowled his left-arm seam-up from one end and young Graham Stevenson plodded away at the other. Occasionally they'd consult. Neither of them were built like athletes: when they stood together they looked like a pair of butchers. When one of them got tired Howard Cooper or Steve Oldham would come on.

Yorkshire's best seamer, Chris Old, had already been on, and likely limped off with some unspecified niggle or knock. We did not voice any criticism. Old was one of the few cricketers who came from our home town of Middlesbrough

(Geoff Cook of Northants was the other one). We wanted to love him. We wanted him to break through the cloud of melancholy dampness that seemed perpetually to hang over his wide but slightly stooped shoulders and do something startlingly brilliant and make us proud, but it never quite happened. Old trudged gamely on, always with the air of a man labouring under the effects of a heavy and insidious cold, greatness like that extra yard or two of pace perpetually just beyond his reach.

Chilly (he was C. Old, you see) had made his Yorkshire debut ten years before at Portsmouth, Derek Shackleton's favourite ground. In those days he was a batsman who bowled a bit, sometimes coming on after Trueman, Tony Nicholson and Brian Close had had a go. Nicholson looked after him. Taught him how to shine the ball properly and swing it. Old's bowling action was easy and natural. Observers thought he'd be the next Fiery Fred. Perhaps even Fred himself thought it, telling the youngster to be more aggressive, to get up the batsmen's snouts. Maybe the rest of Yorkshire believed it too. 'People always expected me to be Fred's natural successor, to bowl as nastily as him,' Old recalled with an air of resignation.

Like Alan Davidson, Chilly was beset by injuries – two knee operations in the early seventies, electric-impulse treatment for a dormant thigh muscle a few years later, a persistent shoulder injury that meant he couldn't throw – but his tendency to dwell on his aches and pains earned him a reputation as a hypochondriac. 'The biggest battle with Chris Old,' Mike Brearley would later say, 'was to get him on the field.'

In 1978 he'd take 7 for 50 against Pakistan at Edgbaston, score a century and take nine wickets against Lancashire in the Roses match; he'd play a small but pivotal role at

Headingley in 1981, scoring 29 in England's second innings as Botham crashed the bowlers about the place and taking the wicket of Allan Border for a duck just when Bob Willis's mad burst from the Kirkstall Lane end looked to be running out of fuel. All these things happened after Old had, by his own admission, 'stopped trying to bowl really quick'. He had reached for the trundler inside himself. If you were English, that was what you had to do. And if Old was not himself great he had, in that Ashes series, been part of greatness, which is probably better. Rumour has it that nowadays Old runs a fish and chip van. I cannot confirm this, but I hope that if it's true the business is called Medium Plaice.

I cannot recall who Yorkshire were playing at Scarborough that day, but whoever it was would have made little difference. A few counties, it was true, had fast bowlers – sexy foreign types like Mike Procter, who were denied to Yorkshire – but most were trundler-heavy. In the first-class season of 1976 dobbers dominated the wicket-taking. Mike Selvey of Middlesex got ninety; Paddy Clift, a straight-up-and-down seamer from what would soon be Zimbabwe, picked up seventy-four for Leicestershire; John Spencer of Sussex took seventy-nine. Even David Gurr of Somerset got sixty-one – the same number as England offy Pat Pocock. The most successful leg-spinner, Mushtaq Mohammad, picked up thirty-seven. (In 1968, the season in which Compton wrote his *Wisden* article, things were markedly different. At Middlesex, for instance, England off-spinner Fred Titmus and Jamaican-born leg-spinner Harry Latchman took 199 wickets between them. Along with Titmus four other spinners broke the hundred-wicket mark, but only three seamers – one of whom was, inevitably, Shackleton.)

The best of the seamers were household names, familiar to us from England's recent hammerings by the Australians and the West Indies. Surrey had Geoff Arnold (nicknamed 'Horse' because his initials were G. G.). Arnold bowled with a chest-on action of the sort that drove Tom Cartwright mad and came in off a twenty-five-yard run that was ostentatious to say the least. As a youngster, Surrey's Peter Loader had taught him to bowl an out-swinger. Horse made his county debut in 1963, wobbled the cherry around and sometimes found the seam. He topped the Surrey bowling averages more often than not from 1965 onwards and took 109 wickets, average 18.22, in 1967. Since in the eyes of the England selectors any wicket taken for Surrey counted double, Horse was inevitably picked to play for his country that same year. In the right conditions Arnold was unplayable and he got lucky against Pakistan at the Oval, when in conditions so humid there was practically a mist hanging over the Harleyford Road, he took five wickets for 58. A huge prejudice existed against him in the north of England, where he was thought to be depriving better bowlers such as Alan Ward (Derbyshire) and Peters Lever and Lee (Lancashire) of their rightful place in the line-up. Since I grew up in this climate I am surprised to find that Horse took 115 wickets in thirty-one Tests. Though as I type these words I can already hear my dad – who had a particular aversion to Arnold – saying, 'Yes, but look who he got them against. India and New Zealand. Pah! And thirty-one Tests? They didn't give Dick Pollard that many chances, did they?'

Arnold had a long, lugubrious face and goofy teeth that suggested the straight man in a comedy duo. In the mid-seventies he shared the new ball at Surrey with Robin Jackman, another RFMer who had the bundling enthusiasm of a terrier pup, scampering to the wicket at such speed you half expected him to carry on after he delivered the ball until he crashed into the sightscreen. Surprisingly for a

Surrey bowler who took a lot of wickets (over 1400) he was only picked for England four times. It probably would have been five, but Jackman's frequent visits to South Africa to play and coach led the Guyanese government to refuse him an entry visa during England's 1981–2 trip to the Caribbean and the Georgetown Test was cancelled as a result.

If it wasn't Surrey then it might have been some other side from the Deep South, maybe one of those that had in their ranks a dobbing-strokemaking all-rounder who John Arlott might praise during a televised John Player League match. The great broadcaster was particularly fond, naturally enough since it was his home county, of Hampshire's Trevor Jesty, whose 21,916 runs and 585 first-class wickets earned him ten appearances for England in one-day internationals back in the days when one-day internationals were regarded as pretty much the beer matches of a Test series. Arlott also had a liking for Stuart Turner of Essex, whose eight-hundred-plus scalps and just under ten thousand runs were not enough to get him any kind of international recognition at all. The heedlessness of the England selectors had at least one benefit for the likes of Turner and Jesty: it meant they were referred to as young and promising until well into their late twenties. Such players, often batsmen who bowled a bit or vice versa rather than true all-rounders like Sobers, Greig or the emerging Somerset wonderboy Botham, were an intrinsic element of any county side, their value increasing as one-day cricket expanded to fill all remaining gaps in the calendar. They were predominantly dobbers. Some – Nash, Barry Wood, Roger Knight – were home-grown, others – Asif Iqbal, John Solanky, John Shepherd – were imported from far and wide. Usually they made the ball swing, though in Wood's case generally only against Yorkshire, whose batsmen he seemed to mesmerise at least once a season.

The counties of the Midlands had almost as many do-a-bit-off-the-pitchers as Yorkshire and Lancashire. Derbyshire, as we have already seen, was a kind of Serengeti of seam, its great beasts trundling unmolested across the green tops of Chesterfield, Ilkeston and Buxton (where 'Snow Stopped Play' was always a possibility, even in June). Sitting on my desk today is the autographed benefit brochure of one of them, Mike 'Hendo' Hendrick. To open it is to stick your head through a dormer window and gaze upon another world. Here is the international sportsman standing proudly before his new patio doors courtesy of Abbey Glass (Derby) Limited, who ask the reader to 'open your innings this summer with a visit to our showrooms'. And here he is looking equally pleased with his Renault 20TS. 'I'm bowled over by its performance,' he assures us. Strangely Hendo has not joined his Derby and England team mates Bob Taylor and Geoff Miller on their trip to the Butler's Office Equipment Showroom to find out what the solution is when you are 'stumped with an office problem', but maybe white-collar work was not his thing. Besides, he was probably too busy elsewhere, in all likelihood visiting the Chapman Sheep-skin Shop, which is apparently the thing to do in Burton upon Trent if you are – what else – 'stumped for a day out'. Many of the articles that dot the brochure mention Gladwin and Jackson, George Pope and Bill Copson ('In his day the fastest bowler in England', Arlott says) and the great tradition of the raw-boned Derbyshire seamer. A few Derby-based journalists even describe Hendo as 'hostile', though to be honest, if they thought he was menacing they must have hidden behind the sofa when Sylvester Clarke or Patrick Patterson rolled into town. Give generously is the general tenor of the thing – cricketers were poorly paid back then, the reason why many played until so late in life – and people did.

Hendrick's benefit raised £30,050 and it's nice to think that the man who originally bought the brochure I'm flicking through now made his contribution.

Hendrick's start in the game had not been easy. He'd been on Leicestershire's books as a youngster, only to be discarded. Derbyshire almost did the same. The turning point came in the winter of 1972 when, like others we have already encountered in these pages, he spent a winter working as a labourer, built up his strength and fitness through manual work and returned to the fray a bigger man. Hendrick had a good action, broad shoulders and moved towards the crease with a kind of loose-limbed gallop. He bowled the classic Derbyshire length – just short of what would normally be thought of as good – and moved the ball both ways off the seam. He could swing the ball too, though his insistence on never quite pitching it up militated against him getting the best from it.

In international cricket Hendo was at his best at Headingley – the nearest Test arena to Chesterfield in more ways than one. He took eight wickets in the game against Australia in 1977 (though returning hero Geoff Boycott stole the headlines). And in 1979 against Pakistan the man from Darley Dale produced a display of one-day bowling worthy of the great Gus Gilmour himself. The tourists were chasing an England total of just 165, but if they thought that was easy they had thought without the bearded Hendo. Swinging the ball both ways in the air and in and out off the track, Hendrick sent back Majid Khan, Sadiq Mohammad, Mudassar Nazar and Haroon Rasheed in the space of eight balls for just three runs. He finished with 4–15 in twelve overs and took a brilliant catch at mid-off as England won by fourteen runs. Little wonder that, a year later, the Shoe Box in Mickleover ('Service by Trained Staff') wished him all the best in his benefit year.

If Hendo provided a link to the past in his style of bowl-ing, then another trundler who regularly hove into the range of my binoculars did so in an altogether more literal way. Leicestershire's Ken Higgs had joined Lancashire from Staffordshire way back in the late fifties (he hadn't wanted to be a medium-pacer. He'd wanted to be a centre-half for Port Vale), taken 7 for 36 in his first Championship match to win the game and become the regular opening partner for Brian Statham, who had done the same job with Alec Bedser in the era when the sight of a banana made people squeal.

Ken Higgs was one of those men who seemed to have been born a veteran. Photos of him in his youthful pomp at Lancashire show a man who even at twenty looks like Steve McClaren's older brother. Gappy teeth, an enterprising swathe of slicked hair curling about his head like a pagri and the complexion of somebody who's stood in front of a wind machine loaded with gravel. Every year for what seemed like decades (because it was), this big broad-based bloke bowled a thousand overs a season, into the wind and up any gradi-ent the captain could find for him. When he'd first appeared many saw him as 'the next Bedser': he was a similar pace to the Surrey ace, bowled a good full length, moved the ball in the air and off the pitch and jarred the batsmen's hands with that infamous heavy ball. Maybe if Higgs hadn't played for Lancashire he might have become just that, but despite taking nearly a thousand wickets in the first ten years of his career he played for England just fifteen times (seventy-one Test wickets at 20.74 – go figure). When he was thirty-two his place at Old Trafford was eventually usurped by Peter Lever (who had to wait till he was thirty to play for England) and the splendid Ken Shuttleworth, so Higgs moved on to Grace Road. In 1968 he was one of that trio of trundlers who broke a hundred wickets.

It was during his Leicestershire days that I used to watch Higgs, with a slightly disdainful expression on my face it must be said. Higgs was a master of his craft and part of a substratum of veteran trundlers who turned up at Scarborough to play cricket even though to the untutored eye each looked more like the sort of bloke who should have been leaning against the side of his luxury coach, an Embassy Regal in the corner of his mouth, waiting for the OAP trip he was driving to come back from their picnic in Peaseholm Park. At Gloucestershire there was Brian Brain, who would go on opening the bowling until he was forty, at Sussex Tony Buss, whose name provided the jokers in the stands with an endless supply of 'he missed a Buss' jokes. Northants, meanwhile, had a twin-pronged ageing dobber attack of left-armer John Dye and Bob Cottam, a remorselessly accurate purveyor of medium-paced cutters who'd opened the bowling with Derek Shackleton at Hampshire before moving north. Cottam – who took 130 wickets in 1968, the third of the trio of trundling centurions – was considered by many to be the best bowler there was in typical English conditions, which probably explains why he only played four Tests, all of them on the Indian subcontinent. Middlesex, meanwhile, had John Price, who was worth the cost of admission for his run-up alone. A tall, slender, balding man, he had the elegance of a ballroom dancer. He'd once been the fastest bowler in England but he'd been born before the war and by the seventies was, if not quite military two-step, then certainly not much above a foxtrot. His approach hadn't altered, though: he came in at an oblique angle from somewhere to the left of long off, running upright around the curve in the manner of the 400-metre star Michael Johnson. By the time he approached the umpire he was facing the batsman. His action was an unfathomable whirl, his arm straight, the ball most usually curving away from the right-hander.

At the time, I resented these ageing dobbers. I thought they were keeping a burgeoning generation of young bowlers out of their county teams. I imagined that these young bowlers would be far more dynamic and exciting. I was in for a disappointment: they would, in fact, be Tim Tremlett, Paul Allott and Steve O'Shaughnessy.

Ken Higgs went on playing first-class cricket till he was forty-nine, by which time he'd taken just short of two thousand wickets at a little over twenty each. He was the menace Denis Compton warned us about. He seemed all right to me.

As it turned out, the game was changing, not because of anything the authorities did, but because of the success of the Australian and West Indian pace attacks. In 1982 the leading wicket-taker in the County Championship would be Malcolm Marshall, who bagged an extraordinary total of 130 for Hampshire. Sylvester Clarke of Surrey and Wayne Daniel of Middlesex both took over seventy and Garth Le Roux at Sussex and Imran Khan at Worcestershire weren't far off. All were genuinely fast; none was English. Spinners too prospered. Febrile googly-merchant Abdul Qadir was the best of them, but the silver-haired former England batting hero David Steele took over seventy, as did Maltese-born Scotsman Dallas Moir. Meanwhile, only four moderates broke seventy wickets. The most successful of the traditional English seamers was Marshall's new-ball partner at Hampshire, Kevin Emery. Emery came from Swindon and had begun his career as an off-spinner; 1982 was his first full season of county cricket. He picked up eighty-three wickets and was picked to play for the England B team. The following season he disappeared. The official reason was injury, but there were rumours that he'd got the yips and that the brain-to-hand shenanigans that are the terror of golfers had seen him repeatedly hitting the side netting in early season training. If that is true, it was a cruel end to a promising career and one that proved that trundling was not quite as simple a process as the medium-pacers' many detractors claimed.

Chapter 14

Trundlers in Sun and Shadow

Australia's mysterious plethora of left-arm medium merchants has already been dealt with, but two Aussie right-arm swing bowlers deserve consideration here. (A third, Max Walker, we will approach in a suitably wrong-footed manner in the next chapter.) Though 'Terror' Turner met with success in his homeland, there's little doubt that he was more effective in England, and that is equally true of Harry Boyle and Bill Johnston. However, none of these men gave quite the same powerful sense of having been born in the wrong place as Bob Massie and Terry Alderman.

Alderman and Massie both came from Perth and played for Western Australia. At the WACA the Fremantle Doctor, that mysterious afternoon sea breeze, helped swing bowlers just as much as the salty Channel fret had aided Tate at Hove and Shackleton at Portsmouth. Back in the fifties the state's bowling attack featured Ray Strauss, who moved the ball both ways in the air as well as off the pitch at medium pace, and was good enough to have taken 7 for 75 against the South Africans in a tour match in 1953. The track at Perth was extremely fast, however, and generally so closely shorn and hard it was said that at times a batsman could see his reflection in it. (In international cricket, possibly only the track at Sabina Park is quicker.) Strauss was good, but the Western Australian fast bowlers Graham McKenzie and Dennis Lillee, who pounded the ball into the rock-hard pitch, were better known.

Though Massie was not a great success in club cricket – twenty-one wickets in ten matches for Bentley – the clear evidence that he had the swing thing was enough to see nineteen-year-old Fergie (after the Massey-Ferguson tractor) selected for his state in 1965–6. He played one match, took no wickets and Western Australia did not select him again that season. Or the next. Or the one after. In the meantime, Massie took the job of professional at Kilmarnock Cricket Club (he wasn't the only Australian to pro in Scotland. Ashley Mallett and Kim Hughes also played there.) As a place to learn his trade as a seam bowler the soft, green wickets of the Western Union were ideal. Massie took all ten wickets for thirty-four runs on his debut against Poloc, a haul that included Pakistan Test opener Sadiq Mohammad. He stayed at Kilmarnock for three seasons, helping them to two league titles and picking up over two hundred wickets and a wife along the way.

His skills honed and his confidence high, Massie finally regained his place in the state side in 1969. The atmosphere in Sheffield Shield cricket was less forgiving than in Scotland in every sense and Massie's performance remained patchy. In the 1969–70 Australian season he failed even to take the fifteen wickets necessary to get in the end-of-season averages. In 1970 Massie got a crack at Ray Illingworth's MCC side when they took on Western Australia prior to the second Test. He failed to inconvenience the English batsmen and was dropped again. Massie was brought back the following month after McKenzie and Lillee had come up against South Australia and Barry Richards, who smashed 325 off them in a single day. He found himself bowling against Queensland on a sprightly Perth track, and with the Doctor helping his out-swing took 8 for 55.

Looking ahead to the next Ashes series in England, the Australian selectors took note, just as they had of Big Bill Johnston's less-than-startling but nonetheless Albion-suitable performances in 1947, and though Massie did nothing particularly noteworthy at the start of the 1971–2 season they picked him to play against Garry Sobers's Rest of the World XI at Melbourne and Sydney. It was this last match that opened the way to Massie's days of glory. He took 7 for 76 in 20.6 overs, including Sobers himself, dismissed by an off-cutter that pitched on the left-hander's leg stump and moved away from him to clip off.

Unlike many Australian bowlers Massie rarely bowled short, pitching the ball up to take maximum advantage of the swing. 'In England, line and length is the absolute key,' he observed. 'As soon as you drop the ball anywhere near short of a good length, the good players put it away either through the cover point area or tuck it away off their pads.'

Massie ran in at a leisurely pace, both hands on the ball in the old 'rocking-the-baby' style. If his action was a little too chest-on to be truly classic that only helped his stock ball, the out-swinger. He also bowled with his first and index finger behind the ball, the classic English seamer's grip.

He had learned at Kilmarnock that the skill in Britain – one that Shackleton had perfected – was finding the right spot on the wicket for the conditions, hitting it constantly and letting nature do the rest. He proved the effectiveness of this and his other attributes in his Test debut at Lord's. Here under a leaden sky Massie, sporting sideburns the size of doormats, found the sort of late swing he'd specialised in back in East Ayrshire.

In the first innings he produced a straight yorker to clean-bowl Boycott, then did a Tom Cartwright on Basil D'Oliveira, bowling him four fullish out-swingers in a row and then, as the Worcestershire right-hander glided into the same forward defensive shot he'd played to those deliveries, swinging one back in to trap him lbw. Mike Smith played across the line and was bowled by a full toss; Alan Knott was caught in the gully wafting his bat as if trying to chase a wasp from a cake; and Tony Greig played a loose off-drive and inside-edged an in-swinger to Marsh. If poor batting contributed to those three dismissals it was an excellent ball that did for Ray Illingworth, swinging in and then straightening off the pitch to catch him leg before. John Snow was clean-bowled by another beauty, a yorker that swung from the direction of leg stump to hit off. The left-handed Norman Gifford was caught at the wicket playing for an in-swinger that turned out to be a straight one. Massie finished with 8 for 53.

There was nothing in the wicket, but when England batted again the clouds were still heavy, the atmosphere moist. If Massie had bowled well in the first innings, he bowled superbly in the second. After having John Edrich caught at the wicket and D'Oliveira pouched at second slip driving at one that moved away, the Western Australian changed the point of attack and started to bowl round the wicket. He had Greig, Knott and Illingworth all caught in the slips off balls that started off looking like they'd fly down the leg-side, then swerved across the right-handers shortly before pitching, and had Snow caught at the wicket trying to leg glance one that didn't 'go'. John Price fell next and the left-handed Underwood was last out, caught in the cordon off one that moved away from him to give Massie his second eight-wicket haul of the match – the first Australian ever to take more than fifteen wickets in a Test, and on his international debut too.

Massie took 4 for 43 in the first innings of the next Test, but after that the summer warmed up and things slowed down for him. He only got past fifty wickets for the tour in the final week.

The swinger was picked for Australia's trip to the West Indies that winter. Many observers thought the Caribbean would be the making of him, teaching him to adapt to different conditions. It proved the opposite. On the flat, hard wickets and under the clear, moisture-free skies Massie started to bowl too short, banging the ball into the pitch to try to extract some life from it. The effort subtly altered his action with the result that he lost the out-swinger in the same mysterious way that Cartwright had found his. 'I was never the same bowler again,' he said a decade later. 'A lot of people gave time trying to help me but it was too late. I used to be able to bowl the "outie" at will. Now I was lucky if I could produce it a couple of times a season.'

Massie's final Test appearance came against Pakistan in 1973. Within the year he had been dropped by Western Australia and was back playing club cricket, his first-class career over at twenty-seven. His 16–137 at Lord's remains the best ever bowling performance on a Test debut and the second best of all time by a medium-pacer. To Massie too falls a unique title: he was cricket's one and only meteoric trundler.

Physically, Terry Alderman was a close match to Massie, taller but with the same solid, broad-shouldered build. In terms of bowling style he was similar too, though he came in off a longer run, meandering to the crease in small trotting steps before delivering the ball with an action that, while not fully chest-on, was certainly nudging that way. Like Massie, Alderman's swingers benefited from a spell as a professional in Scotland and he too flourished in English conditions, taking eighty-three wickets in two Test series here. Even more remarkably, they were eight years apart.

Alderman had begun his career as an out-and-out pace bowler and, as a raw eighteen-year-old, was good enough to force his way into a powerful Western Australia team then in its Lillee-and-Marsh-led heyday. Unfortunately for Alderman, at this point his career took a rather Massie-style nosedive. He was in and out of the side, pulled a hamstring, performed inconsistently and was twice dropped from the state squad. Along the way he'd slowed down and begun to bowl within himself, concentrating on swinging the ball into the Perth breeze. In 1980 he took the job of pro with Watsonian Cricket Club in Edinburgh.

Back in Australia and back in the Western Australian starting eleven, Alderman did well enough, taking thirty-two Shield wickets, to get picked for the 1981 Ashes tour. In England his role was support for the great but ageing Dennis Lillee and the nippy Geoff Lawson. As such Alderman was expected to bowl long spells into any headwind and up any slope.

Oddly, given those circumstances and the local conditions, Alderman attributed much of his success on that tour to the fact that he bowled a couple of yards faster in the UK than he did back in Australia. He hit upon the idea during a spell in the nets at Edgbaston: 'Dennis told me to bowl off a long run and see what I could do. I tried to hit the seam and was unplayable. That was the first time I realised I could do more as a seam bowler than as a swing bowler. What I did after that was to try and do more off the wicket.' In the end he did both, swinging the ball late and getting it to deviate off the strip.

On his Test debut at Trent Bridge he took 4–68 in the first innings and 5–62 in the second as England were skittled out for 125. A nine-wicket haul in his first Test wasn't quite up to Massie's standard but it was good enough, and unlike his Western Australian predecessor Alderman sustained it, picking up nine wickets in the third Test at Headingley, eight in the next one at Birmingham and another nine in the fifth Test at Old Trafford. He finished the series with forty-two, the fourth-highest aggregate of all time. Unfortunately for the bowler, his deeds had been rather overshadowed by those of Ian Botham. Australia's dramatic collapse at Headingley and the destruction that followed tainted the entire side.

England's unexpected fightback under the leadership of Mike Brearley had left Alderman feeling deflated, despite his personal triumph. Worse was to follow eighteen months later. The Ashes series that winter began in searing heat in Alderman's native Perth. On the second day a group of England fans invaded the pitch. One of them struck Alderman and ran off. He gave chase and rugby-tackled his assailant, and as the medium-pacer fell to the ground he dislocated his shoulder At first it was thought he'd miss only the second Test, but the injury proved more serious than it had originally seemed. It was twelve months before he could bowl again.

If that absence was unfortunate, the next was self-inflicted. Alderman had been selected for the Ashes tour to England in 1985 when word leaked out that he had recently signed a deal to go on a rebel tour of South Africa the following winter. He was immediately banned from international cricket for three years.

When Alderman finally returned to England in 1989 he was a different bowler from the one he'd been eight years earlier. He'd spent three summers in county cricket with Kent and Gloucestershire, was appreciably slower and had gone back to what he'd originally done best: wobbling the ball about in the air. He may have lost several yards of pace, but in English conditions he remained as tough a proposition as ever. Graham Gooch in particular was baffled by him, so often caught rooted in front of the stumps that his answer-phone message reputedly said 'I'm out right now ... Probably lbw to Alderman'. In total the Western Australian trundler accounted for the Essex man seven times, five of them leg before. Gooch became so paralysed with indecision when he faced him he asked to be dropped, an ignominious surrender. He wasn't the only batsman to suffer, though. At Lord's in particular Alderman was Massie-like in the way he swung the ball in and out, late and at will. In one devastating spell he ripped out the England middle order in sixteen extraordinary deliveries.

Alderman took a hundred wickets in the Ashes, an incredible return for someone who played in only seventeen matches. He was never anywhere near as effective against other nations. More than that, he was at his best in British conditions. His Test average in his own country was 30.11, in England 19.33 and he took ten five-wicket hauls here in just twelve matches. If he'd been born in Todmorden or Buxton (or even Auckland) there would have been no stopping him.

Chapter 15

Here We Go, Dobbing All Over the World

While India is plainly the home of spin, and the Caribbean's status as the circuit of speed has recently come under threat from South Africa and Pakistan, England has always been the undisputed nest of trundling. Or so you might think. But if we were to look at per-capita military-medium distribution globally we might well feel that New Zealand deserves some kind of prize. The Land of the Long White Dobber, as it is unofficially nicknamed, has generally placed greater emphasis on seam than – oh, I don't know – a stocking factory. The recent arrival of the top-class spinner Daniel Vettori has only emphasised the fact.

From their first arrival in Test cricket in 1930 New Zealand have displayed a frankly heroic commitment to trundling that no other nation – not even England – can match. Local conditions plainly play a part. A combination of heavy rainfall (roughly 50 per cent higher than in Manchester), a temperate climate, damp summers and high humidity mean that no other Test nation plays its domestic cricket in an environment that comes quite so close to August in Leeds.

Yet it is more than merely precipitation that has influenced the Kiwis. It is something to do with the national character.

New Zealanders have no time for ostentation or showing off. The average Black Cap cricketer is so humble, so reluctant to emphasise his achievements as to make Maurice Tate seem like peak-period Muhammad Ali. Just as England's ingrained conservatism has fostered trundling, so New Zealand's diffidence has done the same. After all, if you hate drawing attention to yourself what other form of bowling would you choose?

The Kiwis signalled their intentions in 1931, arriving in Britain for their first tour with an attack based around the dobbing skills of Mal Matheson, Ronald Talbot, Ian Cromb and the classically self-deprecating all-rounder Lindsay 'Dad' Weir, who scored ten first-class hundreds, took over a hundred wickets and played high-class rugby, but was likely to take umbrage if anybody had the temerity to praise him for it.

Auckland's Matheson took forty-four wickets on the tour but strained a leg muscle, which limited his effectiveness in the three-Test series. Cromb, a right-arm swing bowler, played in all of those matches and also took wickets against the MCC. Douglas Jardine, at least, was impressed, claiming that the Canterbury player's deliveries came off the pitch so quickly 'the ball hits the bat before the bat can hit the ball'.

When the Kiwis returned to England six years later they brought with them the first of their truly international-class trundlers. Jack Cowie came from Auckland, was big and powerful enough to have earned himself the nickname Bull and, according to a much-quoted – well, in New Zealand anyway – line from *Wisden*, 'Had he been Australian he might have been termed a wonder of the age.'

Like Weir, Cowie couldn't abide that sort of fuss, preferring to get on with his job of bowling right-arm quickish medium pace for the sort of lengthy, consistent spells that led *Wisden* to conclude he was 'impervious to fatigue'. Physical fitness was something Cowie emphasised. He didn't smoke or drink, and in the days when most bowlers warmed up with a pipe and a pint of ale (Harold Larwood lived off beer during Test matches), and 'got fit by bowling', Cowie advocated 'two long runs in the hills per week' to build up stamina, and three hard sessions in the nets too. 'Too many bowlers turn up at nets, bowl at a couple of batsmen, put their sweaters on and go home,' he said. 'That sort of thing will not do you any good.' In Cowie's eyes, constant practice was essential: 'Practice makes perfection whether you are a pianist, violinist or even a cricketer.'

Cowie had begun his career as a batsman who bowled a bit of leg-spin, turning to the faster stuff as his physique developed. He'd been something of a prodigy, playing in the national under-21 competition at the age of fourteen. The Auckland side was well stocked with decent batsmen, so Cowie decided to focus on his bowling. Fittingly for a man who would later be a senior figure in an insurance firm, his approach was one of moderation. After retirement, when asked what advice he would give to young bowlers, Cowie responded, 'Bowl within yourself. Too many bowlers try for that extra yard of pace that they have not got.'

Cowie ran in about fifteen yards ('Do not run further than is necessary. Even a few extra yards will add considerably to your workload during the course of the day,' he counselled sensibly) and delivered the ball in the classic manner of a Cartwright, left shoulder pointing down the wicket, head still, right arm so high in delivery it brushed his ear. In conversation Cowie emphasised the importance of the non-bowling arm: 'Aim is given by the left shoulder,' he said, the right just delivers the ball.

Cowie generally swung his deliveries away, and he got movement off the pitch in both directions. His line and length were never less than tidy. The approach was simple and methodical and very effective. On that 1937 tour he took 114 wickets in first-class matches, nineteen in the three Tests (the next best New Zealand bowler, slow left-armer Giff Vivian, got eight). Cowie's best performance was in the second Test at Old Trafford, where he had match analysis of 10 for 140, but his most remarkable came in the final game of the tour, against Ireland in Dublin. On a pitch so lively that a match scheduled for three days was completed shortly after tea on the first, Cowie helped dismiss the hosts in their second innings for just thirty runs (ten of which were extras). He bowled eight overs, conceded just three runs (all of them singles) and took six wickets.

Like Tate and Bedser, Cowie was said to get extra lift off the wicket. He explained that the key to this was the grip on the ball. To bowl an off-cutter Cowie placed his first finger to the left of the seam and his index finger on the right outer edge of it. He reversed the positions to bowl one that cut away from the right-hander. To bowl his kicker he had his first and index finger *across* the seam and his thumb tucked under the ball. The kicker was not bowled short but full, the lift coming from hitting the seam. Len Hutton was impressed.

In those days opportunities for top-class cricket in New Zealand were limited – more than half of Cowie's eighty-two first-class matches were played in England – and touring teams tended just to stop in briefly on the way home from Australia. A single Test was the norm. In 1945–6 Australia dropped in and, in the same game in which O'Reilly and Toshack ran rampage dismissing the home side for 42 and

54, Cowie bowled brilliantly, taking 6–40 in Australia's only innings. When England stopped in the following winter he took 6–83 in a rain-affected match. By the time New Zealand came to England again in 1949 Cowie was thirty-seven and starting to feel his age. He'd dropped a yard or two of pace and was perpetually troubled by the kind of pulls, strains and niggles that had once been unknown to him. He still bowled with remarkable consistency, though, always aiming at middle or off stump, making the batsmen play. His best performance came against Scotland where he took six wickets, all clean bowled. Denzil Batchelor, who watched and admired Cowie, commented that he was a man who displayed 'a bovine contentment in his lot'. Despite playing for a team that often struggled to force the opposition to bat twice, Cowie took forty-five wickets in Tests at 21.53 each. By all accounts this solid, unexcitable man would not have wanted to be a 'wonder of the age'.

Nor, I suspect, would the men who followed him, although to be honest no one was likely to give them the chance. Perhaps because they do not have so many players to choose from ('Only sixty-six,' according to Ewen Chatfield) or maybe because they are not given to change for change's sake, or indeed for any sake at all, New Zealand tend to stick with the same group of players. Once a man is wearing the black cap he tends to keep it on for some while. In the fifties a constant figure in the line-up was right-arm fast-medium merchant Tony MacGibbon, generally backed by a combination of Harry Cave, John Hayes, Bob Blair and Don Beard. Of this quartet Hayes was genuinely quick and is mentioned here solely because he is the only fast bowler in history ever to have served as an honorary consul-general of Morocco. Probably.

New Zealand waited twenty-six years for their first victory in a Test match and these unheralded trundlers were instrumental in bringing it about. The West Indian tour of 1955–6 had not gone well for the hosts. The visitors – who in those days relied heavily on the spin of Ramadhin and Valentine backed by the dobbers of Clairemonte Depeiaza and Dennis Atkinson – had hammered them in the first three Tests, twice by an innings and once by nine wickets. As they moved on to the fourth and final encounter at Eden Park, Auckland, John Reid's team must have feared more brutalisation was in store. At the same venue two years earlier England – with Tyson, Statham and the seamy-spinners of Appleyard – had dismissed them for just 24.

Batting first and with the belligerent Reid in rugged form the Kiwis posted what seemed a moderate total of 255. Then Harry Cave and Tony MacGibbon went to work. The former was a tall, ram-rod straight farmer from Central Districts who'd lost his ability to bowl the out-swinger after tearing an elbow muscle in 1947, so now focused on seamers and cutters. A keen gardener, I suspect he may be the only man in these pages to have a variety of camellia named after him.

MacGibbon was from Canterbury, broad-shouldered, whole-hearted and with the ability to swerve the ball away from the right-hander and move it off the seam. The Canterburian was the quicker of the two – bowling at around 75mph – and the more erratic. In a game against Essex on the 1958 tour he would deliver a ball so wide it struck second slip on the right shin.

At Auckland MacGibbon was at his best, his late swing accounting for Garry Sobers and Everton Weekes as the Windies' cavalier middle order collapsed. At the other end Cave was a good foil. He bowled at military medium pace and was renowned for his sparing accuracy. Like Derek Shackleton, it was said he only bowled one half-volley per season. Hitting the right length and line and letting the ball and the West Indies batsmen do the rest, he snapped up four wickets for 22 as the visitors were dismissed for 145.

In their second innings New Zealand scrabbled their way to 157 before declaring with nine wickets down. The West Indies needed 267 to win. For a batting line-up containing Sobers, Weekes and Colly Smith that should have been achievable, but Cave and his Central Districts team mate Don Beard had other ideas. Like Cave, Beard was a tall man who bowled trundlers with a high arm and was noted for his immaculate control. Between them the pair from Wellington got a stranglehold on the Caribbean batsmen. New Zealand wicketkeeper Simpson Guillen stood up to both bowlers and was rewarded with a stumping off Cave as the West Indies collapsed to 77 all out. Beard finished with 3 for 22, Cave 4 for 21.

As the fifties gave way to the sixties a new batch of Kiwi medium-pacers dropped off the production line: the left-armer Dick Collinge, whose lengthy run saw him pawing the air with both hands like a man trapped in a net; Bruce Taylor, who smashed a century and took five wickets in an innings on a Test debut that was only his fourth first-class match; and the late Bob Cunis, who is probably best remembered for Alan Ross's joke about him in the *Observer*: 'A funny name, Cunis. It is neither one thing nor the other.' Early on they were backed up by the classic stock bowler Frank Cameron, a tenacious medium-pacer who swung the ball late and, according to the Pathé News commentator, could 'peg away for hours'. By his own account Cameron had been taught how to grip the ball by an anonymous 'old fellow' in the Dunedin park where he and his friends played as teenagers. He bowled the out-swinger naturally and though he could also bowl an in-swinger he felt that the extra twist in the back required to do so was more likely to cause him injury than take him wickets so he ditched it. On the tour of South Africa in 1961–2 New Zealand took only three seamers, and Cameron lived up to his billing by sending down 721.4 overs.

The beefy Collinge's career extended into the late seventies and he played his part in the Kiwis' first ever Test victory over England, at Basin Reserve, Wellington in 1978, dismissing Geoff Boycott with an in-swinger as England were dismissed for 64. By then he'd been joined by Richard Hadlee (too quick to detain us) and briefly by another Hadlee brother, Dayle. Dayle Hadlee had suffered a back injury that precluded him bowling at the speeds of his younger sibling and instead he concentrated on nagging line and length with a little bit of swing here and there. Dayle played in twenty-six Tests, didn't give much away and didn't take many wickets either.

By the eighties the Kiwis had entered a trundling Golden Age. Aside from Richard Hadlee, who continued to insist on bowling at over 85mph, the Black Caps' attack was made up of deluxe dobbers such as left-armer Gary Troup; Martin Snedden, the first bowler to concede one hundred runs in a one-day international; Lance Cairns, who bowled with a chest-on action and generated such booming swing it sometimes seemed the ball might fly in a complete circle and hit him on the head; all-rounder Jeremy Coney, whose barely medium-paced wibbly-wobblers were a thing of beauty; and Ewen Chatfield, who by his own admission was too slow to bowl a bouncer, could not swing the ball at all and focused purely on hitting the seam and hoping. As you may judge from this Chatfield, who now works as a taxi driver, is in the best self-effacing tradition of New Zealand cricket.

When the Chatfield generation shuffled off an even greater one replaced them. In the nineties Chris Harris became a cult hero in his native land, bowling looping slow-medium wafters. Gavin Larsen, Rod Latham and Willie Watson accompanied Harris in his endeavours. The attack was so bland David 'Bumble' Lloyd once referred to them as 'Dibbly, Dobbly, Wibbly and Wobbly'. Though we were not to know it at the time, it was a high water mark.

Like Pakistan, South Africa seem to have been rather seduced by pace and leg spin. In the latter case a trundler is to blame. Reggie Schwarz was bowling military medium pace for Middlesex when, in around 1904, he fell under the spell of his county team mate Bernard Bosanquet. Bosanquet had just invented the googly. In the spirit of Monty Noble he taught the new and mysterious delivery to his international adversary and Schwarz quickly trained his international team mates Ernie Vogler, Aubrey Faulkner and Gordon White. Between them this quartet of leg-spinners would destroy England in 1905 and 1907. Trundlers did not get a look in, though a few medium-pacers did make a limited impact thereafter. We have already heard of Blanckenberg and Nupen, and mention should be made of Sid Pegler, who moved the ball off the deck and whose cricket was so disrupted by his day job as a district commissioner in Nyasaland that he only ever seemed to play for his country when they were touring England. During the South Africans' 1912 visit he appeared in thirty-four of the thirty-seven first-class matches and took 189 wickets, including twenty-nine in the Test series. In 1924, aged forty-two, he turned up in England on leave at the same time as the South

African team arrived and joined them on tour. It is perhaps a sad comment on the weakness of the South African attack – in which bright hope Buster Nupen was struggling – that the middle-aged trundler proved the visitors' most potent weapon. Pegler finally retired in 1930, by which time he had not played a first-class game in his own country for nigh on twenty years.

We might also make mention of Sandy Bell, who in the thirties swung the ball both ways and was sometimes described as the South African Tate; the bespectacled trundler Geoff Chubb, who made his Test debut against England in 1951 aged forty and celebrated by bowling forty-six overs and taking 4–146; and Sydney Burke, who came into the team to play New Zealand at Cape Town in the penultimate Test of the 1961–2 series and finished with a match analysis of 11–196. Mysteriously, Burke was made twelfth man for the final Test and was not selected to tour. He made just one more Test appearance, three years later, and took no wickets.

Diverting though their tales are, it is fair to say that these men are rarely mentioned in the same breath as Hugh Tayfield, Neil Adcock, Peter Pollock, Mike Procter or other South African bowling giants of the past, nor do they rank high in the list of great trundlers. The Cape is and remains a dobbing backwater.

While the newly independent Pakistan found its first great bowling hero in Fazal Mahmood, India's came in the shape of Vinoo Mankad, a brilliant slow left-armer. In many ways Mankad and Mahmood set the template for the attacks of their two neighbouring nations – broadly one would favour speed, the other spin.

The Indians' obsessive focus on spin and the preparation

of dry, dusty wickets designed to encourage it meant that, until the arrival of Kapil Dev and later Javagal Srinath, Ajit Agarkar and co, there was little room in their game for genuine speed. Instead the new ball fell into the hands of a succession of trundling all-rounders, and batsmen who dobbed a bit. In the fifties that invariably meant Dattu Phadkar and Ram Ramchand. A hard-hitting batsman and handsome heart throb, Phadkar had been coached by the great Surrey bowler Al Gover and could swing the ball both ways. He took 7–159 against the West Indies at Madras in 1948–9, but arguably cost his side the match when he irritated the tourists with some innocuous bouncers, provoking a barrage of altogether spicier throat-ticklers from Prior Jones in response. The Karachi-born Ramchand was tall and powerfully built and – as one Indian cricket writer observed – 'looked every inch the fast bowler, until he actually bowled'.

In 1958–9 India called up specialist seamer Ramakant Desai for the Test against the West Indies in Delhi. He was just nineteen. The lad was also very small. Indeed, at just five feet, four inches tall Desai must be the shortest opening bowler in international cricket history. Inevitably nicknamed Tiny, Desai's main weapons were out-swing and raw courage. With little in the way of medium-pace support the little youngster was forced to bowl prodigious spells. On his debut against Jerry Alexander's men he sent down forty-nine overs, finishing with 4–169 and – such was India's shortage – was immediately tasked with leading the attack on that summer's tour of England. Here he was partnered by another youngster, Raman Surendranath. Surendranath played for the Indian army and bowled with great accuracy and control, though *Wisden* claimed he spent most of the summer aiming at a spot just outside the right-hander's leg stump and grumbled that 'there was much dull cricket to watch' while he was bowling.

While trundlesome Surendranath created little but yawns and irritation (he took seventy-nine wickets), Desai was widely admired, even if his direction was a bit erratic. A plucky little chap who tried his heart out in a losing cause was always likely to find favour with a British public who had recently made Norman Wisdom a superstar.

In England Desai continued to bowl marathon spells, sometimes to just reward – as at Lord's where he took 5–89 – but mainly not. At Leeds he toiled for so many hours as England piled up a massive total the crowd feared he might need to be carried from the field on a stretcher. Gamely Desai soldiered on, but the workload and India's bounce-sucking wickets wore him down. In New Zealand in 1967–8 he confirmed his bravery by batting with a broken jaw at Dunedin, but it was the last Test he ever played. He was just twenty-five. In his twenty-eight Tests he had sent down 5597 deliveries and finished on the winning side just four times.

With Desai broken by drudgery and lifeless pitches, India entered a new phase of seamer-deprived desperation that at one point saw wicketkeeper Budhi Kunderan taking the new ball. Relief, however, was at hand.

When it comes to determining which bowlers helped create India's 'world champion team' of 1971–3 the statistics cannot be argued with. In three series in which the Indians defeated the West Indies in the Caribbean and England first away and then at home, the twirlymen – Bedi, Chandrasekhar, Prasanna and Venkataraghavan – took 156 wickets of the 193 that fell.

However, not even the most blinkered spin-romantic would overlook the telling contribution to those victories made by two wibbling-wobbling all-rounders, Abid Ali and Eknath Solkar.

Hailing from Hyderabad, Abid began life as a wicket-keeper batsman before throwing off the gauntlets and adopting the role of unabashed trundler. Abid was in some ways the Cec Parkin of Asia, eccentric, lively, inventive and comical. Over the years he added a cornucopia of variations to his basic style that was sufficient to keep a batsman guessing no matter how long his innings. On Indian wickets Abid had the often undervalued skill of making the ball keep low, a trick less celebrated than the one of making it kick, but which on slow strips was arguably more effective. A physical fitness fanatic who bubbled with such enthusiasm it is said that when batting he often set off for a run without first taking the trouble to actually hit the ball, or even wait for it to arrive, Abid bustled about the field like a man with business to finish. His appeals were so loud that at times they threatened the stability of Bishan Bedi's patka.

Solkar was an altogether different character; though he appeared flamboyant his antics on the field seem to have masked a mounting anxiety. Brought up in a one-room shack next to Bombay's Hindu Gymkhana ground where his father was groundsman, Solkar was a difficult batsman to dislodge, a great close fielder who, according to *Wisden*, 'leapt about like a hungry salmon' and bowled left-arm wobblers that among other things sent Geoffrey Boycott into temporary international retirement. In India people referred to him affectionately as the poor man's Garry Sobers.

Abid made his Test debut in 1967 – a time when the new ball was sometimes entrusted to middle-order batter Ajit Wadekar, whose bowling was barely faster than that of Chandrasekhar and who never took a Test wicket – and true to his character did it in hyperactive style, taking 6 for 55 against Australia at Brisbane and following that up with two brilliant fifties. Solkar's first appearance two years later, against New Zealand at Hyderabad, was altogether less spectacular – he bowled just three overs and made 0 and 13 not out.

India's unexpected series win in the West Indies in 1970–1 was largely the result of brilliant batting by the young Sunil Gavaskar and the bowling of the spin quartet, but Solkar and Abid Ali chipped in. In the second innings of the first Test, with West Indies forced to follow on, Solkar denied Garry Sobers a century by trapping him for 93 and then brought victory agonisingly close by dismissing Arthur Barrett, but the home side held on. Abid set the tone for the decisive second Test win by bowling Roy Fredericks with the first ball of the match, and in the final Test at Port of Spain, with the West Indies chasing a massive target for victory, the pair combined. Abid got opener John Shepherd early and then dismissed Rohan Kanhai and the danger man Garry Sobers in successive deliveries; Solkar snapped up David Holford a few balls later. The West Indies clung on desperately to finish with eight wickets down.

A similar minor yet important role was played by the trundle twins during the historic tour of England in 1971. At the Oval Solkar hit 44 and picked up three wickets in India's first Test triumph in this country. Then on the opening morning of the Manchester Test Abid – who had made the winning hit at the Oval – took the first four England wickets as the home side were reduced to 41 for 4 at lunch, effectively scuppering a series fightback.

On India's return to England in 1974 Abid Ali and Solkar were joined by Madan Lal, another dobbing bits-and-pieces man who was to play a key part in Indian triumphs yet to come. Madan bowled what is sometimes described as nippy medium pace, though in truth the impression of speed was created more by the haste of his run-up than the pace of his deliveries. (Indeed, some unkind observers have suggested that if he had kept on running Madan Lal would have overtaken them.) Like Abid and Solkar he could bat a bit – he scored over five thousand runs in Ranji Trophy matches – and hit five Test fifties, often quickly and at vital times for his team. Like his batting his bowling tended towards the short, decisive burst.

The 1974 tour started brightly enough, Solkar establishing his hex over Boycott in a tour match – winning a bet of a pint of lager that he couldn't get the great man out – and carrying it on into the Tests, getting the Yorkshireman's wicket four times in five innings, at which point the opinionated opener could take no more and asked to be dropped. Boycott would not return to international cricket for three years. Some – including the late Tony Greig – blamed his absence on a fear of fast bowling, though it was the terror of a trundler that precipitated it.

Despite this early excitement the Test series and the tour as a whole rapidly turned into a total disaster for Wadekar's team. They lost all the Test matches, were bowled out for 42 at Lord's – Chris Old and Geoff Arnold doing the damage – and opening bat Sudhir Naik was accused of shoplifting from Marks and Spencer.

Abid Ali's Test career came to an abrupt end the following summer, after he had top-scored with 70 and taken 2 for 35 against New Zealand in the 1975 World Cup. He went on playing first-class cricket for another four seasons. In 1990 Farokh Engineer announced on Indian radio that Abid had died. He hadn't, and so became one of those rare men who get to read their own obituaries. Two decades later he is still going strong.

Solkar's career stuttered to a close shortly after that of Abid; his final Test was against England at Calcutta in 1977. Some blamed the stress of close catching – he so rarely dropped anything that when he did it tended to make newspaper headlines in India – for the premature end (he was twenty-eight), others the battering of West Indian and Australian pace attacks. He died in 2005.

At roughly the time that Solkar was being discarded by the Indian selectors, so too was Madan Lal, who was dumped during the 1977–8 visit to Australia. His role as new-ball partner for the truly waltz-paced Mohinder Amarnath was taken by the slow left-armer and occasional seamer Karsan Ghavri.

If the selectors did not much favour Madan Lal, the view was not shared by Indian players, particularly new star Kapil Dev, and he was brought back for the series against England in 1981–2. The five-year rest from international cricket seemed to have sharpened Madan's appetite, and on a sunny afternoon in the second innings of the second Test at Bombay he bowled unchanged throughout the England innings, brilliantly exploiting the low bounce of the crumbling wicket to pepper the visiting batsmen's ankles and finish with 5–23 as India ran out winners by 138 runs.

By the time of the 1983 World Cup Madan had found his Solkar in the shape of all-rounder Roger Binny. With Mohinder Amarnath still dobbing gainfully with his in-dippers, this gave India a three-pronged trundling unit that most observers considered a tragically laughable impediment to Kapil Dev's side progressing beyond the group stage (in which they found themselves in section B, alongside the West Indies, Australia and Zimbabwe). The doubters were very wrong for, against all the odds, in the era of Marshall, Holding, Thomson, Hogg, Hadlee and, erm, Paul Allott, and in a summer that by English standards was not at all bad, the world was about to witness what was arguably the greatest devastation wrought by medium-pacers since Barnes, Foster and Douglas eviscerated the Australians before the Great War.

During the course of the World Cup Binny took an extraordinary eighteen wickets (then a record for the competition). The all-rounder from Karnataka – the first Anglo-Indian to play Test cricket – was tall enough to get a bit of extra bounce from the wicket and the fact that he could swing the ball both ways was a particular bonus in English conditions, as he'd demonstrate at Headingley three years later when under low cloud he took five wickets for 40 and England were skittled out for 102.

The Indian wobblers sent out their message early when Binny took 3–48 against the West Indies at Old Trafford to set up an unexpected win. Against a game Zimbabwe side that had just beaten Australia thanks to the niggly seamers of a certain Duncan Fletcher, Binny and Madan shared five wickets as India won again. They then combined to destroy the Australians at Chelmsford, Madan taking 4–20 and Binny 4–29 as Kim Hughes's team was humiliatingly bundled out for just 129.

In the semi-final against England at Old Trafford Binny nipped out openers Fowler and Tavare, and Amarnath did away with Gower and Gatting as the hosts were brushed aside by six wickets with five overs to spare. What was becoming plain was that when sides were chasing runs India's trundlers, apparently so innocuous, were often much harder to hit than the quicker bowlers. It was a pattern in the tournament as a whole. Sri Lanka's far-from-fast Ashantha de Mel took seventeen wickets – more than Lillee, Thomson and Hogg put together – while Jeremy Coney, New Zealand's answer to Amarnath, finished with a better bowling average than Andy Roberts.

In the final India struggled to 183 against the ferocious pace of Roberts, Garner, Marshall and Holding and the West Indies seemed to be cruising to victory when they reached 50 with just one wicket down. Viv Richards had been giving Madan a bit of a pasting, but far from deterring the trundler it only encouraged him. 'The more he hit me the more I thought I could get him out,' he said afterwards. Sure enough, the masterblaster mistimed a swat off a long hop and was brilliantly caught by Kapil Dev. Seven runs later Madan got the obdurate Haynes and then trapped Gomes. Binny claimed the scalp of Windies captain Clive Lloyd, caught by Kapil at cover off a loose drive, and just as Dujon and Marshall looked to be stabilising things Amarnath came on and dismissed them both. Against an attack that in terms of firepower was a peashooter to their broadside of grapeshot, the West Indies folded for 140.

Binny would continue to bowl well and make decisive contributions for several more years. At Headingley in 1986 he did much to ensure his country's victory and the following winter against Pakistan he bowled brilliantly in Calcutta, taking four Pakistan wickets for nine runs in just thirty deliveries. Madan too plodded on as a regular member of the side till 1985. Off pro-ing in Lancashire League cricket he returned briefly in 1986 when India, beset by injuries, called him into the side for the Headingley Test. He showed that there was life in the old dob yet by taking 3–18 in the first innings.

India's commitment to the military-medium option wavered after that. Kapil Dev had demonstrated that Indians could bowl fast and the great all-rounder inspired a new generation of youngsters determined to ping the ball down at speeds Abid Ali and Dattu Phadkar couldn't have reached with a hurricane behind them.

Medium-pacers have had many fine moments over the centuries and I think it is fair to say that at Lord's on 25 June 1983 Binny, Madan Lal and Amarnath provided what is undoubtedly one of the greatest. It was the Day of the Dobber.

Chapter 16

Going the Other Way

In the nineties something happened that has threatened to wipe trundlers off the face of the earth for ever. The wibbly-wobbly men were already under threat – mainly from food. And not in the way W. G. Grace or Mike Gatting were either. Improved diet, including larger amounts of protein, had increased average height and added to potential muscle mass: nowadays even Englishmen are built like Australians, and Indians once routinely and patronisingly characterised as 'supple' (meaning skinny) are too. Allied with more scientific sports fitness plans this produced bowlers who were bigger and more physically powerful than ever before. The days when the six foot, fourteen stone Chub Tate would be thought of as a man-mountain were gone. We had entered a world of giants. Increasingly the fast-bowling rosters of England, Australia, West Indies, Pakistan, India and South Africa resembled second-row rugby forwards (who had themselves increased to the size of juggernauts). Across the board the speed of bowling increased. Had he been born in the forties Jimmy Anderson would, I feel confident, have been at least three inches shorter and bowling at the same pace as Barry Wood.

The thing that really threatened to call time on the dobbers, though, was a technical breakthrough, a new and dangerous weapon in the bowler's armoury: reverse swing. Conventional swing had been the trundler's tool for the simple reason that, using the methods perfected by George Hirst, it was very difficult to swing the ball if you bowled at speeds above 80mph. Indeed, tests carried out at Imperial College, London in 1983 found that the optimum speed for swinging the ball conventionally was around 70mph – slap in the dobber zone.

Reverse swing is different. While any bowler can use it, tests suggest that the ball reverse swings most effectively at speeds of 85mph and above (at over 90mph physicists say that reverse swing is the only swing possible). At one time fast bowlers – Ray Lindwall, Fred Trueman and Richard Hadlee would be good examples – used to slow down to take advantage of cloud cover and humidity. With the discovery of reverse swing that was no longer necessary. In fact, many bowlers had to speed up to catch the new wave.

Even more has been written about reverse swing than conventional swing. At first it was thought that reversing had something to do with one half of the ball being made heavier – by soaking it in sweat and saliva – but that proved to be a red herring. Basically it all comes back to the old chaotic boundary layer business. While conventional swing tends to be associated with the shine of the ball, reverse swing is all about its roughness. This is why it generally only comes into play with older balls. The beauty of reverse swing is that a bowler who could only bowl out-swingers with the new ball can bowl in-swingers with an older ball and vice versa without any change in grip or action.

Everyone knows how to produce shine on a ball; producing roughness is another matter, which is why reverse swing has so often been associated with tampering. Gouging one side of the ball with a bottle cap – as we saw earlier – is probably the most popular method, alongside the prising open of the quarter seam and the use of soil, often stuck to the surface using sugar-impregnated saliva.

Bowlers looking for reverse swing generally favoured the Alfred Reader ball, feeling that the Duke's didn't swing as much and took longer to work into a condition when it would. Seamers traditionally favoured a soft grassy pitch to help the ball move and a lush outfield to preserve the shine. Purveyors of reverse swing generally clap their hands with delight when faced with a rock-hard wicket that's the colour of Weetabix and an outfield as bald as Isaac Hayes. Abrasion is the key to their sorcery.

The discovery of reverse swing is generally credited to the Pakistan team of the eighties, with Imran Khan and Sarfraz Nawaz high on the list of the men behind the dramatic new phenomenon. Imran was far too quick to be given space in these pages, so suffice it to say here that he was an in-swing bowler who noticed that late in an innings he would sometimes find the ball boomeranging outwards instead. Predictably, when he raised this topic with scientists they initially discounted the possibility altogether.

Imran may have been the first man to draw the attention of the boffins to reverse swing, but he was not the first bowler to use it. In all likelihood that was a gentleman we encountered earlier, Eric Atkinson, the fifties West Indian seamer with the fondness for hair-care products. Atkinson was from Barbados and began life as a tearaway paceman before slowing down and starting to use the swing-bringing properties of the Caribbean breeze. Hard though it is to imagine now, back in those days West Indian cricket wasn't as dominated by lightning speed as it would be in the coming decades. In fact, in the early fifties opening bowling duties in the West Indies team were done by batsman Frank Worrell (a useful trundler who had honed his skills in the Central Lancashire League) and the very moderately paced Gerry Gomez. The duo's main job was simply to wear some shine off the ball for the spin twins Ramadhin and Valentine; if they took a wicket it was a bonus. Sometimes West Indies skipper Jeff Stollmeyer would give them a helping hand, rubbing the ball in the dirt. Even in the early seventies the bespectacled Clive Lloyd – with his slingy long-armed medium-pacers – would often come on first change.

Atkinson's skill as a swing bowler eventually earned him a call-up to the Test team at the Tate-ian age of thirty. In total he played for the West Indies eight times and took twenty-five wickets at 23.56 apiece. His best performance was against Pakistan at Sabina Park in 1958 when he took 5–42, a feat that might have garnered more attention had not Garry Sobers hogged the headlines by scoring 365 not out.

Around the time that Atkinson was apparently reversing the ball in the Caribbean (and passing the skill on to his protégé Richard 'Prof' Edwards, who made a handful of Test appearances in the sixties), a number of bowlers were doing something similar in club cricket in the Pakistani city of Lahore. One of the men who regularly faced such bowling was Nazar Mohammad, one of those limpet-like batsmen in which Pakistani cricket specialised in the fifties, occupying the crease with such obduracy the bowlers must have been tempted to lob dynamite at them. Nazar registered his nation's first Test hundred and at Lucknow in 1952 became the first player in cricket history to spend an entire Test match on the field of play. Nazar Mohammad has little part to play in our narrative beyond the fact that he fathered a son, Mudassar Nazar, who many have credited with educating the Pakistani Test team in the arcane ways of reversing.

Mudassar was a batsman in the same doughty mould as his father. He had perfected his swing bowling as a teenager, playing in the leagues in Lancashire. Mudassar was a true trundler, loping to the wicket off a short run and delivering the ball with an elastically swinging arm at a military clip. He looked innocuous, but for an out-and-out wibbly-wobbly man who was primarily in the side for his sturdy batting he put in a surprising number of match-turning performances with the ball. At Lord's in 1982, for instance. Pakistan were hunting their first victory over England in an away series for twenty-eight years. The home side had been forced to follow on, but Pakistan's attack – already handicapped by an injury to pace bowler Tahir Naqqash – was further weakened when Sarfraz Nawaz limped off the field with a strain during his opening spell. That left captain Imran with few options, so he threw the ball to Mudassar. Up to that point in his Test career the opening batsman had taken eleven wickets at 43 apiece. He'd done reasonably well in one-day internationals, though, a format that often suited bowlers who didn't give batsmen too much pace or movement to harness to their advantage, and had been effective the previous winter in the tour matches in Australia.

Mudassar bowled Derek Randall in his first over, then in the space of ten deliveries trapped Allan Lamb lbw and had David Gower caught behind for a duck. What he lacked in pace he made up for in guile. He wobbled the ball both ways, changed pace and line subtly and occasionally produced the leg-cutter he'd been taught to bowl by Dennis Lillee. Chris Tavare – a batsman so rock-like you could tell which direction was north by checking where the moss grew on him – and Ian Botham took England safely through to the close.

The next morning Mudassar was back. He had Botham caught in the deep and then removed Mike Gatting and Ian Greig (sometimes when you read the names of the England Test line-up in those days you almost want to cry) in quick succession. Imran and the febrile leg-spinner Abdul Qadir wrapped up the innings and Pakistan won by ten wickets. Mudassar was the hero. He'd taken 6–32 in nineteen overs and made the old ball loop around in a manner many observers found inexplicable. In Pakistan the newspapers dubbed him the Man With the Golden Arm.

Batting remained Mudassar's full-time occupation, but when conditions were right he still got his chance with the ball. Against New Zealand at Lahore in 1984 he actually took the new ball, bowled an eleven-over spell and took 3 for 8. He finished his international career with sixty-six Test wickets and he'd taken over a hundred in one-day matches.

Sarfraz Nawaz had a centre parting, a drooping moustache and the general look of the bass player in an Eagles tribute act. He was a familiar figure to English cricket fans, having signed to play for Northamptonshire in 1970 – spotted by county skipper Roger Prideaux on an MCC tour – after he'd played only handful of first-class matches. Sarfraz had a stuttering tippy-toe run-up and was on the brisker side of medium pace. He was very accurate, had a twitchy off-cutter and even as a youngster could swing the ball both ways apparently without much change in his action. In the mid-seventies he opened the bowling for his country with another impressively coiffed trundler, Asif Masood, the bowler whose low-slung run-up John Arlott likened to 'Groucho Marx chasing a waitress'.

Sarfraz was a fiery eccentric whose fallings-out with the Pakistan Cricket Board occurred with the regularity of apple blossom. In the middle of the 1977–8 series against England he vanished, turning up in wintry Northampton apparently having got the hump over pay and conditions. He was omitted from the 1979–80 tour of India apparently because Pakistan skipper Asif Iqbal couldn't cope with his moods, and he caused a series of minor scandals throughout his career over everything from appealing successfully to have Australia's Andrew Hilditch given out when he handled the ball at Perth in 1978, to pinging down ten-foot-high bouncers in a one-day international against India (when the umpires took no action Indian captain Bishan Bedi forfeited the match in protest) and bowling a beamer at Tony Greig at the Oval in 1974, via delivering a string of bumpers to a singularly unimpressed Joel Garner in the Gillette Cup final.

His greatest performance came against Australia at Melbourne during the two-Test series of 1978–9. The entire series was played out in a festering atmosphere created by the fall-out from Kerry Packer's World Series and some comments by Asif Iqbal about the childishness of the Australian players. In that first Test Australia were set a target of 388 to win. Shortly after lunch on the final day they were 305–3 with Allan Border and Kim Hughes having built an unbroken stand of 177. Pakistan had taken the second new ball, but Imran Khan was off the field with food poisoning. With 77 needed for victory Sarfraz, who had been bowling off a truncated dash of nine paces, decided to waste a bit of time by going back to his full run-up. Bowling with the seam upright to extract any possible movement in the air or off the strip he quickly dismissed the resilient Border with one that cut back in to him sharply, and in the next thirty-three balls took six more wickets at a cost of one run. Australia were all out for 310 and Sarfraz had figures of 9–86, which at the time were the best ever achieved by any non-spinner.

Like Mudassar, Sarfraz learned his cricket in Lahore, and is credited with being one of the first exponents of reverse swing. He has done little to dampen this idea, claiming that he kept the secret to himself for several years before eventually passing on his skills to Imran. What is certain is that Sarfraz did reverse-swing the ball as well as swinging it conventionally and that he was a very fine bowler who, had it not been for his frequent disagreements with the Pakistan hierarchy, might have got far more than the 177 Test wickets he ended up with in an international career that ran through three decades. After retirement he moved into sports politics and remains as feisty as ever, denouncing everything from gambling to ball tampering to Darrell Hair.

As to how he came upon reverse swing Sarfraz is reticent. It's possible that he stumbled across it – much as Hirst did the conventional variety – or that he learned something about it from Saleem Altaf, with whom he opened the bowling in Australia in 1972–3. In *Wisden*'s account of the Tests on that tour there are comments about the late swing Saleem obtained in unpromising conditions. On that tour Sarfraz also encountered an early master of the reverse, the goofily grinning, giant Tasmanian Max Walker. Walker was a medium-pacer who played for Victoria and delivered the ball with such a convoluted, wrong-footed, windmill action the other players nicknamed him Tangles.

Back in the mid-seventies, when the Australian team was characterised by its gum-chewing, shark-eyed aggression, Tangles stood out. As my father remarked, 'I can't stand any of them except for that Walker. He seems decent enough, like a big, genial idiot.'

With his gap-toothed smile, broad hooter and wild rustic hair, Walker certainly had the look of a man who ought to have been leaning up against a gate with a straw between his teeth. The appearance was at least in part deceptive, because while Walker was indeed an easy-going funny bloke, he was no idiot. He was a qualified architect, an entertaining writer and enough of an all-round sportsman to have played eighty-five games for the Melbourne Australian Rules football side.

Walker lolloped up to the wicket and delivered the ball chest-on and in a blizzard of swinging limbs, or as he himself put it, 'I bowl right-arm over left ear-hole with legs crossed at point of delivery.' His stock ball was a booming in-swinger that started out aimed at first slip before looping back towards the stumps. Aged twenty-seven he added an out-swinger, though as he explained he only bowled that delivery for show: 'I didn't expect to take a wicket with it. I just wanted the batsman to know I could do it, if I wanted to.'

Walker's mentor at the Melbourne Cricket Ground was the veteran trundler Alan Connolly. Connolly had played for his country sporadically from the early sixties until the start of the seventies and been good enough to pick up over a century of Test wickets. He'd started out, predictably, as a straight-ahead, pawing-the-ground paceman, but soon shaved his run-up, cut down his speed and increased his fitness and his accuracy so that he could bowl long, diligent spells of probing medium pace. Connolly moved the ball in the air both ways by conventional methods, but in the Sheffield Shield matches of the early seventies he and Victoria wicketkeeper Ray Jordan began to notice how the ball would start to wobble about late in an innings. After various experiments the pair decided that the way to enhance this weird swing was to soak one half of the ball with sweat and saliva. They believed that the swing was something to do with weighting one half of the ball. As we know, their reasoning was faulty, but there was no mistaking the fact that the treated ball now dipped around in previously unheard-of ways.

Connolly taught the new skill to his protégé. By then Walker had been called up to the Australian Test team to play Pakistan – and Saleem and Sarfraz – during that 1972–3 series. According to Walker, his introduction to the teeth-baringly macho Australian dressing room was unhappily savage: middle-order batsman and partnership-breaking trundler Doug Walters had apparently dumped the debutant's kit in the toilet after finding it in what he regarded as *his* locker.

After the Pakistan series Australia travelled to the West Indies where Walker, using Connolly's reverse swing and an out-swinger taught to him by the soon-to-be-neutered Bob Massie, caused a minor sensation by picking up twenty-six wickets, a record for an Australian bowler in the Caribbean that would stand until Glenn McGrath took thirty a quarter of a century later. Tangles's best moments came in the first innings of the first Test at Sabina Park where, opening the bowling with Dennis Lillee, he took 6–114. Shortly after that match Lillee was diagnosed with a severe spinal problem and left the tour, leaving Walker to lead the attack alongside the fast-medium Jeff Hammond. The two were supported by the leg-spinners Kerry O'Keefe and Terry Jenner and the medium pace of Walters and Greg Chappell. I must add that if that sounds like a fairly innocuous attack for an Australian side, it should be borne in mind that in the Test at Port of Spain Clive Lloyd *opened* the bowling for a West Indian team that included three specialist spinners, one of whom was Elquemedo Willett – a piece of information with no particular relevance, but it is nice to be reminded of the name.

For the next few years Walker took the new ball with various partners including Gus Gilmour, but in 1974–5 Lillee returned and was paired with a raw, slingy but stunningly quick newcomer named Jeff Thomson. Walker found himself shuffled down the bowling order. He became the uncomplaining workhorse of the Australian team, coming on after Lillee and Thomson had pounded the new ball into the ground and it was as soft and shine-less as an over-ripe russet apple, and inevitably bowling up the hill and into whatever wind was available.

Walker's ability to swing the ball meant he was never merely a stock bowler. In the final Test of the 1974–5 series, with Lillee and Thomson both injured and the Ashes secured, he returned to new-ball duties and took 8–143 in the first innings.

In the first five Tests of that series Lillee and Thomson had battered the English side into submission, destroying several careers as well as numerous abdominal protectors along the way. When Ian Chappell's team came to England in 1975 people expected more of the same. For the first Test at Edgbaston the country geared itself up for the sort of casualty list normally associated with a George A. Romero movie. Instead, in damp conditions with heavy overcast skies it was the medium-paced Walker – a springer spaniel to Lillee and Thomson's pit-bulls – who caused most of the trouble, boomeranging the ball all over the shop to take 5–48. After that, normal service was resumed.

Walker carried on as Australia's first-choice first change for a couple more years before he was lured away by the World Series. The early master of reverse swing took 138 Test wickets and was one short of his five-hundredth first-class victim when he finally retired from Shield cricket in 1982. The last time I stumbled across him was on YouTube, where I found him grinning out at me and extolling the laxative virtues of cartons of iced coffee. Bowel problems notwithstanding, he appeared as genial as ever.

Walker, Connolly, Saleem, Atkinson, Mudassar and Sarfraz are all thought of as pioneers of reverse swing. However, there is a possibility that they were actually at the forefront of something else entirely. According to the sports aerodynamics consultant and NASA scientist Rabindra Mehta, there is a third type of swing: converse swing. This occurs when a bowler holds the seam upright – as he would when bowling conventional swing – but finds the ball swinging 'the wrong way' (i.e. towards the shiny side rather than away from it). Mehta suggests that genuine reverse swing only happens at very high speeds – over 85mph – and with the seam held at an angle. If he is correct (and his explanation is so bamboozling to an idiot such as myself that I'm pretty sure he must be) then none of the illustrious trundlers named above would actually have been quick enough to reverse it. Imran Khan would have been, of course, as would other later Pakistan quicks such as Shoaib Akhtar, English bowlers including Andrew Flintoff, Simon Jones and Darren Gough, and West Indians like Kenny Benjamin.

Mehta tells us that converse swing results from the usual rough/smooth combination but is caused by side forces created by asymmetry. There's always one more thing with swing. As Michael Corleone famously remarked, 'Just when you think you're out, they pull you back in.'

Epilogue

Where Have All the Dobbers Gone?

Over the centuries cricket romantics have constantly called for the obliteration of the medium-pacer. Incensed by the trundler's lack of panache, his stolid insistence on line and length, his dogged adherence to values that are, in sporting terms, the equivalent of magnolia emulsion, they have tried to do away with him, from outlawing the sort of calculated leg theory that propelled Fred Root to the top of the averages to flattening the wickets that so benefited Barnes and covering those that Shackleton and Shepherd brilliantly exploited. None of these had much effect; the dobbers simply adapted to the new conditions and got on with it as they had always done.

Nowadays, however, the trundler is genuinely under threat. And it is not the lawmakers who have brought the situation about, but reverse swing. Jimmy Anderson is a worthy successor to Barnes, Tate and Bedser as an England new-ball bowler of guile and craft. But Anderson is no trundler. His wicketkeepers stand well back. The Lancastrian bowls consistently at around 85mph. The swing he extracts is of the newer, fancier kind.

Old-style swing has gone out of fashion, much as leg-spin

did in the eighties. One-day cricket had long been the natural habitat of trundlers who batted a bit and vice versa. In 1983 dobbers had played an integral role in India's unexpected World Cup win. Yet thirteen years later the World Cup was dominated by spinners, not just the ones you might expect like Shane Warne, Anil Kumble and Mushtaq Ahmed, but the likes of West Indian Roger Harper and Zimbabwe's Paul Strang. The nearest to an outright dobber to take more than ten wickets that winter in India and Sri Lanka was Kenya's Rajab Ali. When the tournament returned to England in 1999 it was dominated by pace – Glenn McGrath, Allan Donald, Shoaib Akhtar, Courtney Walsh and the New Zealand left-armer Geoff Allott who, ignoring the advice of Jack Cowie, threw everything he had into each delivery and had the speed gun wobbling up towards the 150kph mark. At least India remained true to their traditions and offered up Robin Singh and Debasis Mohanty. Unfortunately, they got nowhere.

And then came reverse swing. Since then things have deteriorated further for the dobbers. Mark Ealham, who took ten wickets in the 1999 World Cup and followed in the heavy yet not-entirely-threatening footsteps of such Kentish dobbing giants as Norman Graham and Richard Ellison, delighting fans everywhere with his fluttering deliveries has retired. So too has that broad-beamed follower of Lancashire trundling traditions, Ian Austin. In New Zealand Wibbly, Wobbly, Dibbly and Dobbly have all gone. South African change bowler Craig Matthews, whose mastery of medium tedium led some to suggest that he literally bored batsmen into submission, has quit. The last Australian to swing the ball the old-fashioned way favoured by Terry Alderman, Bob Massie and Gus Gilmour was Damien Fleming.

Praveen Kumar of Uttar Pradesh and India keeps the

flame alive, swinging the ball conventionally both ways at a speed that doesn't frighten the horses (Mohammad Asif was similarly gifted but his brushes with bookmakers have absented him from the scene) and Australian all-rounder Andrew McDonald may yet turn into the sort of run-throttling medium-pacer the wider world is crying out not to see, but these are isolated voices in the wilderness. England's team is chock-full of gigantic men who can bounce the ball round the batter's ears from just short of a length. Even Kumar's international team mates such as Zaheer Khan seem more intent on mimicking Shoaib Akhtar than Madan Lal.

When Alderman was asked about the situation seven years ago, he answered that his type of swing-and-seamer was now an endangered species and pointed to England's Matthew Hoggard as the sole survivor of a formerly vast and apparently endless herd that spread across the north and midlands as bison once did on the Great Plains. 'He might not take any wickets, but he'll bowl all day,' the Western Australian observed approvingly. Because Alderman was a true trundler and as such knows deep within his soul that turning your arm over for hours on end with no material reward is what cricket is all about.

With his wild hair and pack of assorted dogs, Hoggy seemed a man out of time in more ways than one. In temperament he called to mind an earlier era of softly eccentric Yorkshire medium-pacers such as Emmott Robinson, who obsessively checked barometers for warnings of potential swerve-inducing summer storms. Hoggy was quicker than George Hirst, Tate and their ilk, but not as quick as Anderson, Flintoff or Simon Jones. He could reverse-swing the ball, but not much. He relied on the early shine and the strange whims of humidity. At Trent Bridge in 2005, when the clouds appeared in the first innings, Hoggy took the wickets of

Langer, Hayden and Martyn for 70 and in the second when Australia looked to be building a big total he found more movement to nip out Clarke and Gilchrist in a manner Robinson would have appreciated.

Shortly after the end of that great Ashes series a friend of mine was on the East Coast Main Line train from Edinburgh to London. As the train headed out of Doncaster he heard something unusual: a ripple of applause gradually moving towards him from the rear of the carriage. My friend looked around to see a slightly embarrassed Hoggy striding down the aisle towards the buffet car. The applause followed the Yorkshireman as he went, stopped while he purchased his sandwich and then followed him all the way back to his seat. It was a touching and spontaneous tribute. My friend was amazed less by the ovation than by the circumstances. 'I can't believe an England Test cricketer was sitting in standard class,' he said. Maybe others were surprised too. I wasn't. After all, where else would the true trundler sit?

On Elysian Fields

When I was teenager I devoted considerable hours to picking imaginary cricket elevens. My inspiration were the various teams that were selected to take on the tourists; Lavinia, Duchess of Norfolk's XI, T. N. Pearce's XI and D. H. Robbins's XI are probably the best remembered. My particular favourite was the Callers Pegasus International XI that played an annual one-day match at Jesmond in Newcastle. Named after the sponsor, a local travel agency, the International XI featured stars such as Zaheer Abbas and Basil D'Oliveira in a limited-overs battle with a combined Northumberland and Durham side. The match was such a big deal in the north-east it was shown live on Tyne Tees Television.

In the long wasted hours of youth I would select World XIs and Rest of the World XIs, Northern Hemisphere XIs and Southern Hemisphere XIs alongside others based on criteria too arcane to be gone into here. After the rigorous selection process I would then pit the teams against one another in matches played using metal *Owzat!* cylinders when I should have been doing my homework. That U in O-level physics was the direct result of a five-match series between the West Indians (a combined team of West Indies and India) taking on Austral-Asia (Australia, New Zealand and Pakistan, obviously). Sadly I cannot recall the result, though I seem to think Trinidadian wrist-spinner Inshan Ali was an unexpected Man of the Series.

In the spirit of my adolescent years I have here selected two all-time trundling greats XIs, England and the Rest of the World. The teams will play one another in a fifty-five overs match in which each player – including the wicket-keepers – must bowl five overs. The game will be played at Chesterfield, a ground which I believe will allow the trundlers maximum expression of their talents.

The selection process for both teams has been tough and has involved a good deal of arguing with myself. Let us deal with England first. The choice of opening batsmen eventually came down to picking two from the excellent trio of Graham Gooch, Jack Hobbs and Barry Wood. The Ossett-born Wood was one of the most valuable payers in the history of the one-day game, picking up armfuls of Man of the Match awards in the seventies. He could swing the ball about all over the place when conditions were in his favour (usually against Yorkshire, the county of his birth) and took close to three hundred first-class wickets. Graham Gooch surpassed Wood's record for gold awards in the eighties. He was not as much of an all-rounder as the Lancashire man, but his slingy seam-up was effective enough to account for over 250 opponents and he did a rather good Bob Willis impression that could entertain the crowd if play turned dull. Jack Hobbs was arguably the greatest opening batsman of all time. He bowled skimming right-arm medium pace with a career best return of 7–56. It was a difficult decision, but eventually Gooch and Hobbs got the nod.

At number three I have opted for the later, larger period W. G. Grace. Aside from anything else his round-arm round the wicket style will add variety to the attack. In at four and five are two members of England's triumphant trundling triumvirate of 1911–12, J. W. H. T. Douglas and Frank Foster. The third member of the trio, S. F. Barnes, is – naturally – also included. He bats at ten.

In at number six comes one of my boyhood heroes, Tony Greig. Putting aside his more controversial comments and his alarming choice of blazers, Greig was a terrific cricketer and a man who never shied from a challenge. One of my happiest memories is sitting on the Western Terrace at Headingley and watching him smash Jeff Thomson for a straight six. He bowled both traditional medium pace from a vast height and also quickish off-spin, a style with which he took thirteen wickets in the Trinidad Test of 1974. I am making him captain too.

Following Greig in the batting order is Maurice Tate. Chub will take the new ball with Barnes. His record as a bowler is exemplary and he also scored twenty-three first-class hundreds. Finding an English wicketkeeper who also trundled was not that easy. Hampshire's George Brown had a good claim to the gauntlets, having taken 568 catches and made seventy-eight stumpings as well as bowling right-arm dobbers well enough to have taken 8–55 in an innings. In the end, though, I have opted for the Right Honourable Alfred Lyttelton, QC. Lyttelton was one of the great all-round sportsmen of the nineteenth century, excelling at all manner of games and pursuits including real tennis and the hammer throw. For Middlesex and England the lanky barrister was a scintillating strokemaker (he hit seven first-class centuries), kept wicket adequately (130 catches and seventy stumpings) and, most importantly, bowled under-arms in the style of Lumpy Stevens. These proved effective against Australia at the Oval in 1884 when – with Grace taking over the gloves – Lyttelton bagged 4–19.

The final two bowling places were subject to heated debate. George Hirst was mentioned, of course, so too Tom Cartwright, Derek Shackleton and Don Shepherd. But finally I reached further back into the past and selected William Lillywhite and George Lohmann. The latter's record speaks for itself and he was also a handy late-order striker. Lillywhite was unfailingly accurate and I believe his top hat would give England a sartorial edge if nothing else. Perhaps the middle order is not as strong as it might have been, but with two round-armers, an under-armer, the left-arm Foster and Greig's medium-paced spin I believe this gives England a positive and varied attack.

One notable omission is Sir Alec Bedser. I offer no apologies for this. After all, he gave me none when he failed to pick Barrie Leadbeater or Richard Lumb for England.

The final selection: Hobbs, Gooch, Grace, Douglas, Foster, Greig, Tate, Lyttelton, Lohmann, Barnes, Lillywhite.

To take on this formidable side the Rest of the World need something a little special. I believe they have it. The Man with the Golden Arm, Mudassar Nazar, is an obvious choice of opener. To partner him I faced a difficult decision. Vijay Merchant was the greatest Indian batsman of the immediate post-war years and bowled medium-paced off-spin; he might have made the cut. So too might a later Indian, Manoj Prabhakar. However, I felt that the notoriously obdurate Mudassar needed a more belligerent opening partner than either of these two and so instead have opted for Sir Clyde Walcott. A brilliant heavy-hitting batsman, Sir Clyde's right-arm fastish medium-pace was effective in the Lancashire Leagues and also earned him eleven Test-match scalps.

Mohinder Amarnath picks himself at three for his courageous batting and even braver wibbly-wobblies, and he is followed in the order by the belligerent Clive Lloyd, whose slingy right-arm medium-pacers earned him 114 first-class wickets. At number five the selector toyed with the elegant flares-wearing Asif Iqbal who swung the ball nicely at a military clip, but then plumped for Doug Walters not just for his electric stroke play and the niggly 'partnership breaking' medium pace that earned him a Test best of 5–66, but also because he is the ideal man to organise a card game during a rain break. At number six I have selected Sir Frank Worrell. Worrell was a great strokemaker and had honed his trundling skills in the Central Lancashire League. He bowled left-arm which adds variety. A man of intelligence and considerable charm, I also make him captain.

When it comes to trundling wicketkeepers the Rest of the World was spoilt for choice. West Indies Test cricketer Clairmonte Depeiaza was a worthy candidate. The Barbadian – who hit a Test century against the Australia of Lindwall and Miller – did not bowl much in first-class cricket but he once took a hundred wickets in a season for Haslingden with what *Wisden* described as 'awkward low trajectory fast-medium'. Former Zimbabwe captain Tatenda Taibu, a world class wicketkeeper batsman who bowled right-arm medium pace well enough to take 8–43 in a first-class match, was also a possibility. In the end, however, I decided to hand the gauntlets to Sir Clyde Walcott and free up another bowling position.

Who should fill the number seven slot? There was a good deal of debate at this point. Sir Garfield Sobers's name came up, but it was felt that the fact the great all-rounder could bowl fast, slow left-arm, chinamen and probably right-arm off-breaks too if he wanted militated against his selection. An argument was made for Mohinder Amarnath's father Lala, a mercurial batsman who bowled in-swingers using a technique so bewildering most observers thought he bowled off the wrong foot even though he didn't. Jeremy Coney's name came up too, largely because he was such a genial character (once, when he was being cruelly flogged by Kapil Dev, Coney took his hanky out of his pocket and waved it like a white flag) and possibly the only international trundler who is also a trained theatrical lighting designer. Monty Noble, that sporting all-rounder, was discussed, though on balance his batting might not have been suited to the limited-overs format. In the end it was decided that the cricketer the public would most benefit from seeing in action was a man eligible for both XIs, the Anglo-Australian Albert Trott. I believe Trott's massive hitting and eccentric swing bowling would be highly effective in the one-day game, which might have set him just the sort of challenges his short attention span demanded.

Leading the Rests attack are Charles Turner and Bart King. The former is the most devastating non-English dobber in history, while the latter was not only an innovative swing bowler and a dashing strokemaker (he scored eight first-class fifties) but will also help sell the game in the US. Which leaves just two places up for grabs. Fazal Mahmood and Amar Singh are both good candidates, so too are Sarfraz Nawaz and Terry Alderman. On balance, though, I feel the attack needs a left-armer. I am tempted by both Ernie Toshack and Bill Johnson, but in the end have, for sentimental reasons, opted to hand a place to Gus Gilmour, whose big hitting may provide useful runs late on and whose rotund outline will give a fillip to many male spectators. For all that New Zealand has given trundling I give the final place to Jack Cowie, a terrific medium-pacer and the sort of sensible fellow whose calming presence might well be needed in a team containing Trott, Gilmour and Walters. Batting-wise, I think this XI has the edge over England, but the bowling is arguably not as powerful.

The Rest of the World XI, then, is Walcott, Mudassar, Amarnath, Lloyd, Walters, Worrell, Trott, King, Gilmour, Cowie and Turner.

If you want to find out who wins you will have to supply your own *Owzat!* cylinders (the prices on eBay are a bit steep, but you can make them out of pencils easily enough) and score sheets.